978.02
O'Ne

D0326991

DATE DUE

DEC 0 2	1998		
DEC 1	6 1998		
DEC 2 1			

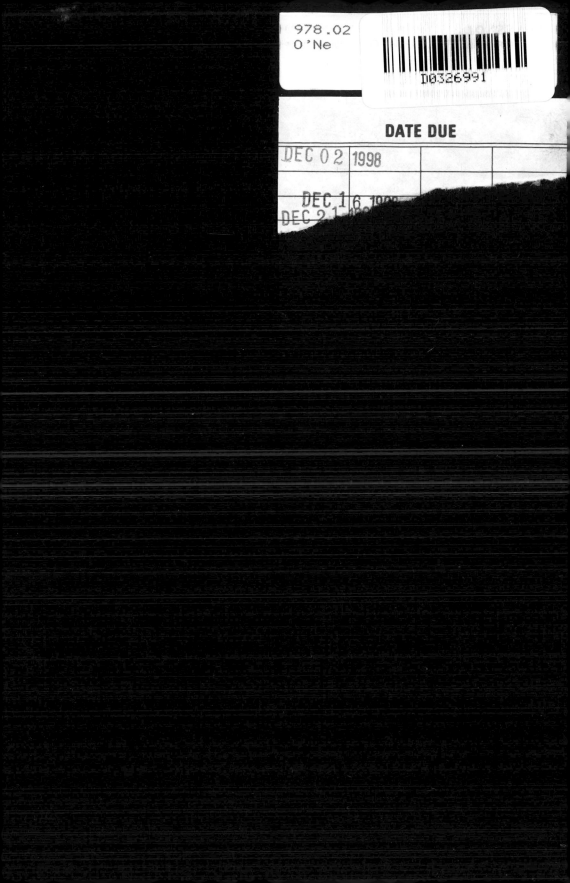

OUTLAWS

OUTLAWS

A Quest for Butch and Sundance

EAMONN O'NEILL

WITHDRAWN
MUSSER PUBLIC LIBRARY

MAINSTREAM
PUBLISHING

Distributed by
Trafalgar Square
North Pomfret, Vermont 05053

Copyright © Eamonn O'Neill, 1997
All rights reserved
The moral right of the author has been asserted

First published in 1997 by
MAINSTREAM PUBLISHING COMPANY (EDINBURGH) LTD
7 Albany Street
Edinburgh EH1 3UG

ISBN 1 85158 931 7

No part of this book may be reproduced or transmitted in any form or by any
means without written permission from the publisher, except by a reviewer who
wishes to quote brief passages in connection with a review written for insertion in a
newspaper, magazine or broadcast

A catalogue record for this book is available from the British Library

Typeset in Bembo
Printed and bound in Great Britain by Butler & Tanner Ltd

To Sarah

OCT 2 2 1998

MUSSER PUBLIC LIBRARY
304 Iowa Avenue
Muscatine, Iowa 52761

Says I, 'Butch, will you-all be comin' back soon?'

'Sure will,' says he, 'and you be here when I get back. I'll be ridin' in one of these days with my pockets full o' gold. You stay right here till you see our dust!'

An' I been waitin' ever since. He ain't never come yet, but I know he will some day. He ain't forgot old Speck!

Some say he got killed in South America; but there ain't 'ary bullet could kill Butch Cassidy! I 'spect he'll be showin' up around here one o' these days . . .'

— Albert 'Speckled' Williams, a former slave and associate of Butch Cassidy, talking on 7 May 1934, two weeks before his own death

Beat the drums lightly, play your fifes merrily,
Sing your death-march as you bear me along.
Take me to the graveyard, lay the sod o'er me,
I'm a young cowboy and know I've done wrong.

— *From 'The Cowboy's Lament', Anon*

*It was hell proper . . . In the daytime we would sweat,
fry, or sizzle under the hot desert sun, or ride for whole
days with our clothes soaking wet in rainy weather, or
sleep in wet clothes on cold nights under one saddle
blanket . . . we would eat this cold, soggy, stale stuff
without coffee in cold dark camps . . . On hot days we
pushed, lickety-split, in desperate, cross-country flights
over mountain and desert . . . The sweat would roll
down our bellies and backs, and the hard, heavy money
belts would gall a raw ring clear around our bodies . . .
While we was frying, freezing, starving and depriving
ourselves of every comfort and pleasure of existence, here
was all that stolen money in our belts that would buy
anything we wanted, and we couldn't go anywhere or
contact anybody to spend it. We just had to leave it
there making raw rings around us, weighting us down
and wearing us out, while we was nearly perishing for
the things it could buy for us.*

*That's what an outlaw had to face. That's the other
side of the adventure and romance of outlaw life.*

— Matt Warner, former Wild Bunch member and friend of Butch Cassidy

Contents

1. A Very Holy Would-Be Outlaw

'Maybe that's where the cowboys live.'

I was five years old and it was my first day at school.

I was surrounded by chaos in the class. Two children had already wet themselves through naked fear at the thought of being separated from their parents, and a little girl had been dragged screaming and kicking into the classroom by her older brother. She had to be practically strapped down into a chair before he could leave. The teacher was an overbearing woman with a big voice who kept rattling a ruler off the desk when she shouted at us. Then there was the owl. A stuffed, staring owl that perched behind her head. Its eyes bored through me. I was scared out of my wits. Alone, without my parents, and utterly terrified for the very first time in my life.

And it wasn't even half past nine.

'I bet cowboys live over there,' I thought to myself. I was staring out of the window, over the rooftops and chimney-pots, at a field that lay in the distance. There was a small hill, some sycamore trees and a pond at one side of it. I imagined cowboys, like the ones I'd seen in films, roaming around on horses, free from the constraints of normal life, free to do what they wanted, free from loud, ruler-wielding teachers and free from staring, evil-looking stuffed owls.

'Whah! I want my mammy!' a shriek went up.

More peeing at the back of the class. Hell was breaking loose again. Other kids started crying and the teacher clattered her wooden ruler off the varnished pine desk. It was no use. Pandemonium reigned.

Needless to say, I felt like crying too, but I didn't. I bit my lip, stared out of the window and thought of cowboys. Afterwards, I realised I'd bitten my lip so hard it had bled down the front of my new white school shirt. When I went home later that day, my parents saw the red stains but said nothing. I think they thought I'd been in my first playground fight. My father slipped me extra pocket-money the next day.

❊

In the West of Scotland real cowboys were very thin on the ground – apart from the dodgy plumber or unreliable electrician variety, that is – but that never stopped my day-dreaming. I used to watch cowboy films, read old western books and hope that one day I'd see the American West for myself.

Of all the hundreds of westerns that I watched when I was young I had one clear favourite: *Butch Cassidy and the Sundance Kid*, starring Paul Newman and Robert Redford. I appreciate I'm not unusual in liking this movie – nearly everyone I know enjoys it. To me, however, it's always had added significance. It stems from a book I read as a boy about the real Butch Cassidy and his Wild Bunch.

When I was a kid my father took me to the famous Barras

market in Glasgow. This was one of his favourite places. Out of earshot of my mother he could talk to his heart's content, tell tall tales without being apprehended and generally be pleasantly anonymous. His favourite stall sold books. One day he bought a pile of paperbacks, one of which was called *The Wild Bunch*. He gave the stallholder the money and we trooped off to speak to an Irish gypsy woman he knew who wore a sleeveless fur coat in the middle of the summer and a bowler hat with a feather stuck in its side.

As they talked and ate scorchingly hot fried donuts I began leafing through the book about the Wild Bunch. It was an old paperback, originally published in the 1950s, and only about a hundred or so pages long. It claimed to tell the whole story of Butch Cassidy, the Sundance Kid and their Wild Bunch. Although by this time I'd seen the Hollywood film a few times, I'd always thought that the whole thing had been made up, that the story was no more than the figment of a scriptwriter's imagination. I never thought for a moment any of it might be true. Yet, this little paperback suggested it was. I was spellbound.

Written in the same shock-horror style as the books I used to see men on trains and buses leafing through, most of this book's claims sounded highly improbable. An uncle of mine used to read such cowboy books on his way to work in Glasgow. The thin, unlikely plot was enough to keep him enraptured for nearly an hour as the train rattled towards the city. He knew his cowboy 'stuff' all right. One sunny summer morning when a small crowd was waiting for a late train to arrive he jumped down on to the tracks and put his ear to the line.

'It's coming now, I can hear it.' He stood up and smiled.

Everyone clapped as he clambered back on to the platform, trying not to dirty his suit. Sure enough, the train gently rounded the bend in the distance. I looked at my uncle in a new light.

'Where did you learn that?'

'In one of these.' He withdrew a cowboy book furtively from

his pocket. 'It's an old trick. Cowboys used to do it all the time when they held trains up.'

In later years I'd learn he was in interesting company reading cowboy books. Both Adolf Hitler and Albert Einstein, for example, loved to read western stories that featured Karl May's hero 'Old Shatterhand'.

In my imagination my pinstriped uncle had assumed another identity during that train journey as he read his book: a gunslinger, sheriff or cowboy on a long cattle-drive. I hated the expression on his face when the train finally shuddered to a stop. He always paused for a moment or two before snapping the paperback shut in anger as he realised we'd arrived. I'd have been annoyed too if one moment I was wearing a stetson riding out on the range and the next I was arriving in Glasgow Central Station at 8.40 a.m. on a wet Wednesday morning with a day's work in an office ahead of me.

One day after he'd put his book away and we'd got off the train, I walked him to his office. He'd been with the same company for almost twenty-five years and was very loyal to his employers. But on this particular morning he was met at the main door by a sorry-looking, pot-bellied security guard. With his head bowed, the guard told my uncle he'd have to escort him up to his office on the fourth floor to collect his bits and pieces. Then he issued him with a small cardboard box that had the name of a leading brand of dog food printed on the side. My uncle had just been fired because of 'cutbacks'. I watched him take the cowboy book out of his pocket and stare at it briefly before dumping it in a bin near the elevator. Then he went up to collect his things.

The paperback which I held in my hands at the Barras market in Glasgow affected me in the same way that cowboy books affected my uncle – they suddenly opened up a whole new set of possibilities.

There was no getting around the fact that Butch and Sundance were outlaws, however, and not the type of people I'd ever come into contact with. I mentally scanned my background for any known criminal reference points. I think at least one much older guy I'd known from the village, a Teddy Boy and big Conway Twitty fan who used to sell cut-price stolen school-dinner tickets, had ended up in prison for resetting lawnmowers one summer. I heard years later that he'd eventually hung himself. Then there was another local guy, a would-be pervert who stole ladies' underwear – but he was more of a sad, basket-case as opposed to a real outlaw. Someone told me that his father, a local politician, used to electrocute budgies for a laugh.

I myself once stopped a criminal act from taking place when I stepped in to dissuade my father and one of his brothers out of digging up a freshly buried uncle. They wanted to rob his grave after they heard he'd been accidentally buried wearing a jacket which had several thousand pounds of his life-savings zipped into it by mistake. This dead relative was the only person I ever knew who really did take it with him.

Personally I hadn't really done anything illegal in my young life, at least not knowingly, and I'd certainly never electrocuted any poor old budgies. I didn't think rubbing the metal Communion plate on my altar-boy vestments until it gave off electric shocks at the throats of pious-looking Mass-goers really counted. I did once witness some friends letting the air out of the tyres of a funeral hearse just before the body was loaded into the back. This was revenge for the dead man always keeping our footballs when they were kicked into his garden. He'd died a few days earlier when he was out cutting the grass on his beloved lawn. One minute he was walking up and down pushing an expensive electric lawnmower and the next he was dead. He lay in the garden for hours without anyone raising the alarm. Everyone thought he was sunbathing.

Disappointingly, as far as I could ascertain, crime didn't run in the family either. So in my young mind I felt that contact with real outlaws was clearly limited. I was slightly annoyed about this for a while. I began having vivid dreams about meeting real outlaws who would show me how to ride a horse and rob a bank. In my dreams I always handed over the proceeds from the robbery to my parents and kept some to put in the church collection on Sundays. You see, I was a very holy would-be outlaw. When I awoke from these fantasies I'd silently dress in the cold dampness of the morning and go to church to serve Mass. The parish priest used to spit on a comb, then attack the knots in my hair, before shoving me out on to the altar in front of three or four bleary-eyed old ladies who were first-service regulars. The altar-boys called them 'coffin dodgers'.

My little cowboy book, however, suggested that both Butch Cassidy and the Sundance Kid did have normal, decent up-bringings. This was tantalising information. The author didn't go into much detail but even the suggestion that outlaws had families sounded interesting. I could hardly believe it. Imagine the scene: a respectable American woman from last century is walking down the street when suddenly she's approached by a nosy neighbour who asks: 'Oh, hello. Tell me, what is your brother – the one that left home a few years ago – doing with himself now?'

The first woman blushes and answers: 'Oh, actually, he's robbing trains and holding up banks. You'll have read about that stick-up in Cheyenne a few weeks ago? Well, that was my brother. He's doing very well for himself!'

I digested the news with amazement. It was good stuff but there wasn't nearly enough of it. I wanted more. I devoured the little cheap map that gave a general idea of where some of the famous robberies had taken place. It even mentioned some of the towns where the outlaws had actually lived and the places they'd used as hideouts.

To some people this old map might have been nothing more

than some lines printed on cheap paper in a battered book found in a second-hand market. It would be at best only glance-worthy. But to me back then it was priceless. I regarded it as a venerable document, a treasure-map. It was the last thing I looked at every night. I would read and re-read the pages by torchlight under the blankets until I knew them by heart. Then, when my eyes were tired from looking at the small print, I'd shove it under the pillow until the morning.

Then I'd read it all over again over breakfast.

2. Going a Bit Funny in the Head

Two decades later I was clearing books out of my life by the boxful. Too many words, too many ideas. I gave hundreds away to my local library. I shipped them round the block by taxi and even gave the cab driver some when he spotted a couple he took a fancy to. He was very grateful and helped me carry some of the boxes in through the library doors. Before he drove off he said, 'Do you want this one?' He pointed to an old paperback lying on top of one of the piles. 'If you don't, I'll take it.' He sounded hopeful.

'What is it?' I didn't know which one he was referring to.

'Something about Butch Cassidy and his Wild Bunch. I like a cowboy book – so if you want, I'll take it off your hands.' He was grinning.

I hesitated for a moment, was suddenly aware of the smell of hot fried donuts, and then decided to keep it. I gave the driver a big book full of maps instead. He seemed happy enough and drove off smiling.

That night I read the old cowboy book for the first time in

years. I read it from cover to cover, looking once again at all the familiar words, chapters and maps. Even twenty years on the stories were still fresh in my mind.

After I'd read it I sat, as I did when I was young, staring out of the window and thinking about cowboys. But my thoughts were interrupted by screams echoing up from the street outside as a man and woman fought with each other on their way home after a night on the town. Their shouts filtered up from the black, rain-washed streets. A few cars drove by under the orange streetlamps. No one paid any attention to them.

Three or four minutes after they'd gone I saw two men stagger into view. They were both very drunk. One was wearing a dress and crying. He had a very thick moustache. The other grabbed on to a lamppost and refused to let go. He looked the younger of the two and was very skinny. It was a freezing cold night and I could have sworn I saw him shivering. While he swung on the post his friend went into the doorway of a department store and hoisted up his dress to urinate. When he finished he turned around, still crying, and proclaimed his love for his very drunk friend who'd collapsed in a heap at the bottom of the lamppost. They eventually clambered into a taxi on their fourth attempt. The driver refused to help either of them in the door. After they'd gone I noticed one had dropped a small silver handbag on the pavement. It sparkled in the darkness as the rain washed over it. It looked like a dead fish with shiny scales lying on the wet ground.

I sat on the edge of the bed for hours holding the book. Then I read it over and over again until my eyes grew too tired.

❊

After that night I began carrying the little outlaw paperback in my pocket everywhere I went. I don't know why really – it was a bit of a childish thing to do, I suppose. But I did it anyway. In between meetings at work I'd snatch a glance at it and at lunchtime I'd read certain parts over again. I wondered about maybe using it as a sort of route-map, a starting point, for a journey of sorts that would see me travelling to America and the West to find out more about outlaws. I'd go on the trail of Butch Cassidy and the Sundance Kid. Then I'd . . . Well, I didn't know what I'd do next. That was as far as my thinking went. I kept hoping something would nudge the project forward, perhaps encourage me to make more definite plans. Instead, I just stopped thinking about it. I left the matter hanging in the air for a while and got on with other things.

But I still carried the little book with me wherever I went. And I kept finding myself staring out of the window at work thinking about what I'd read in it. Occasionally I'd stop and think how patently stupid I was – had nothing changed since that first day at school? I decided I was pathetic and needed to grow up.

A few weeks later I was driving in the countryside. As the car sped along I noticed a solitary figure ahead. He was walking along at the side of the road all by himself. His stride was purposeful, he looked neither left nor right, and his eyes were fixed on some point far off on the distant horizon.

Bizarrely, this lone figure was dressed from head to toe as a cowboy. I thought for a moment that I was seeing things. He looked ludicrously out of place. It was a freezing cold Scottish afternoon, grey and overcast. The trees were bare and the grass in the fields blew this way and that in the strong wind. Here was I driving along a back road in the middle of this typically Scottish landscape, and the last thing I expected to come across was a cowboy. It was preposterous. And yet, there he was.

As I got closer I instinctively eased my foot off the accelerator, dropped my speed and took notice. The cowboy was dressed entirely in red. He wore red leather boots, a red felt stetson, a red silk shirt with fringes, red jeans and a red leather gunbelt. I slowed down almost to walking pace as I drove past him and saw clearly that in his holster there was a child's small plastic gun. It looked exactly like the sort of thing I had played with as a boy. At the exact moment I looked at him our eyes locked for an instant and I could see he had a thin, lined face and deep, intense eyes. Time seemed to stand still. Quite unexpectedly in that mere fraction of a second I found myself thinking of a story my father had once told me about a strange event he'd witnessed in a working-men's club in Scotland many years ago. It was a story I hadn't thought about in over a decade and a half. Apparently, a very successful stage hypnotist had put several people in a trance. One of them was a dour local undertaker who, under hypnosis, was told he was in fact a renowned and feared gun-fighter from the Old West called the Moonlight Kid. Moments later, my dad said, the normally sullen undertaker jumped around the stage, firing off imaginary shots at anything that moved. The audience hooted with laughter and applauded. Shortly afterwards the hypnotist, an ex-miner who'd learned his routine from an American College correspondence-course, counted to three and snapped his fingers. All the people on stage who'd been hypnotised came out of their trances at once and looked around in bewilderment, unable to understand why everyone was clapping and laughing. The dour undertaker especially looked baffled and dazed, said Dad.

The next time the hypnotist was booked to appear at the club he was surprised to find the undertaker waiting for him in his dressing-room. The hypnotist listened sympathetically as the man explained that he'd been having flashbacks for weeks and weeks of the night he was told he was a gunfighter from the Old West. Suddenly having the urge to pull out an imaginary six-gun and shoot mourners halfway through one of his funerals was no joke, he said. He'd enjoyed being a cowboy for a time but enough was enough. His life was in ruins; he couldn't even sleep. He asked the performer for help; in fact, he *begged* him for help. And so the hypnotist put him in a trance again and then counted to three and told him to wake up. When the under-taker opened his eyes the hypnotist asked him how he felt.

'I feel unbeatable, fantastic, like a tiger,' smiled the perplexed undertaker. 'Thanks!'

'That's great! You feel unbeatable . . . excellent!' said the other man with relief.

'Yeah . . . unbeatable!' repeated the undertaker grinning. The two men shook hands and the undertaker got up to leave the room. He paused in the doorway for a moment or two, the smile fading from his face. Then he turned to face the hypnotist: 'Unbeatable – 'cause I'm the Moonlight Kid . . .'

He disappeared out the door and into the night.

Two days later the undertaker closed his business, sold it off and bought himself a cowboy outfit from a costume shop near Glasgow Cross. Then he vanished into thin air, never to be seen in the area again.

My dad told me that the hypnotist quit putting people into trances for a living and returned to his old job. Working in the cold, claustrophobic darkness of the Scottish coalmines, the former hypnotist spent the rest of his life in fear of the Moonlight Kid who, he was convinced, would one day return to take his revenge.

❈

I drove slowly past the man in red. He blinked, averted his eyes and stared ahead again. I also looked away, put my foot on the accelerator and kept going. But as I watched this cowboy in my rear-view mirror, I began to wonder. Perhaps, I thought to myself, I should go back and ask him some questions: Why was he dressed like a cowboy? Had he ever heard of the Moonlight Kid? What were his favourite cowboy films? Then I thought better of it. Why he chose to dress like or what he did with his life was none of my business. After all, one man's dream can often be another man's nightmare.

But I did think about that man in the weeks that followed. The image of him walking along that road, kitted out like an extra from a Hollywood western never left me. It stuck in my mind and again I found myself staring out of the office window instead of working.

I decided one morning, without any fanfare, that it was time I grew up. Time to take responsibility. Time to sort out this cowboy nonsense once and for all.

So I left my job and rented a copy of *Butch Cassidy and the Sundance Kid* on video.

The following day I called the removal people.

❁

I bought the cheapest airline ticket to the States that I could lay my hands on – to New York via Iceland – and began doing research into the history of the American West. All the book-reading and phone-calls were crutches to reassure me that I had half an idea about what I was getting into. As always, research tends to raise more questions than it answers. But at least I'd refined my questions down a bit. I wanted to know things about outlaws in general and Butch Cassidy and the Sundance Kid in particular: What had their real names been? Had they any wives or families? How accurate had the Hollywood film been? Were they more cold-blooded and vicious than their respective screen characters? And, perhaps most intriguingly of all, how had they died? Did they really go down in a hail of bullets in Bolivia as the movie had suggested?

I also wanted to know more about the American West itself. TV programmes, movies and books had papered the walls of my mind with clichéd images – saloons, gunfights, hangings, out-laws – how precise were these? Was there a grain of truth in any of them? I was curious about the locations, the famous towns whose names I read in my little paperback book, in countless movies and in black and white TV shows – were they still there?

Only by getting on a plane and going to America could I hope to find answers to some of these questions. There was a fair chance of course that many would remain unanswered but I decided that didn't matter. What was important was that I at least try. Hopefully I'd lay a few old ghosts to rest in the process and, if I was lucky, I'd resurrect a few new ones.

❀

When I told my colleagues and friends about my plans to go to America they listened patiently and smiled understandingly. They couldn't understand why I was restless.

One colleague, constantly on the verge of divorce, who was the same age as me and from a similar background, said bluntly: 'You're mad. At our age we should be settling down and raising kids. Your feet should be on *terra firma*.'

He was the only person I knew who used the phrase *terra firma*. He used others like that too. I sometimes thought he manipulated conversations so he could hear himself say these things. But I couldn't be certain.

'Don't you think that by leaving your job you'll miss that feeling of always having money on hand in the cash machine? You have a little *pied-à-terre* just now so why throw all that away to go off and chase cowboys in canyons? You must ask yourself that.' He sounded very sincere and serious.

Then he added, with great gravitas, that his wife had grave concerns about me too. (I didn't know his wife very well but I had once overheard her holding a polite conversation with another female guest at a dinner party about how the gussets in ladies' underwear weren't made to the same high standards they used to be.) He told me that his wife knew I was doomed when she spied me wearing a cowboy hat in the city the day before. 'He's not very refined at the best of times,' was the way she put it after seeing me with the hat, 'but that hat business was the first sign he was going a bit funny in the head.'

3. Mr Onion's Arrival

'What's your name, honey?' The large black customs officer didn't even look at me.

I had arrived in America.

The customs officer had the largest breasts I had ever seen in my life but my eyes were drawn to a huge revolver at her waist. She sensed I was apprehensive – I think that was why she called me 'honey'.

'My name is Eamonn O'Neill.' I spoke very clearly so she understood my accent.

She nodded politely and shouted across to another official: 'His name is Ian Onion.'

I hung my head in despair. I'd been on the road for over fourteen hours.

I'd flown in to America via Iceland and our plane had just managed to land for a quick refuel at Reykjavik because a volcano had been erupting. Everything looked steamed up and muddy when we'd flown over it.

Some of my fellow passengers weren't too pleased with

mother nature's display. 'They might have stopped that thing erupting until after the *American* plane had taken off,' said an American woman with candy-floss hair and a mouth that turned down at the corners. She was seated two rows in front of me and had complained several times during the flight about it being all non-smoking. Her husband agreed enthusiastically with this and every other complaint she made.

I noticed he was always wearing earphones when he nodded.

❀

Seven hours after seeing the volcano I was seated with about forty other people in a small glass-fronted room at JFK airport in New York. A long wood-panelled desk-cum-bench affair was in front of me. Behind it was a steady stream of officials, all coming and going, absorbed in somebody's passport or paper-work. I approached the bench and handed my papers, my passport and my X-rays to a man wearing a brown nylon suit with very wide lapels. He had long hair and looked faintly Middle-Eastern.

The X-rays had caused much worry and confusion. The Embassy in London insisted I have them taken during my medical and I had to agree to carry them with me into the USA. So I lugged a huge envelope with me on the journey, which contained X-rays of my chest.

'What do *I* want with *your* X-rays?' The guy behind the desk looked as if he'd had a long day. He chewed gum and shrugged a lot.

'You tell me,' I smiled, trying to look pleasant.

'Are you bein' smart, huh?' He turned sour and leaned over the desk until his face was inches away from mine. 'Take a goddamn seat and wait till your name is called!'

I sat down in the front row next to a guy with blond hair. We were the only two white faces in the room. Behind us there was chaos. A woman wearing a turban sat whimpering softly to herself. She kept wrapping and unwrapping a bandage around her lower left leg. I caught a glimpse of a terribly infected open sore – I could smell it too. Every so often she'd look up imploringly and raise her hands as if in prayer. No one paid even the slightest attention to her.

'Hey, you!'

I looked up. The guy in the nylon suit was pointing in my direction.

'Me?'

'No, him! Yeah, you.' He flicked his finger at the blond man next to me. The guy stood up slowly and approached the bench with great apprehension.

'Mister, you are going to prison, you understand me. I can do that. Yeah, me, yeah, I can have you arrested because your goddamn paperwork ain't in order. Are you listening to me, mister?'

The blond guy stared back at him. His lip visibly quivered.

'Take a goddamn seat. You people disgust me . . .' The nylon suit walked off carrying lots of passports.

The blond guy stood for a moment regaining his composure, then slowly sat down beside me again. I asked him what had happened.

'I forgot my Green Card. They hate that more than anything. It makes it look like you aren't grateful for the chance to live and work in America.'

I nodded and he shrugged. Then he leaned over and took a paperback from his bag. He leafed through the pages, thought better of being seen relaxed enough to read, and replaced it in his bag. He stared into space. 'Maybe he doesn't like my type.' He made a slight gesture in the direction of the man behind the desk who was still pacing back and forwards with handfuls of passports.

'What's your type?' I asked.

'German.' He sounded depressed.

'Yeah, I'll arrest you too – vanish, disappear, don't be here anymore! You understand that much? . . . '

The nylon-suited guy was bellowing at an old Greek couple who looked like my mother and father with suntans. They backtracked slowly, clearly scared of this man who kept staring at them while he took another pile of passports behind a makeshift screen at the far end of the room.

Every so often a name would be called and a person would eagerly go behind the screen followed by the man in the nylon suit. There would be some shouting until finally the person came back out looking scared and lost.

I watched all this for an hour. The place filled up until the pace of events got more and more frantic and the atmosphere became increasingly heated. We all smelled of stale sweat and old soup. Travel smells. Many who arrived had no luggage, no money, couldn't speak English, claimed to have no friends who were meeting them and didn't have a return ticket back to where they came from. Some had literally just got on a plane to America hoping for the best.

One very black man with a wonderful smile who was wearing an old purple velvet jacket hung rakishly over one shoulder, was speaking in heavily accented English to the man in the nylon suit. 'But sir, I have read *The Great Gatsby* many, many times. I know America extremely well! I feel at home, so to speak.'

Still smiling and repeating the sentence like a prayer he was waved away by the incredulous official. He waved at me and smiled broadly like an old acquaintance when he saw me watching him from the front row.

'O'Neill!' My name was bawled out by the guy in the nylon suit. He looked angry. I turned around. 'Yeah, you! Need a special invitation? Move it right here, c'mon!'

He gestured for me to go behind the screen. As I gathered my bits and pieces I noticed he was silently pointing at the German who was pretending not to notice him.

I went behind the screen and was met by a short, worried-looking man wearing a uniform and holding my passport. 'Irish?' I nodded. Then added: 'By way of Scotland.'

The guy in the nylon suit looked me up and down then glanced at the passport. The official looked over my paperwork and then stared at me again. I noticed he had lots of freckles.

'We need to take your fingerprints.' He snapped the passport shut and handed me back my papers. He rubbed my fingers on an ink pad while the loud guy watched. The freckle-faced official scratched his nose and then slowly stamped my papers and passport. 'I went to Jesuit school in Ireland,' he said looking at me blankly. His face suddenly broke into a smile. 'Welcome to America, Mr O'Neill.' He held out his hand and I found myself shaking it.

'Yeah – have a good one, won't yah?' Mr Nylon-Suit smiled and shook my hand warmly.

As I walked out from behind the screen I heard the loud official behind me saying to the freckle-faced guy: 'No, the German, he ain't goin' anywhere, put his papers over there . . .'

I approached the blond guy and collected my remaining bag. He smiled at me. 'Good luck.' He stared at me blankly for a moment, then smiled.

I heard the familiar voice of the nylon-suited inspector hissing from behind the desk. He was pointing at the German. 'Long night mister, real long, take it easy.' My friend shifted in his seat and lowered his eyes. He looked like he was about to cry.

As I left the glass-fronted office I passed the black man in the purple velvet jacket who was talking to the large-breasted security guard at the door. 'Yes, I've read that book too,' she said politely as he waved a strangely colourful edition of *The Great Gatsby* under her nose. 'Now please take a seat.'

'Thank you, I feel already at home, so to speak!' He retreated smiling and waving at everybody. I smiled and waved back at him and he responded by nudging an Indian who'd nodded off next to him before blowing me a very enthusiastic kiss. I grinned and kept on going, sure I would be called back and deported at any moment.

I was still clutching my chest X-rays like a child.

4. A Very Dysfunctional Family

After a few weeks of research in the USA – many long-distance phone-calls, red eyes from reading old books, endless tacky videos, several worthy documentaries, too many wrong numbers, numerous false leads and memorable long chats with various small-town museum curators – I finally picked up the trail of Butch and Sundance. The latter, I discovered, made his criminal début about a hundred and ten years prior to my arrival in his homeland.

On the morning of 7 June 1887, the *Daily Yellowstone Journal* offered its readers the following front-page headlines:

HE PLAYED 'POSSUM'
HOW DEPUTY SHERIFF E.K. DAVIS
FOOLED A FLY YOUNG CRIMINAL
HE HAD IN CHARGE

THE ASTONISHING RECORD OF CRIME
PERPETRATED BY HARRY LONGABAUGH
IN THREE WEEKS

A FLY KID
AND THE WAY HE WAS CAUGHT UP BY OFFICERS
DAVIS AND SMITH

The 'Fly Kid' mentioned in the article was known in those days as Harry Longabaugh. When he was arrested for horse-stealing near Sundance, Wyoming, the twenty-one-year-old Longabaugh was going under the alias 'Kid Chicago' – later he'd be known throughout the United States and the world as the 'Sundance Kid'. This headline was the first time the American press-reading public had heard of him. It wouldn't be the last.

From my digging I knew the Sundance Kid's present-day relatives lived somewhere on the east coast of America so I thought it would be wise to speak to them before I headed out West. After some foraging in the phone book I eventually managed to locate Donna Ernst and her husband Paul, the latter being a great-great-nephew of Sundance. They lived in a little town called Souderton in Pennsylvania and said they'd be happy to meet me.

Souderton is in the part of Pennsylvania that was heavily populated by Dutch and German settlers. And that's where Harry Longabaugh traced his roots to – Germany. His forebears came over to America, one as an indentured servant, on Christmas Eve 1772, and they settled in Pennsylvania.

Photographs of Harry's parents show hearty German peasants. His mother, Annie Place Longabaugh, was plump and plain-looking, while his father, Josiah, with a moustache-less beard and thinning hair that hung over his ears, looked severe and tired. Even in an old tintype photo Josiah's hands looked as if they'd always carried out rough work. The Longabaughs weren't rich people but, like good peasants, they produced a large family – five children in all. There was Elwood, Samanna, Emma, Harvey and, finally, Harry. The last-named was born in the spring of 1867 somewhere in Pennsylvania. According to Donna Ernst, who's done most of the research into the Longabaugh family, it's anybody's guess exactly where and when he was born. Records weren't a big priority back then.

As I drove down to Souderton from upstate New York where I was living, I passed many, many churches. I was in big-time Christian country. One sign, just outside the town simply said in huge letters: 'Thou Shalt Not Kill'. Across the road from the sign I watched as a dozen or so little Mennonite children, all wearing aprons and headscarves, ran around playing in the early winter sunshine. They looked like the kids from *The Sound of Music.*

The Amish people who'd brought to America from Germany their hard-line and more austere version of Christianity also lived in the area. The Amish devoutly eschew any modern conveniences and still use horse-drawn carriages to get around in. Motor cars are outlawed. In recent months, however, they'd decided it was okay to use a new form of transport – they'd been spotted whizzing down lonely lanes and ancient roads wearing heavy wool clothes, straw hats and hi-tech rollerblades.

✸

'Grandpop in his last few years alive used to mutter something about having "two uncles who were like Jesse James who'd died in South America" but he wasn't keen to talk much about them,' said Donna Ernst to me as we sat in her living-room in Souderton.

'So you never knew your husband was related to Harry Longabaugh until relatively recently?' I asked.

'That's right!' said Donna excitedly. 'We'd even been out West a couple of times to areas we later found out that the Sundance Kid had been to, yet at the time we were there we didn't know anything about him.'

Donna looked like everybody's favourite aunt. With her permed hair and sparkling eyes, she looked just like a million other happy middle-aged women all over America. She was friendly and modest about her achievements in digging up her husband's famous ancestor.

'But in 1976 someone saw a magazine article written by Robert Redford which mentioned the name of the Sundance Kid as being "Longabaugh". And because that's such an unusual name, that was where our trail began,' said Donna.

'What was the family's reaction to finding this out?' I enquired.

'Mixed – indeed mortified might be more accurate,' she said flatly. 'This is a good Christian family. Outlaws, famous or otherwise, weren't good news. In fact, Sundance's immediate family even partially disowned him – one of his sisters even changed the spelling of her name so that people wouldn't associate her successful business with a well-known outlaw.'

That sister was Emma T. Longabaugh born in 1863, who'd died unwed on 23 January 1933. By that time the family hadn't heard from the Sundance Kid for many years. In a family photograph Emma looked fat, matronly and glum. She'd disinherited her brother in her will by adding the following stinging paragraph:

> Note: On account of my not knowing whether or not my brother Harry Longabaugh is living, and to avoid any difficulty in settling my estate, I made no bequest to him. This note is merely explanatory, and whether my said brother Harry be living or dead is not to change or affect this will.

We were joined by Donna's husband Paul, a tall, very quiet man, who watched much and said little. Apparently his famous relative had been much the same. In her later years Butch

Cassidy's sister pieced together reports which formed the basis of her description of Sundance as being of a 'rather ugly disposition and was morose and moody, while Butch got along with everyone . . . Sundance drank a great deal, and his tongue was often in a slick place'.

Another outlaw writer, however, wrote that 'in disposition he was similar to Cassidy – pleasant, friendly, and cool in any emergency'.

'They say I walk like Harry,' said Paul when I asked if there was any family resemblance. 'They called him "The Straddler" because he walked with bow-legs.'

Paul demonstrated the walk as we drank coffee and watched. I thought his legs looked fine but maybe it was the low lighting in the kitchen. We all headed downstairs to the office from which Paul and Donna ran some of their small businesses, including a real-estate business called 'Sundance Properties' and a local laundry operation. An old sign hung on the wall advertising the Longabaugh Carpentry business. It had once belonged to Sundance's brother.

'Like the poster?' said Donna unfolding an advertisement for beer which showed the Sundance Kid and Butch Cassidy wearing fancy hats and suits. 'Our daughter found it when she was travelling out west – the barman gave her one.'

She dutifully rolled up a copy of the poster and gave it to me as a gift. We chatted for a while. Donna told me as much as she could about Sundance's background, explaining that as a child he'd even been hired out to another family as a servant and how, as he grew older, he'd became restless, wanting to travel and see more of the US.

I would have stayed longer but it was late and I could tell the Ernsts were tired talking about Sundance. We said our goodbyes on their doorstep. Just as I was about to leave Donna added, like an enthusiastic guest psychologist on a daytime chat-show: 'There's one thing to bear in mind.'

'What's that?' I asked.

'I think that Sundance's family were very dysfunctional.'

❀

I drove through the night to a nearby motel where I hoped to stay. The surly Pakistani manager wearing a bright Mickey Mouse tie stood behind the counter checking everybody in. Two female truck-drivers stood in front of me. Both wore dirty padded trucker's shirts and had worn oily leather gloves hanging out of the back pockets of their jeans. The taller of the two, a very masculine although extremely attractive woman with blonde hair, turned to me abruptly and said: 'Take one of the bigger rooms. For five bucks more you'll get a large hot-tub.' She nudged her friend who was chewing tobacco in the side of her mouth. 'We had a great time in ours the last time we were here, didn't we?' said the attractive blonde suggestively in husky tones.

The friend looked me up and down, said neither yes nor no, then looked away.

I took my key and trudged off to a cheap room that didn't have a large hot-tub thinking about a friend who'd remarked that Butch Cassidy and the Sundance Kid sounded like 'the name of a lesbian rockabilly band'.

Later that night in my cramped room I watched a TV programme about the Actors Studio in New York. Paul Newman, the guest speaker, talked about all his movies and experiences in making them. The audience listened in reverential silence but when the interviewer mentioned *Butch Cassidy and the Sundance Kid* they spontaneously burst into a long round of applause.

'Brando was supposed to play Butch – did you know that?' said Newman. 'Even when I turned up I wasn't exactly sure which character I was going to play. Jesus, when I think back on that movie,' said the actor scratching his head, 'I can no longer separate fact from fiction.'

❀

I left early the next morning, keeping an eye out on the misty back roads of Pennsylvania for high-speed rollerskating Amish people, and followed the leafy, winding roads through the countryside towards a place on my map called Phoenixville. Donna and Paul Ernst had suggested I go there to view the graves of Sundance's parents and sister and to see where the outlaw had once lived.

After about an hour I eventually found Phoenixville: it was a curious little town. Small and neat and perched on the banks of a river, it felt very European, very insular. I stopped a road-sweeper who gave me directions to the local cemetery where Sundance's family were buried.

The fat woman behind the desk at Morris Cemetery wasn't in a hurry. I tried to look very sad but that didn't seem to concern her either. Finally, she focused her attention on me and I asked for help in locating the Longabaugh graves. She turned to a large wooden board and, with a long, painted fingernail, pointed out the family plot to me. As I was about to leave she said: 'Where are you from?'

'Scotland,' I answered.

'My father goes there all the time, he's in the business . . . ' she said, twirling her hair with her fingers and waving the other hand in the direction of the cemetery.

I imagined a man selling state-of-the-art coffin-handles from a large suitcase. 'That's nice,' I replied. 'Which part of Scotland does he go to?'

'Dublin,' she replied. 'He says it's great.'

❀

The last of the afternoon sunlight bounced off the marble gravestone which bore the names of Harry Longabaugh's parents and sister. I squinted and shaded my eyes to make out the dates. It was a cold day and my fingers nipped. The headstones were small, respectable and compact. To the right was the grave of Harry's sister Emma. At the turn of the century Sundance had donned a suit and fancy hat to come home to Phoenixville to visit his parents' graves in Morris Cemetery. Small farms dotted the green hills that lay behind the graveyard. The streets were narrow and neat. Old-world customs and courtesies still prevailed. It was a world away from an outlaw's life.

I left the cemetery and walked off down one of the backstreets looking for the house where the young Harry Longabaugh had lived as a boy. It started to snow lightly, then more heavily.

Eventually I found it. It was nothing remarkable – just a two-storey house on a street. There was no plaque, no marker to tell you that a famous outlaw had once lived there.

As I looked at the modest building for a minute or two, a mother walked by with two children. The little girl held a large blue balloon in her hand. Her elder brother trotted alongside his mother wearing a padded ski-parka and jeans. Earphones were jammed over his ears. On top of his head was a cowboy hat made of black felt with red fringes around the ends. I noticed he had a little sheriff's badge pinned on to the bright jacket.

When I was four years old my mother and father bought me a cowboy outfit for Christmas. I have no memory of wearing it on Christmas morning but one of my sisters told me years later that I could hardly speak that day because I had the mumps. My throat was so swollen I could barely even swallow. She said I looked like the 'world's saddest cowboy'. The only time I smiled that day was when I trotted off, chaps, guns and hat and all, to look at the snow which was starting to fall. I didn't know what it was called apparently, so I pointed to it falling and croaked in a faint voice: 'Look! It's the black and the white!'

That's what was falling to the ground and on to this little boy's black cowboy hat as I stood outside the house where the Sundance Kid once lived as a child. The black and the white.

As I padded down another street I saw a couple of old shops that had gothic lettering in the window. I stopped, snowflakes swirling around me, and peered into one of them. It was an ancient old bespoke tailor's shop with a torso-dummy in the window which displayed a half-made suit. 'All Customers Very Welcome', said a sign. I noticed a pin had fallen out of the suit which was on display. It lay shining on the floor near the window. A spider had built a web using it as a starting point.

Across the street and further down was an old barber shop, again it had gothic lettering in the window. Inside a bored-looking bald man was reading the *National Inquirer*. The newspaper's headline screamed: '*Jesus is Back! He's Been Spotted in Several Parts of the USA! We Reveal What He's Wearing!*' When he saw me looking in the window, the man smiled and waved, then went straight back to reading his newspaper.

❋

As I slowly paced the deserted, wintry streets of Phoenixville I realised that Harry had probably played Cowboys and Indians just like me. I had watched old movies about my heroes and their dubious activities, while he had read dime-store novels and highly colourful press reports in Phoenixville a century earlier about his.

I could imagine why the young Harry Longabaugh would want to leave a place like this. It was small-town USA. It was heavily Christian, probably very moralistic and, at a time when the West was opening up, very stuffy. Joining the Young Men's Literary Union Library for a dollar as Harry did in 1882 wasn't the most exciting thing in the world, I suppose. Not when you could read cheap, colourful novels about gunfighters. The most popular of these when Harry was growing up would have been the infamous Jesse James. When the Sundance Kid had been a young boy in the 1870s the exploits of Jesse James were shocking American sensibilities.

Not only did Jesse, together with his Shakespeare-loving brother Frank and the Younger brothers, rob banks left, right and centre, he even robbed fairgrounds, delighting in telling his victims that they were being robbed by the 'famous' Jesse James. On 26 September 1872, for example, Jesse, brother Frank and Cole Younger rode up to a cashier at a fairground near Kansas: 'What if I was to say that I was Jesse James and I told you to hand over that tin box of money? What would you say?' enquired Jesse.

'I'd say I'd see you in hell first,' answered the cashier.

'Well, that's just who I am and you'd better hand it out pretty damned quick or –' replied Jesse, grinning and shoving a gun under the hapless cashier's nose.

The gang rode off into the night with $978 to show for their trouble. Jesse, the supposed hero of the time, managed to pull out his gun and accidentally shoot a female bystander in the leg as he escaped.

On 31 January 1874 Jesse had better financial luck when he and his gang robbed a train called the Little Rock Express near Gadshill, Missouri. They removed about $22,000 from the train's safe and proceeded to walk through the passenger coaches stealing money and valuables from the startled occupants. Just as the outlaws were about to leave the scene, Jesse tossed a stick with a note tied to it to one of the guards with the shout, 'Give this to the newspapers!' The note read:

THE MOST DARING TRAIN ROBBERY ON
RECORD!

The southbound train of the Iron Mountain Railroad was stopped here this evening by five heavily armed men and robbed of _____ dollars. The robbers arrived at the station a few minutes before the arrival of the rain and arrested the agent and put him under guard and then threw the train on the switch. The robbers were all large men, all being slightly under six feet. After robbing the train they started in a southerly direction. They were all mounted on handsome horses.

PS: They are a hell of an excitement in this part of the country.

Jesse was doing his own public relations. He'd even left a blank space for the railroad to fill in the exact amount he'd stolen from them. No wonder the papers thought he had charisma.

Without a doubt, Harry Longabaugh would have known all about Jesse James and his ilk before he ever set foot in the West himself. He might even have had a thought somewhere at the back of his mind that he would one day fill the shoes of the legendary outlaw who was killed in 1882, the same year Harry left Phoenixville for the West. James, the son of a Baptist preacher, lay beneath a gravestone which read:

Jesse W. James
Died April 3, 1882
Aged 34 years, 6 months, 28 days
Murdered by a traitor and a coward
Whose name is not worthy to
appear here.

Bob Ford was the man whose name was 'not worthy' to appear on Jesse James's gravestone. Both Bob and his brother Charlie had been sometime criminal associates of Jesse and his ragged, dwindling gang. Ford shot Jesse in the back when the outlaw was fiddling with a picture on the wall of his house, collected the reward money for his trouble and went on to tour with a Wild West stage show in which he re-enacted his famous murder every night for paying audiences. The large crowds he played for booed when he pulled the trigger at the fatal moment of his act. Bob had nightmares and drank heavily, wandering the West until he was finally gunned down himself after an argument in a cheap saloon he'd bought in Colorado. A photograph taken after he'd killed Jesse James shows Ford as a handsome young man with side-parted swept-back dark hair. He is sitting holding a large gun, said to be the very weapon which he'd killed Jesse with. His face looks relatively lean and open with no hint of the alcoholic puffiness or the clouds of tormented doubt that witnesses say marked his features in later life.

Bob Ford's brother Charlie also came to no good. Plagued by even worse nightmares than his brother, he developed acute long-term insomnia. Night after night he sat up in bed unable to close his eyes without imagining the putrid body of Jesse James rising out of a shallow pebble-covered grave to take revenge. Charlie tried to overcome this by drinking himself into a stupor every night. The stress eventually took its toll on his body and mind. No one close to him was surprised when he committed suicide.

The legend of Jesse James grew, rather than diminished in death. Every young boy in America read dime-store novels about the outlaw, some of which had the most unlikely of titles: *The New York Detective Library – Price Ten Cents: 'THE MAN ON THE BLACK HORSE or The James Boys' First Ride into Missouri!'*; *'Log Cabin Library – New Stories of Startling Adventure by the Best Authors: 'JESSE THE OUTLAW – A Narrative of the*

James Boys by Capt. Jake Shakelford, The Western Detective'.

For a time the US postmaster general refused to deliver these books which some blamed as being behind rising juvenile crime in many eastern US cities. (Ironically, Jesse himself had taken to ordering and collecting such books shortly before he died. He enjoyed reading about the fantastic exploits he was supposed to have been involved in and revelled in the fame his crimes brought.)

Jesse's devoted mother, Zerelda James Samual, who never did see any wrong in her boy, began holding tours of her wayward son's burial place in the family home's backyard. For twenty-five cents, the outlaw's mother would regale gawkers with tales of her son's heroism; they also had to listen to her equally colourful condemnation of the Ford brothers, the 'vile cowards' who'd killed him. For an extra quarter she'd sell the eager tourists a pebble from her son's grave. Later in the evenings, when the visitors had gone, she'd quietly go down to a nearby stream, reach in to the cool, fast-flowing water and gather up new pebbles to replace those she'd sold earlier in the day.

❦

In the early 1880s the young Harry Longabaugh growing up in Phoenixville must have been influenced by the growing cult of Jesse James. Almost every schoolboy in America during that period had heard of his exploits and his dramatic death. James had fulfilled all the prerequisites to become a fully fledged mythical hero to the impressionable youth of America – he was a bad boy who'd lived fast and high, dying young in mysterious and tragic circumstances. A lot of people quickly wrote some very bad songs about him. One example, popular in the eastern states in 1882, the summer young Harry Longabaugh left Phoenixville, went:

Jesse James was a lad who killed many a man,
He robbed the Glendale train.
He stole from the rich and gave to the poor,
He'd a heart a hand and a brain.
It was Robert Ford, that dirty little coward,
I wonder how does he feel,
For he ate of Jesse's bread and he slept in Jesse's bed,
Then he laid Jesse James in his grave.

The people held their breath,
When they heard of Jesse's death
And wondered how he ever came to die.
It was one of the gang called Robert Ford,
Who shot Jesse on the fly.

The youthful Harry Longabaugh, aged only fifteen, no doubt grabbed at the chance to travel west with a relative in the late summer of 1882. It was a chance to see the place everyone was writing and talking about. It was a chance to see the places where the likes of Jesse James had once lived. It was a chance to grow up out of sight of his strict family. It was a chance to march to the beat of his own drum.

If he'd waited a few more months, however, he would have read that the handsome, educated Frank James, Jesse's equally infamous brother, had given himself up to the authorities. If the young Sundance Kid had heard what Frank had said when he surrendered then he might have put his dime-store novels aside during his trip west and turned instead to the more peaceful task of homesteading. In October 1882, just six months after Jesse was killed, Frank had walked into a sheriff's office looking pale and drawn, to deliver through clenched teeth what would become one of the most famous speeches a criminal ever made. It served as a rare insight into the stark and brutal world that real outlaws inhabited:

I have known no home, I have slept in all sorts of places –
here today – there tomorrow . . . I am tired of this life of
taut nerves, of night-riding and day-hiding, of constant
listening for footfalls, cracking twigs and rustling leaves
and creaking doors; tired of seeing Judas on the face of
every friend I know – and God knows I have none to
spare; tired of the saddle, the revolver and the cartridge
belt . . . I want to see if there is not some way out of it . . .

He then unbuckled his gunbelt and holster and handed his
weapon to the startled sheriff. His life as an outlaw was over;
he'd had enough.

A sympathetic jury didn't convict Frank when he stood trial. In
later life he became a shoe-salesman, the doorman of a brothel, a
race-starter at county fairs and a store detective. He tried very
hard to settle down. He read lots of Shakespeare and the essays of
Francis Bacon in the hope of gaining some perspective on his
troubled life.

Then something disturbing happened. As he grew old Frank
inevitably began following in his mother's footsteps by leading
tourists around his dead brother's grave for the price of an
admission ticket. On seeing the visitors' stunned faces when he
was introduced as the famous Jesse James's brother, Frank started
to realise that in death the same tacky fate might well await him.
He became obsessed by the prospect. People say he was a
changed man, withdrawn and secretive. He began to believe
that his corpse would become the object of fascination and that
his soul would never truly rest in peace.

Consequently, he left strict instructions in his will stating that
he was to be cremated and his ashes locked away from prying
eyes. In a bank vault.

❋

If he had designs on becoming an outlaw, these were the type of men Harry Longabaugh would one day have to emulate. And he did just that.

Within five years of leaving Phoenixville Harry's name and the infamous Jesse James were being mentioned in the same sentence. The *Daily Yellowstone Journal* may have called Harry Longabaugh 'a fly kid', but it also quoted someone drawing comparisons between him and the famous dead outlaw: 'Talk about the James boys, this fellow [Longabaugh] has all the necessary accomplishments to outshine them all . . .'

This prompted the young Harry, still languishing in a cold cell for swiping a horse near Sundance, to put pen to paper. Like all great outlaws, both past and present, he had a youthful weakness for self-publicity. He wrote to the editor of the *Yellowstone Journal*, which printed his letter on 9 June 1887:

> In your issue of the 7th inst. I read a very sensational and partly true article, which places me before the public not even second to the notorious Jesse James. Admitting that I have done wrong and expecting to be dealt with according to law and not by false reports from parties who should blush with shame to make them, I ask a little of your space to set my case before the public in a true light. In the first place I have always worked for an honest living; was employed last summer by one of the best outfits in Montana and don't think they can say aught against me, but having got discharged last winter I went to the Black Hills to seek employment – which I could not get – and was forced to work for my board a month and a half, rather than to beg or steal. I finally started back to the vicinity of Miles City, as it was spring, to get employment on the range and was arrested at the above named place and charged with having stolen a horse at Sundance, where I was being taken by Sheriff

Ryan, whom I escaped from by jumping from the cars, which I judged were running at the rate of 100 miles an hour.

After this my course of outlawry commenced, and I suffered terribly for the want of food in the hope of getting back south without being detected, where I would be looked upon as I always had been, and not as a criminal. Contrary to the statement in the Journal, I deny having stolen any horses in Canada and selling them near Benton, or anyplace else, up to the time I was captured, at which time I was riding a horse which I bought and paid for, nor had I the slightest idea of stealing any horses. I am aware that some of your readers will say that my statement should be taken for what it is worth, on account of the hard name which has been forced upon me, nevertheless it is true. As for my recapture by Deputy Sheriff Davis, all I can say is that he did his work well and were it not for his 'playing possum' I would now be on my way south, where I had hoped to go and live a better life.

Harry Longabaugh had left Phoenixville to travel west five years before he'd written this letter. He'd already toured some cities in the north-east in the summer of 1882 and had probably developed a taste for freedom. This, after all, was the era in which the *New York Tribune* editor Horace Greeley had written in his editorial: 'Go West, young man, and grow up with the country' – sentiments which, although Greeley hadn't set foot in the West when he wrote it, had encouraged tens of thousands of young men like Harry Longabaugh to leave home.

Donna Ernst's family records revealed an entry in Harry's sister Samanna's business books which stated: 'Phoenixville, August 30th, 1882. Harry A. Longabaugh left home for the West. Left home at 14 Church St, Phoenixville, below Gay Street.'

It's anyone's guess whether Harry had set out from Phoenixville in Pennsylvania that August day with the intent of becoming the outlaw that would later be known as the Sundance Kid. As I walked down the street towards the railway station, past a large mural painted on the side of a dilapidated building, I was retracing a journey that Sundance had taken many times.

He may well have been bursting with hope as he walked down to the railway station; he may well have been full of innocent joy, already making plans about what he'd do when he joined his cousin George who'd invited him along to join his young family start a new life in Colorado.

I tried to imagine what it must have been like leaving this little town full of immigrants still clinging to old traditions, with their strict moral codes and small-town gossip, their starched collars and predictable jobs and bleak futures for the un-educated, and I couldn't help thinking that young Harry, decently brought up as I'm sure he was, was probably thinking of other, more adventurous things.

Over a century later I stood on the same empty station plat-form where the young Sundance Kid had waited to leave Phoenixville to head West in 1882. It was a freezing day. The station was boarded up but I could still see how it had once been a beautiful building – all gingerbread woodwork and stained-glass windows. Against all the odds it had kept an air of dignified optimism and hope about it. Travelling on trains back then was still an exciting thing to do. Even just waving someone off was a bit of an adventure. As I poked around, looking in through windows, construction workers pounded the tracks with drills and hammers, sending clouds of smoke and dirt into the snowy air. The noise echoed around the trees. The heavy banging and rattle of progress brought small puffs of dust, as if in defiant protest, from the old wooden beams of the station roof. It wanted to be left alone; frozen in winter and in time.

I returned to the truck, turned on the heater and stared at Phoenixville railway station for a few minutes before driving off slowly and silently. The road out of town was completely deserted. The ground was already covered in a thick carpet of fresh snow. Winter was coming.

5. Go West-Pac, Young Man!

The snow kept falling for weeks. It swept in from the north-west of the United States, dipped down across the Great Plains, then whipped back up across the Great Lakes before being funnelled into the north east with a dry, unyielding ferocity the likes of which I'd never seen before.

The weather stopped me from driving across the country in my truck. In the time I had I knew I could never drive thousands of miles through an endless series of blizzards. I opted to fly to the West instead. Neither as scenic nor as interesting, but at least I got there in one piece.

I boarded a plane at Newark airport in New Jersey bound for Colorado Springs. I should have guessed what was in store for me when I saw that the outside of the plane had been painted to resemble a giant Bart Simpson cartoon. The airline staff on the Western Pacific ('Call us West-Pac!') flight were cheerful in the way that people on American TV tend to be cheerful. That is, they've had their brains removed and a permanent smile attached to their faces. They dressed in nondescript, stained and ill–fitting 'casual' clothes – no airline uniforms here – with polo-shirts instead of shirts and ties. Their conversation with the passengers was a sort of forced folksiness, usually starting off with an insincere, 'Hi! How ya' doin'?' said in a sing-songy sort of way that quickly got on your nerves. I tried to blank it out and read my newspaper.

I came across a column in the 'news digest' section headed: 'Colorado Springs: Squirrel Danger'. Three local squirrels had been caught and tested and found to be infected with the bubonic plague. This brought the total number of infected squirrels captured at our destination to ten in the last month alone.

I left my seat and queued up for the toilet. As I stood in line I mentioned the squirrel story to another passenger.

'Wow! No kidding, huh!' said Steve, a computer programmer from Aspen. He thought for a moment. 'Bubonic plague – that was like a medieval kind of Aids, wasn't it? Like, without the sex part, though,' he said. Then he added earnestly, 'Not that I've a problem with alternate lifestyles, you understand.'

As the plane landed, our stewardess DeDe screamed, 'Hey! Hey! Hey! Was that a great landing or what, huh? Let's hear it for the guys driving this thing!'

All around me people clapped and whistled.

❋

It had taken me about four hours in a plane to do a journey that the young Harry Longabaugh took many, many weeks to complete a century ago. He'd started his journey in comfort on a train from Phoenixville. Then, once he'd reached Illinois, he'd joined his cousin George Longabaugh and his family and from there they'd all travelled by covered wagon to Colorado.

The Longabaughs were very much part of a general trend. The whole demographic picture in the US was shifting westwards during this era. In the 1870s nearly two million people headed on to the plains and the prairies. Some had heard rumours that the railroad expansion had altered the weather and that rain was now more commonplace than before. Others simply believed that 'rain followed the plow'. Even Europe had heard about the opportunities opening up 'out west' – by 1875 more than half of Nebraska's 123,000 settlers were from households that had been established by incoming foreigners. One English settler wrote home to say that, 'good land dog-cheap everywhere and for nothing, if you will go far enough for it'. By 1890 the cities in the west were growing faster than any other region in the US, apart from possibly the north-east.

Harry, George and the family travelled from Illinois to Colorado by wagon. A general lack of means probably forced them to undertake the arduous journey in this very uncomfortable and time-consuming way. If they'd had enough money they could have travelled by train. In 1882, when the Longabaughs undertook their journey to Colorado, the Pacific and Atlantic coasts of the US had already been united by railroad tracks for over a decade. The ticket prices for such a journey, however, were still beyond the budget of most migrants.

A ceremony to mark the completion of that epic trans-continental railroad was held on 10 May 1869 at Promontory Summit, Utah. The men who'd financed the operation turned up in their fancy railroad cars, their two respective legions of workers – the Chinese from the Central Pacific and the Irish from the Union Pacific – facing each other after hauling the last pieces of rail into place. Four spikes – two gold, one silver and the fourth a mixture of gold, silver and iron – were presented to various dignitaries and then gently tapped into the ground.

A special fifth spike – ordinary in every respect except it was wired to a telegrapher's key – was organised for Mr Leland Stanford, President of the Central Pacific Railroad. This bigwig's job was to drive the last spike into place thus sending the message out that the two sides of the continent had at last been linked by rail. The whole ceremony was relayed coast to coast by telegraph. Massive crowds gathered in New York, San Francisco and all the other major US cities to await the news. With great pomp and much fanfare the proceedings began. Just after noon the first message came through from Utah:

ALMOST READY. HATS OFF. PRAYER IS BEING OFFERED.

After the lengthy prayer, the next message followed:

ALL READY NOW; THE SPIKE WILL SOON BE DRIVEN.

A reply came through:

WE UNDERSTAND; ALL ARE READY IN THE EAST.

In Utah another message was tapped out:

WE HAVE GOT DONE PRAYING; THE SPIKE IS ABOUT TO BE PRESENTED.

The replete Mr Stanford was then presented with the final spike and a special silver-headed hammer to whack it into place. Everyone clapped and cheered. A band played. With much huffing and puffing he hoisted the large hammer above his head, swung it down towards the spike and . . . missed.

'What a howl went up! Irish, Chinese, Mexicans and every-body yelled with delight. "He missed it! Yee!"' recorded one witness.

Stanford wasn't alone. The next bigwig up to hit a spike in

also missed. The same witness commented: 'Then Vice-President T.C. Durant of the Union Pacific took up the sledgehammer and he missed the spike the first time. Everybody slapped everybody else again and yelled, "He missed it too, yow!"' It didn't matter. The hapless bosses were saved some face by the fact that the loyal telegraph operator in Utah tapped out the word 'DONE!' to each coast.

And so, as the useless dignitaries shuffled off to a dining-car to finish their champagne lunches the final spike was professionally walloped into place by the chief engineer of the Union Pacific. It was a fitting end. The real work had been done by the sweat of ordinary labourers – Irish, Chinese, Mexicans – and the graves of their fellow workers lined the route. Throughout the venture, from beginning to end, the financiers and politicians had creamed money off to line their own pockets. As they toasted one another on that historic day in Utah, they knew that the best was yet to come. They had opened up the West and now all they had to do was await the hordes of fare-paying migrants, who would bring industry, labour, money and 'civilisation' to the West. And make them a fortune in the process.

It was, in many ways, a dubious achievement. As one commentator noted, when referring to a location the railroad had already passed through, 'The place is fast becoming civilised – several men have been killed there already . . .'

❀

Had I arrived in Colorado Springs in the same year as the teenage Harry Longabaugh, I may well have crossed paths with another visitor who, when questioned by a customs officer on entering the US, had replied: 'I have nothing to declare except my genius.' Oscar Wilde was in the States in 1882 for several months giving readings, lecturing, going to endless dinner parties organised by his colourful devotees and generally being himself. Towards the end of his tour of the eastern states he was persuaded to add on an extra twenty-one lectures for eager audiences out West. Dressed in his usual outfit of Byronic collars, knee breeches, silk stockings, shiny buckles, cloak and carrying flowers, Wilde dutifully set off to see the Wild West for himself. It was a sight to behold.

The Great Plains didn't impress him – 'like a piece of blotting paper', he remarked as they shot by – and he headed straight across the country to San Francisco. Having arrived in the port city he was delighted to see how many people turned up to welcome him complete with flowers and wearing what they thought were similar outfits to his outlandish garb. In turn, he bought some cowboy gear – a stetson, trousers, boots and a neckerchief – which he began wearing immediately. 'The western people are much more genial than those in the east,' he told a local reporter. He was, in fact, a great deal happier in the west because people here didn't make fun of his hair-do. His hair was so long that many observers in the East thought he was wearing a dodgy, rarely washed wig. In the West, however, things were different. The appearance of the legendary General Custer with his long blond locks and Buffalo Bill Cody with his flowing mane were all the rage on the Frontier. If Custer and Cody, two undisputed and manly western heroes, could have long hair, then Oscar was safe enough.

After drinking everyone in San Francisco's Bohemian Club under the table Oscar headed east again towards Colorado Springs. *En route* a brief stopover allowed Wilde almost to throttle a young boy he caught flogging cheap, bootleg poorly bound editions of his poems.

Next stop was Leadville, where a cool reception encouraged Oscar to dress himself down in his cowboy gear before heading off to visit some of the saloons. One place in particular caught his eye because above the resident piano-player's head hung a sign saying: 'DON'T SHOOT THE PIANIST, HE'S DOING HIS DAMNEDEST'. 'That's the only rational piece of art criticism I've ever come across in my life,' spluttered Wilde as he tried some Red-Eye whiskey at the bar. Later that night, at two in the morning in fact, a nervous Oscar, dressed in a rubber suit for protection but still wearing his cowboy hat, was lowered into a nearby mine. On reaching the bottom Wilde found himself standing in a dark puddle of water surrounded by twelve dirty, smiling men. They each produced a bottle of booze for the new arrival. 'Within a few minutes all have had twelve snorters. The miners without exception are rather dizzy, but Wilde remains cool, steady, and went away showing neither fatigue nor intoxication,' reported the admiring local newspaper the next day.

The Wilde roadshow lurched on to Colorado Springs, after which the Irish writer's next stop was supposed to have been Denver. Wilde, however, missed the train from Colorado Springs – by all accounts his boozing had caught up with him and he was hungover. A quick-thinking Denver newspaper editor, however, decided to dress up as Wilde complete with flowers, cravat, breeches and wig – before hopping on the very train Wilde had missed one stop before it pulled into Denver. Consequently, as the train arrived, a huge audience of Wilde fans dutifully waved and applauded the man they thought was their beloved hero. The impostor had much fun bowing and scraping, before being driven off in a stately carriage casually reading a book of obscure Danish poetry. Much fun was had by all – except the real Wilde followers. They eventually rumbled the hoax later that day when the newspaperman bowed too deeply causing his wig to fall off.

When news reached the real Oscar that some grumpy fans were waiting on him in Denver, he hastily departed Colorado Springs and arrived to a markedly smaller and less enthusiastic crowd than had greeted his impostor several hours earlier.

Knowing that his lecture was doomed, the canny Wilde raced through it, bowed hastily, waved and threw less flowers around than usual, before retreating quickly to his train carriage which whisked him eastwards.

His next stop was Kansas where, according to contemporary reports, his lecture on the 'Uses of Art in the Home and Dress', was spectacularly upstaged because its date clashed with the arrival of an extremely popular and long-awaited travelling circus which contained some very athletic Russian dwarfs who did an amazing trapeze act.

It was all downhill from that point on.

✿

Downtown Colorado Springs goes out of its way to cater for tourists who like cowboys or Indians. I walked down the main street in the older part of town and found numerous shops selling Native American goods. Most of the sellers didn't look very ethnic. Then I spent some time chatting to an old guy who sold cowboy boots. He'd been a professional rodeo rider for seventeen years before retiring after incurring some bad injuries. Now he sold boots.

'See that pair there?' he said pointing to a pair that looked like they were made of black tar that had hardened. 'Sting-ray. Tough as hell!'

I pointed to the pair he was wearing.

'Ostrich skin – finest you can buy.'

I lifted out another pair.

'Ah, now, they're custom-made, son. You're talking three thousand dollars at least and it takes a few hours to have them properly fitted.'

I nosed around the shop for a while. 'Do you like the West?' I asked him.

'God's own country, boy. Yessir.'

'Could you ever see yourself somewhere else?'

'Sure. Every morning I envisage myself in another place. I stare out of that window and dream of it.' He winked and bent down behind the counter. Then he reappeared with a golf club. He waved it at me like a magic wand.

I smiled. 'The golf course . . .' I said.

'Noooo, not just *any* old golf course. *The* golf course.' He came out from behind the counter and swung the club silently and slowly. 'I'm talking about St Andrews, Scotland, boy . . .'

❀

By 1884 the Longabaughs had left Colorado Springs and moved to a place called Cortez, in Colorado. Harry, about seventeen years old by then, was already working with horses on the nearby LC ranch. The ranch had about 5,000 head of cattle on it and young Harry was by all accounts a fast learner. Becoming a cowboy was also a natural thing for him to do. The US government was buying about fifty thousand head of Western cattle a year just to feed the Indian tribes who'd been robbed of their land and herded into reservations. The year before Harry moved out west, 1881, saw 110 million pounds of meat per annum being exported in refrigerated cars to England alone. Where there was beef there was money, it was as simple as that.

In the winter of 1886, Harry signed up with the N Bar outfit which was trailing a large cattle drive to Montana from Texas. He was doing what thousands of young men before him had done. The herds were usually driven to mining towns and railheads and from there the beef was distributed to forts, reservations and smaller settlements. The bulk of it was shipped east to feed the big appetites of the growing urban population.

The average age of the cowboys was twenty-four and most of them burned out quickly after riding a few trails. They travelled light, often slept out in the elements and ate the same diet every day – beef, biscuits, beans – washed down with gallons of scalding black coffee. Herd sizes could range from 2,000 head of cattle to 15,000. There were usually about a dozen or so men on a trail, all under the thumb of the tough trail-bosses. They often covered up to fifteen miles a day – although bad weather, stampeding cattle and any number of other problems could hold them back. Each cowboy was responsible for himself and his gear. Contrary to popular belief, very few actually rode with their guns in holsters – their weapons were usually stored in the chuck wagon. Many hated to ride wearing guns anyway, simply because they were too bulky and uncomfortable to carry when trying to do a hard day's work in the saddle. The saddle, of course, was extremely important – it was the cowboy's seat all day long, his workbench if he needed to repair anything and his hitching-post when he was roping livestock. It was also, needless to say, his rather aromatic nightly pillow.

Rules on a trail were basic and strict. One old-timer said: 'Before starting on a trail drive, I made it a rule to draw up an article of agreement, setting forth what each man was to do. The main clause stipulated that if one shot another he was to be tried by the outfit and hanged on the spot, if found guilty . . .'

The cowboy's life wasn't as carefree as the dime-store novels made it out to be. But it did have its rewards which Harry Longabaugh must have soon discovered. It gave a young man a chance to stand on his own two feet, learn self-reliance, earn some money and see the growing country. As well as, of course, get drunk on bad whiskey, buy some gaudy clothes and boots, gamble most of his wages away and then, if he'd any money left, jump into the sack with a 'soiled dove' to lose his virginity. And, frequently, proceed to shoot the town up.

One disgusted editor from a bullet-ridden town commented: 'Morally as a class [cowboys] are foulmouthed, blasphemous, drunken, lecherous, utterly corrupt. Usually harmless on the plains when sober, they are dreaded in towns, for then liquor has an ascendancy over them.'

Cowboying was a never-to-be-repeated phase of a young man's life. Some hated it; others thought it was the greatest job they ever had. For some the sheer hard work and drudgery, not to mention the low wages, simply depressed them. Disgruntled cowboys often resented the fact that while they did all the work, the owners – the so-called 'cattle barons' – took all the big profits. Some young men simply took off after one trail too many, never to be seen again. Others, like Harry Longabaugh, looked around for other, quicker ways to make a buck.

When Harry left Colorado in 1886 to head north with the cattle trail, he'd probably already made contact with more than one cowboy who'd dabbled in rustling. Certainly in the area of the LC ranch, where he'd worked prior to travelling north, he'd been near men like Bill Madden, the McCarty brothers and Matt Warner. They all lived within a day's ride of his home in Cortez and, like Harry, were all fond of fairs and races where good horseflesh was on show. Two other brothers, Dan and Robert LeRoy Parker, likeable characters from Utah, were also in the area at the time. Both had probably met, socialised and talked over the problems of cowboying with Harry Longabaugh on more than one occasion.

The latter, Robert LeRoy Parker was already, when the occasion required it, going under an alias – 'George Cassidy'.

❋

I was planning to leave Colorado Springs and head north, following roughly the same route that Harry Longabaugh took when he left the state in 1886. I packed my bags and went downstairs to the hotel reception to check out. Once I'd paid my bill and checked my map, I crossed the hallway to browse in a little gift shop. Several large parrots stood near the main doors.

They loudly yacked and squawked in broken English like drunken football hooligans. The guy behind the counter at the gift shop looked like a man on the edge. Every time the parrots screeched his left eye twitched involuntarily and he adjusted his horn-rimmed glasses.

'Does that bloody thing not drive you up the wall?' I said, asking the obvious and pointing to the loudest and most obnoxious-sounding of the two parrots.

'Oh, yeah,' he answered with mock casualness. His eye twitched again. 'And they make as much of a stinking mess as they do a loud racket,' he added, 'which the boss makes me clean up every morning at the start of my shift.'

I shook my head in sympathy. 'I'd ring their necks,' I said.

He looked at me, sizing me up and mentally deciding whether or not I was trustworthy. His eye was really twitching. He carefully adjusted his glasses, looked around to make sure no one was watching us, then reached below the counter. He pulled out a small blue package: 'I just give them two Alka Seltzer when they annoy me,' he said quietly. 'It blows them up, makes them froth at the beak and they fall off their perch at four in the morning when the place is empty.'

His eye had stopped twitching.

6. The Man from Laramie

'I once spent a night in Stranraer *en route* to Northern Ireland,' said Craig the Hertz car-rental man in Colorado Springs when I went to pick up my car. 'There isn't a whole lot there as I recall.'

From Craig's demeanour I was impressed he could remember his name never mind a trip he'd taken to Scotland as a student a decade before. He looked completely stoned and throughout our conversation he also shook like a jelly. I couldn't work out if he was on his way up or on his way down.

'Glasgow was great,' he went on. 'Some pubs, huh?' His eyes lit up at the thought of the pubs. Then he went quiet again. He looked out of place in his neat yellow and grey uniform. He didn't wear it; it sat on him.

'Did you enjoy Ireland as well?' I asked.

'What? Oh, Ireland . . . Yeah . . .' Craig answered dreamily. The lights in his eyes had gone out again. He stared off into the distance, shook some more and slumped into his chair. He twiddled a pen between his fingers, then shoved it behind an ear. His body was working for Hertz but his mind was clearly somewhere else. I decided to leave him in his half-dream world, so I thanked him for the car keys and headed on my way.

As I walked off I heard Craig's voice shout my name. I turned round. His eyes looked alive again. 'London was shit,' he said defiantly. 'Yeah – really shit. I remember it was really shit! Have a great trip man, you have yourself a great trip! Y'hear me! A great trip!'

'I'll try,' I said waving.

Craig was clearly a man who knew all about trips.

❀

I drove north towards Wyoming. Wyoming is the least populated state in the US. There's only about half a million people in it, and no big cities either – the largest centre of population is the capital, Cheyenne, which is home to about 50,000 people.

After driving for about an hour and a half the grey industrialised suburbs of Denver gave way to larger and larger stretches of land. The watery half-light of the weak winter sunshine coloured everything blue and green. Darkness started to fall at four o'clock in the afternoon. I noticed all the drivers wore cowboy hats. A large wooden billboard loomed up on the distant horizon. As I got closer I read its message: 'Wyoming – Like No Other Place On Earth!' Underneath it was a cowboy who looked slightly mad.

Near Cheyenne I pulled over to refuel the car. A green truck full of people wearing cowboys hats stopped in front of me at the lights. The signal changed to green but the truck stayed put. I honked my horn. It didn't move. Eventually I swung around it. Steam was pouring out from its engine. As I pulled into the petrol station I looked back at the truck. Its occupants were all throwing themselves out of it like madmen. Bags went flying in every direction, hats fell to the ground and jackets were grabbed hastily. Then they all stood back and waited.

The truck exploded.

I watched it burn as the occupants all walked away shaking their heads and laughing. They didn't look too bothered. I couldn't believe it. How often do you see a truck exploding into a ball of flames, I wondered? Within a minute it slowly started to fizzle out. As I paid for my fuel I watched a fire-truck slowly drive towards the burned-out vehicle. It wasn't flashing its lights or sounding its siren – the driver didn't seem too concerned. Tough people out west, I thought to myself.

'Did you see that?' I said to a huge guy serving me. I tried not to sound too shocked.

'Yeah,' he said casually.

'Bad luck, eh?' I said craning my neck to watch the action. Some firemen were slowly unravelling a hose. Others were lazily leaning against the engine chatting to the survivors.

'Yeah, messy . . .' drawled the large guy behind the counter, 'especially when you consider the fact that it's the fire-chief's new truck and that those guys in hats and jeans walking away from it are all firemen on their way to another call out.'

❀

My destination was Laramie. The history books said it had once been 'a hell of a place'. I'd never heard of it before I'd started researching Butch and Sundance. Other people clearly had though. '*The Man from Laramie!*' someone had exclaimed the night before when I told them I was heading for Laramie in south-east Wyoming. 'That was a cowboy series on TV years ago. Before your time probably.' They were right. Repeats of Clint Eastwood in *Rawhide* and grainy episodes of *Bonanza* were as far back as I went.

The wild town of Laramie grew up out of 'hell on wheels'

tent cities which had followed the growing Union Pacific rail-road as it lurched across the country in the 1860s. Hundreds of labourers, gamblers, saloon-owners, hustlers, pimps, fledgling industrialists, goldrush speculators fallen on hard times, itinerant newspapermen, hookers, thieves, rustlers, legions of cowboys and general hucksters-at-large had all passed this way at one time or another. Those that stayed on formed a place called Laramie which was named after a French-Canadian trapper called Jacques La Ramie. This handsome trapper, who'd broken more than a few hearts in the hot summer of 1817, went off hunting beaver pelts only to be found scalped and dead under a thick sheet of ice the following winter.

Laramie flourished with the coming of the railroad, but it also gained itself a dreadful reputation for violence and frontier summary-justice. One old illustration I'd seen showed a riot in progress in a bar, while another showed a black man being hung from a saloon's rafters while masked white men raped some half-naked Chinese workers nearby. Another account I'd traced referred to life in Laramie in 1868:

> I stopped in Laramie City and as there was no place to sleep some friends begged me to stay with them in their bullet-proof apartment consisting of sacks of flour piled one upon another in the centre of the store, inside of which they had beds. They had a bunk against the wall of the dance and gambling house, but advised me not to use it, calling attention to the lights from lamps showing through the bullet holes in the wall. Directly after retiring I heard several pistol shots and the voice of a woman shouting, 'Sam Duggan, you shall not hold up this man!' to which it seemed no attention was paid.

The reason I'd driven to Laramie was to see the only prison that had ever held Butch Cassidy. He'd been incarcerated in the state penitentiary from the summer of 1894 until January 1896 for allegedly stealing a horse worth five dollars. I thought it was a bit like Al Capone being put away for tax-evasion.

I arrived in Laramie at the foot of the Laramie Mountains the same time as the wind started to get up. My four-wheel-drive truck from Hertz shook when I parked it outside the old jailhouse building. It was late afternoon and I'd driven hundreds of miles just to get to this place because it held an open day only once in the whole winter. A small family with a little girl wrapped in a tartan blanket ran out of the building, whipped by the wind, towards their car. The father carrying the little girl fumbled and dropped the keys on the ground. His hands were raw with the cold.

I left the truck and stepped out into the wind. I went blind. The wind felt like spikes being driven into my eyes. It was stronger than anything I'd ever felt anywhere else in my life. I squinted eastwards around the bare land, the low empty hills and threadbare fields. No wonder the wind had such ferocity – there was simply nothing to stop it blowing. There were no hills of any real height for miles, no dense forests, no significant natural barriers – nothing. This was wind heaven. It could do whatever it wanted.

Construction on the state penitentiary began on 15 July 1872. To show 'all evil-doers of all classes and kinds' how resolute they were, one of the founding-fathers, a stiff-upper-lipped character who suffered from lumbago during wet weather, deposited a bottle of 'highest-quality Old Bourbon' into the wet cement of each cornerstone. It was built in Laramie because, as one contemporary newspaper editor stated, 'probably there is no other town in the United States in more need of such an institution'.

The penitentiary itself looked like a Victorian asylum from the outside. While other nineteenth-century settlers scraped together houses from local materials and using rough timber wind-breaks to enclose their land, the builders of the prison had opted for solid bricks and a formal, squat design that defied the elements. It could rain, blow, snow or bake: nothing would interfere with the due process of law. This thick brick building could withstand anything.

I walked around the front of it. The most elaborately decorated part of the penitentiary's structure faced straight into the wind. Underneath my feet the iced-up scrub of grass was scraped bare by the gale. I turned round, screwed up my eyes and stared into the distance with my back to the prison windows. A hundred years ago the inmates all looked out on what I saw. An endless landscape, a huge sky and an old rusted train line. The first two were symbolic of the freedom they'd lost. The last dangled the merest prospect of leaving this place bound for somewhere better.

The building was fortified by a wooden stockade fence that was frosted and snowed up. Guard-towers were placed high up on each corner. It felt bleak, miserable and, above all, forgotten. It may have looked like an insane asylum all right, but it wasn't a place for madmen. There's a difference which nineteenth-century architects knew all too well. What they'd built was a place specifically designed to drive men mad.

I walked across the vacant yard at the back of the penitentiary and entered the building through a large heavy door. Once inside I was hit by a blast of warm air, making me feel as if I'd just crossed the threshold of a supermarket. A woman wearing a red sweatshirt with a sparkling Father Christmas print on the front jumped up from behind a wooden desk to greet me. I noticed Santa had an electric red nose which lit up every so often. I also caught sight of the book she had been reading – *Women are from Venus, Men are from Mars.*

'Hi! I'm Marge and this is the old historic Wyoming State Penitentiary. Entrance fee is three dollars . . .' she rambled on in a sing-song voice.

I paid my entrance fee. 'Is the book any good?' I asked.
'Yeah.'

'I don't know if I'd believe all that stuff,' I said.

'That's because you're a man and you're from Mars.' Marge wasn't smiling, so I moved off quickly.

Across from her desk a huge print of a former prisoner gazed down from the wall. He was a homesteader who'd raped and killed his Indian wife after a drunken argument. He'd served four years in this prison for the crime.

At the entrance to the door into the prison a huge sign laid down the rules. It said:

Rules Regulating Prisoners of United States Penitentiary at Laramie, Wyoming Territory

These Rules are as follows:

You will not be allowed to converse with each other on any subject whatever. Conversation is allowed only when you work out of doors and then only in relation to the work you are performing.

You will not hold any conversation with visitors unless they are accompanied by either the Warden or one of the Guards, and not then without permission.

You will be required to keep your cell clean and in perfect order, and each morning, immediately after rising, fold your bedding and place it on the head of your bed.

You will air and dust your bedding twice per week and at such times as you are ordered to do so, and will keep your bedding in perfect repair.

You will be permitted to smoke and chew in your cell so long as you do not deface the floor or walls. Each cell will be provided with a spitbox which must be cleaned every day.

When you are permitted to exercise out of your cell, you will in no case step beyond the width of the cell door. If you have any request to make, you will remain within the limited space until you have an opportunity to make the request.

At meal hours, you will be ordered by the guard to step from your cell and, when the command is given, march around the table in single file taking the dishes numbered to correspond with your cell number and then return to your cell in the same order.

You will be allowed to write one letter per month and to receive letters every Sunday. All mail to and from you must pass through the hands of the Warden.

Reading matter will be furnished by application to the Warden and must be returned in good condition.

You will change your underclothing every Sunday and wash them at such times as you may be ordered. No excuse will be taken for not keeping yourself clean and in a healthy condition.

The hours for arising weekday mornings is 5.30 prompt and Sunday mornings 7.00.

In case of sickness report to the Guard at once.

You will be expected to understand the above rules. Any point not understood will be explained. Any deviation from these rules will meet with punishment. Good behaviour is to your interest as a record is kept of good and bad behaviour.

Butch Cassidy had looked at these rules when he entered the prison on 15 July 1894. He had been questioned on arrival but he didn't go out of his way to give the prison authorities personal information.

His prison 'Description of Convict' form that I'd unearthed in my research stated that his name was George Cassidy and that he'd been sentenced in the nearby town of Lander in Wyoming for 'grand larceny' on 12 July of the same year. The sentence was two years. He was twenty-seven years old, gave his occupation as 'Cow Boy' and stood five foot nine inches tall. His hair was 'dark flaxen' and he had blue eyes. He said he didn't have a wife or children and when asked who his parents were he'd answered: 'Don't know'. Equally when asked what his relations' address was, he said 'Not known'. His 'habits of life' were judged 'intemperate'.

Under the 'Marks, Scars and General Remarks' section it said:

> Weight 165 lbs.
> Features regular. Small deep-set eyes.
> Two (2) cut scars on back of head.
> Small red scar under left eye.
> Red mark on left side of back.
> Small brown mole on calf of left leg.
> 'Good Build'.

This information wasn't exactly all true or accurate. Butch had, in true criminal fashion, mingled truth with lies. His real name, as mentioned earlier, was in fact Robert LeRoy Parker and he'd been born in Beaver, Utah, on 13 April 1866. Both sides of Butch's family – his mother's line and his father's – came from Great Britain and, importantly, they were all Mormons.

The leader of the Mormon Church in the USA, whose members called themselves 'Saints', was Brigham Young. After leading his foot-weary followers across America he'd seen the arid, woe-begotten Great Salt Lake Valley in Utah and proclaimed: 'This is the place.' His poor followers had pushed handcarts the entire distance. For years they'd been persecuted and scorned in other parts of the States. Now this apparently godforsaken place in the middle of a desert was to be their new home. Privately, many were appalled – this wasn't what they prayed for or expected. Milk and honey was conspicuous only by their absence. But Young held firm. He sent out a message through missionaries that the future of the new Church depended upon skilled workers and tradesmen leaving their homes in the Old World and joining the Salt Lake Valley settlement. The Saints would build their own future and a great city would rise out of this place.

Butch's paternal grandparents came from Burnley in Lancashire. By all accounts his grandfather Robert Parker was well educated, good-looking and a highly skilled weaver. He was also president of the Mormon Church in Preston. Missionaries from the US had arrived in the northern English town where the Parker family had put them up and listened to their stories of life in Utah. On 22 March 1856 the Parkers, having sold up everything, boarded a boat named the *Enoch Train* and set sail for the States and a new life. They arrived in Boston five weeks later. On 12 May in New York City they climbed on board a train for Iowa. A month later the family left Iowa City pushing a handcart with about two hundred other 'souls'. There were six in the Parker party – the two parents and their four children: Maximilian, the oldest, was eleven, Martha Alice was nine, six-year-old Martha and the eight-month-old baby Ada. Young Maximilian would grow up to marry another immigrant, a Scot named Annie Campbell Gillies. Their son was Robert LeRoy Parker.

Annie was born in Edinburgh, the eldest daughter of Robert and Jane Sinclair Gillies, a Scottish couple who had joined the English Mormon Church. An early photograph of Robert Gillies shows him wearing a Scots hat with a feather stuck in the side and a silver clan crest badge on the front. He has a round, full face and a thick dark beard. He looks like a ruddy-cheeked Highland clansman. The Gillies family left Liverpool on the ship *Horizon* on 25 May 1856 to undertake exactly the same voyage that the Parkers had started a few weeks earlier. On the rough seas Robert Gillies apparently lost his Scots bonnet to the high wind. Their emigration records reveal the following details of their party: 'Gillies, Robert (36) from Scotland. Jane (35). Moroni (10). Annie (9). Daniel (7). Christina (3)'. They didn't reach Salt Lake City until November, by which time they'd lost almost one hundred and fifty members of their five-hundred-strong party. Scores had died during terrible blizzards, some had starved on the mountain crossings and reports also speak of several pioneers going completely insane.

Maximilian Parker and Annie Campbell Gillies were married on Annie's birthday 12 July 1865. Robert was born almost nine months to the day later. Shortly afterwards the little family moved to a small cabin in a nearby area known as Circle Valley – also known as Circleville – in Utah.

Butch's upbringing was nothing extraordinary for the time. The family expanded and the little house had to be extended to keep them all under the one roof. The Parkers worked the land and at a young age LeRoy, also known as Bob, was hired out to help on other people's land. At home, he happily helped his father and mother – assisting Annie, for example, to plant five little poplar trees in the garden. Even at a very young age he displayed the qualities that would become his trademark, being regarded as affable and very dependable. In his later outlaw years, Butch consistantly impressed people. Even righteous Mormons stated their affection for him, one 'Saint' openly stating to more than one enquirer that Butch Cassidy 'was simply the finest man I have ever known'.

The Parkers had modest ambitions. Butch's father worked hard, season after season, to develop his land. He even homesteaded some additional property near by, only to discover that another settler had been awarded this land by a local bishop. When he learned he'd been 'jumped' by another 'Saint', Maximilian Parker seriously considered giving up the Mormon religion but his wife persuaded him to carry on and not lose faith. Thereafter he attended church on an irregular basis and defiantly broke one of the religion's taboos by smoking his pipe.

In summer of 1882, strapped for cash, Butch's mother hired herself out to a nearby ranch to do some work. She did everything from working the land to churning butter. These were hard times. Fifteen-year-old Butch accompanied her when she worked at this place, the Marshall Ranch, which lay twelve miles south of Circleville. During that summer young LeRoy started hanging around with an older character named Mike Cassidy. Cassidy was a cowboy: he had drifted on to the Marshall Ranch and was lucky enough to secure a job there for a while. Young LeRoy took full advantage of being around Mike and other cowboys to learn about what life on the range was really all about.

Mike Cassidy was, by all accounts, already taking advantage of any 'stray' cattle he happened upon in the course of his long working days in the saddle. Large cattle companies kept their herds in this region *en route* to their destination. It was easy enough to steal a few steers, re-brand them and call them your own. This is what Mike Cassidy did to make money and it's what his teenage pupil watched him do. To young Parker it looked like a good way to put some cash in your pocket. And, importantly, it didn't involve the soul-destroying, back-breaking labour he'd seen both his parents endure.

By the end of that summer LeRoy knew enough to hire himself out as a cowboy or to go into business for himself as someone 'on the rustle'. The smiling, affable, genial Mike Cassidy, had already vanished towards Mexico after getting caught once too often with cattle that weren't his. Two years later, in 1884, LeRoy himself got into some trouble as a result of his continued friendship with one or two erstwhile associates of Mike Cassidy. Before the law caught up with the eighteen-year-old LeRoy, he left home quickly, carrying a blue blanket his distraught mother insisted he take in case the weather turned cold.

His old mentor at the Marshall Ranch had clearly made a strong impression, because after young Parker left Circleville in 1884 he began introducing himself as George Cassidy. A decade later, in 1894, he'd ended up inside the Wyoming State Penitentiary using the same alias.

The metamorphosis of the young, likeable ranch-hand into the outlaw and inmate who called himself George Cassidy and who denied he had a family, began almost as soon as LeRoy left Utah in 1884.

He had first headed south-east into Colorado to the town of Telluride to be exact. Telluride, according to legend, got its name from the phrase 'to hell you ride', though how accurate that is is anybody's guess. When LeRoy rode into town in the mid-1880s it was undoubtedly a rough, mining camp. He joined the legions of men who sweated and grunted their way through a day's work hauling minerals out of the earth in the mines below various nearby mountains. It couldn't have been easy work.

Things turned sour when the young LeRoy was charged with stealing a horse. This was probably a false accusation and his sister claimed in her book that he was highly indignant about being labelled a horse thief. But it wouldn't be the last time. Embarrassingly for LeRoy, his father turned up at his trial and vouched for his wayward son's good character in court. The judge was duly swayed and the young rustler managed to get an acquittal. Free again, LeRoy refused to accompany his father back to Circleville in Utah, though he did send Maximilian home with some money which he instructed him to give to Annie.

For the next couple of years there are only sketchy reports about exactly where Robert LeRoy Parker went or what he did when he got there. Some research suggests he may have spent some time working near Miles City, Montana, in 1887. The trail heats up again during 1888–89 when he turned up once more in the Telluride area of Colorado. It was around this period that he seems to have developed a friendship with two cowboys who were already operating on the fringes of the law, Matt Warner and his brother-in-law Tom McCarty. The latter had a cabin seventy-five miles away near Cortez – this was less than two miles from where Harry Longabaugh periodically stayed with his cousin's family. By the late 1880s it's fair to say that the men who would become Butch Cassidy and the Sundance Kid were probably on more than nodding terms with each other.

The three men – McCarty, Warner and Parker – shared a love of horses. They apparently spent a lot of time training their horses to race at fairs and local races whenever they got the chance. A personal account written by McCarty testifies to the fact that they drifted from one crackpot race to another, their only rule being that they had to enjoy themselves in the process. On one occasion things turned nasty when McCarty won a horse from an Indian who refused to accept that he'd been beaten fairly in a race. The horse, which had only one eye and was called White Face, was taken by McCarty and his two accomplices back to Cortez in Colorado. The Indian turned up the next day and demanded the return of the fast, albeit half-blind, horse. An argument ensued, tempers rose, and the dispute was finally settled when McCarty drew his gun and blew the horse's previous owner out of his saddle.

The similarities between LeRoy's background and that of his friend Matt Warner were striking. Both came from very strict Mormon backgrounds – indeed Matt's father's name was Christian Christianson – and both came from Utah. Warner, like Parker, changed his name – from Willard Erastus Christianson to the easier-to-remember Matt Warner. For a while Warner even called himself the Mormon Kid. Both men also began their outlaw careers in cattle-rustling before moving on to play for higher stakes.

Evidence strongly suggests that Matt Warner and Robert LeRoy Parker may have teamed up for a botched train robbery on 3 November 1887. After stopping the train, they and their several accomplices (who probably included a couple of the McCarty brothers), were confronted by a guard who refused point-blank to open the safe. One of the outlaws wanted to kill the guard but young Parker suggested they take a vote instead. It was duly decided to leave the guard and the passengers alone. More care would be taken in selecting their next target and Warner probably had bigger ideas.

On 30 March 1889 a bank robbery took place in Denver, and may or may not have been carried out by Matt Warner and one of the McCarty brothers. Whoever it was had casually walked into the First National Bank of Denver and asked politely to speak to the manager, Dave Moffat. The stranger was carrying what looked like a bottle of water. On being shown into Moffat's well-appointed office the outlaw suggested that the manager hand over all the money in the bank or else he might accidentally drop his bottle of nitroglycerine on the floor. Moffat panicked and produced twenty-one thousand dollars in cash – an enormous sum of money even by today's standards and a staggering amount at the end of the nineteenth century – for which the well-dressed stranger thanked him before vanishing out of the front door with his equally smart accomplice. Newspapers from the period say Warner and his brother-in-law Tom McCarty were the perpetrators.

By June the outlaws were becoming restless again, and in a memoir written by Tom McCarty he describes the reasoning behind the gang's next move:

> In that part of the country were men of all grades, and I soon joined up with some that longed for excitement of

any kind, and having been quiet for such a long time, my restlessness began to annoy me. Times being now rather dull and becoming acquainted with men that had no more money than myself, we thought it time to make a raid of some sort. Our plans were accordingly laid very carefully to go to a certain bank and relieve the cashier of his ready cash.

That bank was San Miguel Valley Bank in Telluride, a town that Robert LeRoy Parker knew like the back of his hand.

On 24 June 1889 Parker and Matt Warner walked into the bank, 'dressed to kill' as Butch's sister Lula wrote in later years, and headed straight for a cashier. They smiled at the man, briefly passed the time of day, then stuck a gun in his face.

They fled with $20,750 in cash. Using horse-relays, similar in style to the Pony Express, the robbers managed to make a very fast getaway on their expensive, fresh horses. Interestingly, LeRoy's younger brother Dan may have been part of the gang who supplied the horses in stages along the getaway route.

But the hold-up wasn't without its problems. LeRoy was spotted by someone who knew him as he sped out of Telluride with the loot from the bank. From that point on he was a known criminal. 'George Cassidy', the smart dresser with the small laughing eyes and easy-going manner, had become a wanted man.

❋

The men who held up the bank in Telluride were Robert LeRoy Parker, Matt Warner and Tom McCarty. Some reports, however, suggest there may have been another accomplice. On 27 June 1889, just seventy-two hours after the hold-up, the *Rocky Mountain News* mentioned a fourth unidentified robber:

The robbery of the San Miguel Valley Bank of Telluride on Monday by four daring cowboys . . . the four rode over to the bank, and leaving their horses in charge of one of the number, two remained on the sidewalk and the fourth entered the bank.

Donna Ernst's research into Harry Longabaugh suggests that the fourth man may have been the young Sundance Kid.

In 1886 Harry had left Colorado to head north working as a cowboy on a cattle drive. He bounced from one ranch job to another in Montana for a couple of years before heading south again in the early spring of 1887. He must have been desperate. That winter, 1886–87, was one of the worst in the history of the United States. As a young cowboy Harry Longabaugh must have been in dire straits. The cattle industry had hit an all-time low. Seven and a half million cattle were now competing for less and less grazing. In some hard-hit regions a steer that used to need only five acres for grazing now needed more than ninety. Good grazing grass became scarcer by the day. Beef prices fell through the floor. A cowboy named Teddy 'Blue' Abbot recalled that terrible winter: 'In November we had several snowstorms and I saw the first white owls I have ever seen. The Indians said they were a bad sign, "heap snow coming, very cold" . . . It got colder and colder . . . It was hell without the heat.'

Referring to the starving cattle herds, Abbot went on: 'It was all so slow, plunging after them through the deep snow . . . The horses' feet were cut and bleeding from the heavy crust, and the cattle had the hair hide wore off their legs to the knees and the hocks. It was surely hell to see big four-year-old steers just able to stagger along. It was the same all over Wyoming, Montana and Colorado, western Nebraska and western Kansas.'

For years afterwards that winter was known to cowboys as simply 'the Big Die-Up'. They never forgot it. For Harry Longabaugh it had added significance.

On 27 February 1887 near the town of Sundance in Wyoming, Harry, desperate, hungry and friendless, stole a light-grey horse, a saddle and a revolver. By 8 April he was arrested in Miles City, Montana, after a sheriff tracked him for over two hundred miles. The resourceful Harry managed to pick some locks during the return journey to Sundance and escape. Once free, Harry, for some unfathomable reason, went back to the scene of his earlier arrest, Miles City.

Two months later a couple of law officers picked him up and placed him under arrest. This led to the headline in which Longabaugh was referred to as a 'a fly kid' and which compared him to the legendary Jesse and Frank James.

The travel-weary sheriff from Sundance arrived some time later to make a second attempt to take Longabaugh back to Sundance. The local newspaper reported:

> Longabaugh was securely shackled and handcuffed, the shackles being made of steel and riveted with steel rivets, and as they got aboard [Sheriff] Ryan informed the kid that he was going to land him or his scalp in Sundance Jail. The kid gave him fair warning that he intended to escape and told him to watch him but not to be too rough on him.

He never did manage to escape. He was tried at the court in Sundance, Wyoming, and sentenced to eighteen months' hard labour. Because Harry was under twenty-one he was not sent to the state penitentiary in Laramie to do his time, rather he was confined to the jail in Sundance for the duration of his sentence. He was given a full pardon, the day before his scheduled release, on 4 February 1889. A few days later the *Sunday Gazette* wrote that: 'The term of the "Kid" Longabaugh expired on Tuesday morning, and the young man at once hired himself to the Hills, taking the coach for Deadwood.'

Three months later Harry was involved in a fracas in South Dakota about thirty-five miles from Sundance. One of his outlaw friends was shot dead by the sheriff who'd come to arrest him. Harry survived the incident unscathed but swore vengeance for the death with enough venom to frighten the scared sheriff into swearing out a complaint against him. This meant young Longabaugh had to make another hasty departure.

By now Harry was known in both law-making and law-breaking circles as the 'Kid from Sundance', soon to be shortened to the 'Sundance Kid'. By the end of May 1889, he was heading for his cousin George's home in Cortez, Colorado, near Tom McCarty's cabin. It was here that McCarty, Warner, Robert LeRoy Parker and others had planned the Telluride bank robbery. If Donna Ernst is right, and Harry was involved in this raid, it would have been the first time that the men forever known as Butch Cassidy and the Sundance Kid worked together.

❁

After Telluride the outlaws split up for a while and went their separate ways. LeRoy headed for Brown's Park, a lush valley forty miles by six. It was right at the intersection of Utah, Colorado and Wyoming. The inhospitable terrain discouraged any brave lawmen from poking around the area and the valley's position meant a quick getaway into any of the three states could be afforded if required.

LeRoy Parker had friends in this area – associates might be a better term – who were the original members of what eventually passed into legend as the 'Wild Bunch'. In the beginning the members of this loosely organised gang were just rustlers and part-time robbers like Parker; men who robbed and ran, who lived or passed through the Brown's Park area on their way to their next hold-up or on the run from their last one. At one time or another the gang comprised: Matt Warner, who was likeable but occasionally displayed a volatile and ruthless temper; the McCarty brothers Tom and Bill who'd first encouraged Robert LeRoy Parker to engage in serious crime; the educated William 'Elzy' Lay; the vicious, cold-blooded killer Harvey Logan, alias 'Kid Curry'; William 'News' Carver, who liked reading press clippings about everyone's criminal exploits; O.C. Hanks; Harry Longabaugh, the Sundance Kid, whom everyone, including Harvey Logan, feared because of his fast-draw reputation; Harry Tracy; Dave Atkins, who was once forced at gunpoint to eat Sundance's favourite cereal, Ralston's, after laughing at him; Jack Bennet, who brought the Wild Bunch its supplies; 'Laughing' Sam Carey, who earned his nickname because he never laughed; Joe Chancellor, who liked his cigarettes so much he used to get up during the night to puff on half a dozen; Frank 'Peg-Leg' Elliot; Bob Lee, a friend of the Logans; Tom O'Day, a cowboy who stank to high-heaven because he rarely washed; and Ben 'The Tall Texan' Kilpatrick, who would be killed in 1912 during an attempted train robbery.

The ringleader of this motley crew was the youthful Robert LeRoy Parker, known to the gang as George Cassidy. His easy-going nature and constant scheming were part of the reason the other men looked up to him – though his friendship and alliances with men like the Sundance Kid, whose lightning-fast draw was much feared by everyone, didn't do him any harm either.

In the early days, the 'Wild Bunch' name had as much to do with the gang's love of carousing and women and drinking in places like Rock Springs, Rawlins, Baggs and Dixon, as it did with their outlaw escapades. Unless they had a specific job planned, the gang did not always stay together at one place. Members simply came and went. Some went off on the run, others split into smaller groups to carry out their own jobs, while others opted to stay put and live off their loot. The beginning of the last decade of the nineteenth century was, more or less, their heyday. They could rob anyone and any-where and be pretty much assured of getting away with it. But, in many ways, they were fashioning a rod for their own back. The law of diminishing returns would eventually kick in. The more they robbed, the angrier their victims became. At some unspecified time in the future they'd all pay in one way or another for their crimes. In the meantime, Cassidy and his gang lived the roguish highlife of infamous outlaws.

If the going got rough, or if the heat from eager sheriffs ever came a little too close for comfort, the Wild Bunch simply went to ground. Cassidy hired himself out to the Bassett Ranch in Brown's Park for a while using the disguise of paid work to hide the fact he was well financed from his earlier robbery. He was well liked and completely trusted on the ranch. Years later one of the family reminisced about the outlaw's time at the ranch: 'I knew [Robert LeRoy Parker] a long, long time and so did my father before we ever believed that he was on that life. My father would never believe for a long time. He said, "That fella is not that kind of man." He was a quiet young man nobody knew. Well, he broke horses for different people, worked with cattle and everything. Never got drunk . . .'

To keep up the front of a man in search of honest labour LeRoy left the safe haven of Brown's Park and went to the nearby town of Rock Springs. Introducing himself as George Cassidy, he managed to secure a job as a butcher in William Gottsche's shop in the town. Many believe that this is how he got the name 'Butch' Cassidy. Other explanations do exist, though. Matt Warner, for example, claimed it came from seeing Cassidy blown off his feet after firing a powerful gun that he'd named 'Butch' – thereafter he called his friend after the weapon that had landed him on his arse in the mud much to the merriment of onlookers. Either way, from about 1889 onwards

Robert LeRoy Parker from Circleville became the outlaw Butch Cassidy.

❀

Coincidentally, as Butch Cassidy was successfully beginning to build himself a lucrative career as an outlaw, his younger brother Dan also tried his hand at various illegal ways to turn a quick profit. He wasn't anywhere near as successful or charismatic as his big brother, though. He went under various aliases including 'Dan Ricketts' and 'Kid Parker' before he managed to get himself arrested. Using the name 'Tom Ricketts', and aided by William Brown, another outlaw, he'd successfully robbed the Muddy Creek stagecoach as it made its run between Dixon and Rawlins in Wyoming on 29 December 1889. In October the following year, Dan was captured after a messy gun-battle with United States Marshal Joe Bush in the La Sal Mountains, near Moab. He was eventually brought back to Wyoming, tried and convicted and sentenced to a long prison term of hard labour in the Detroit House of Corrections. Dan wrote to his relations asking for help but because the family were too poor and Maximilian was ill at the time, no one was able to either assist him or attend his trial. He spent seven tough years in prison.

After quitting the butcher's life in Rock Springs, Butch headed to Wyoming to do some more ranch work on the EA Outfit in Wind River. The ranch was owned by Eugene Amaretti, an Italian immigrant who owned about forty thousand head of prime cattle. Together with another fellow, Al Hainer, Butch invested some of his ill-gotten gains in the horse business. It was around this time he also got a letter from little brother Dan informing him he'd been sentenced for robbing the stagecoach. On 13 March 1890 Butch put pen to paper and wrote the following letter to express his support:

My dear Brother,

It has been so long since I have written I suppose you have done looking for a letter from me but do not despair for you shall have one after so long a time. You must forgive me for not writing before. I have no excuse to offer only my negligence and I will try to be more punctual for the future. I was very sorry to hear that you are in hiding again, but you know that I am not one to point a finger only to be careful for I am inclined to think as Grandfather Parker did about the wild cat in Duncan woods. I do wish I could come and see you all and I intend to if nothing happens to prevent this summer coming for I almost feel homesick when thinking how long it is since I saw my Mother it seems almost an age since I saw any of you. When you get this letter you must write and tell me all the news and what prospects are for a safe reunion. I hope we may have a grand revelry but I should think it doubtful according to your letter. I am now located at a good house about 18 miles from Lander and have taken to raising horses which I think suits this country just fine. Hainer and I have thrown our lots entirely together, so we have thirty-eight horses between us and we would have more but it has been a cold winter with plenty of wind and snow. (And you must excuse the pencil but the ink froze.) Business here is very dull and money hard but you know I am well. I should be in perfect health if I did not have such a good appetite and eat so much three times a day. I must draw my letter to a close. Give my love to Uncle Dan and family and tell them I should be happy to see them. Give my love to Father, Mother, Brothers and Sisters and receive the same yourself –

This from your Brother,

Bob.

P.S. Direct all your letters to George Cassidy as before
and burn this up as you read it.

The postscript said it all.

Butch might have been ranching horses with Al Hainer but
he wasn't exactly going straight. The two men had been stealing
horses left, right and centre then selling them on the side. To
subsidise their lifestyle they also ran a small-time protection
racket amongst local ranchers – homesteaders noticed that if Al
and Butch looked after your stock the rustling immediately
stopped. It didn't take a genius to work out why.

At some point over the next year or so a horse was allegedly
stolen and an official complaint was made. Local patience with
Al and Butch had run out. Inevitably the two were brought to
trial. A complaint dated 15 July 1892 charged George Cassidy
and Albert Hainer with stealing one horse on 1 October 1891
valued at forty dollars from the Grey Bull Cattle Company
based in Wyoming. Another legal notice dated 14 March 1893
informed Cassidy that he had to appear in court in June. Both
men were found not guilty and freed. However, a second
criminal trial in June 1893 charged both men with stealing a
horse valued at either five dollars or fifty dollars, the records
suggest two values, on 28 August 1891. Notably, both cases refer
to thefts dating back a couple of years suggesting the people
involved had either long memories or bitter scores to settle.

In any event, both men paid their four hundred dollars bail
money and walked free to await the verdict. After a series of
legal wrangles the judgement was eventually delivered on 4 July
1894. Al Hainer walked free, but Butch Cassidy was found
guilty and sentenced to two years in the Wyoming State
Penitentiary in Laramie. Before he left to begin his sentence,
Butch asked to be given some time to settle his personal affairs.
This request was granted without hesitation. He left the
courthouse and rode off into the distance.

Other outlaws would have taken advantage of the situation and vanished. But they weren't Butch Cassidy. He returned, as promised, by midnight. The next morning, smiling as always, he began his journey to Laramie and his sentence. Some say the sheriff who took him to the prison didn't even bother to bring a gun with him.

Butch Cassidy might have been an outlaw, but he was always, at the very least, a good Mormon outlaw.

Butch served his time inside Laramie a model prisoner. He did what he was told, never caused trouble and seemed to get along with everyone he met. On 19 January 1896 he was brought before the Governor and offered a proposition. He would be set free if he would promise never to commit another crime. Cassidy thought for a moment or two then answered that he couldn't accept the offer. He said he knew it was a promise he couldn't keep, so he wouldn't lie and accept it. However, he added, he could promise never to commit another crime in the State of Wyoming.

The Governor accepted the deal and duly signed a pardon allowing Butch to walk out of the prison a free man after serving eighteen months of his two-year sentence.

Never again would the outlaw see the inside of a prison cell.

❊

I walked around the penitentiary alone. I seemed to be the sole visitor during this, the only open-day of the winter. It wasn't a big prison; it certainly wasn't designed to hold hundreds of men – more like dozens. As I walked down the hallway towards the cells I could still hear the wind outside. It howled and whistled against the brickwork. The cells were painted in predictable shades of grey. Heavily barred iron doors locked the prisoners inside. I was unprepared for the tiny size of the cells, however. Standing inside one I was easily able to reach the ceiling and

stretch out my arms to touch both walls. It felt very claustrophobic. A hundred years ago they put three men to a cell when
the place was busy.

I went into the cell I'd been told Butch probably slept in – the
records weren't precise but they'd narrowed it down to two or
three small steel-encased chambers. A white heavy cotton hammock was strung up from the wall to the door. I decided to try
it out. I casually threw myself into it, hoping to see what it felt
like to lie in the cell and look through the same bars that Butch
had. Instead I hit the floor with a painful crack. The hammock
was a mock-up for tourists, hung on the door and wall with
little bits of thin wire. The sound of me landing echoed through
the empty prison. I looked up and saw Cassidy's prison photograph, blown up to five feet by four feet, staring down at me.
He looked older than his twenty-seven years, tight-eyed and
thoughtful. But still intimidating.

Apart from the sound of the wind outside, there was silence.

All down the walls of the prison other photographs of
inmates from a century ago glowered down at visitors. Like
Butch they all wore grey striped uniforms. For the most part
they looked desperate and unhappy. Some looked like guys I'd
been at school with. The occasional one looked really dangerous. Many had shaven heads and scars. There was prisoner
number 357, for example, William N. Nash, who looked like a
teenage boy when his mug-shot was taken. His head had been
shaved into a tidy crew-cut, his eyes were wide and knowing.
He looked hungry. His record said he'd been convicted of
forgery and sentenced to three years and 'costs'. He was released
after two years and seven months for 'good conduct'. Then
there was prisoner number 59, Michael Foulk, who was
convicted of murder in the second degree. In his prison
photograph he looked unshaven and wild-eyed; his lips betrayed
a slight smile, as if he'd shared a joke with the photographer
seconds before his image was captured. Foulk was sentenced to

twenty years for this crime but was severely wounded in a violent fight with two other prisoners during his term in Laramie. After this incident, which almost cost him his life, he 'learned his lesson and improved his conduct'. His sentence was subsequently commuted to ten years and he was pardoned in 1902 by Governor DeForest Richards. In total he served nine years and eight months.

I took my time viewing their images, voluntarily touring the place they'd longed to leave. Like Butch Cassidy, these men would have had to do some work when they were in here. They made candles and leather goods, they harvested potatoes and manufactured musical instruments and saddles. Broom-making was particularly lucrative by all accounts. Brick-making also reaped high profits. The prisoners were herded out to a quarry a few miles from the penitentiary in all weathers to do this arduous, back-breaking work. They produced over a million bricks a year, which brought in $1,500 in profits for the prison trustees. But some prisoners saw the journey to the quarry as an opportunity to escape. The instant the quarry managers looked the other way many seized the chance to run and were never seen again. The brickwork owners blamed the prison; the prison blamed the brickwork owners. The governor and his trustees were keen not to lose their profits so they suggested that the quarry owner pay for two security guards to watch over the men as they sweated and toiled. But the brickwork management balked at the thought of paying out $52.50 per month for the two guards so the whole deal was called off. When other industrialists heard about this, they were keen to get hold of the prisoners and the cheap labour they represented. Lunches were arranged, dinners consumed and sherry drunk. The convicts had to be made use of and a proper rate for their muscle-power had to be secured. The alternative to using them was unthinkable for the people of Laramie. As one local industrialist said in a crawling letter to the governor and trustees: 'If I can't arrange for Convict Labor, I will have to arrange for Chinamen!'

In the town of Laramie I later visited an elegant house that had some beautiful wooden furniture in the drawing-room which a prisoner from the penitentiary had carved by hand. The detail of his work was exquisite. The owner of the house was on the penitentiary's board of trustees. I could just imagine his wife and all the other middle-class tea-drinking ladies of the frontier running their hands over the furniture and marvelling at the savage's carpentry skills.

I wandered through the deserted prison, the grey walls around me painted with dark curtains of shadows. Hidden corners creaked and splintered when a rare shaft of weak sunlight illuminated them. The slightest noise echoed throughout the whole building. The careless clearing of a throat or the scuff of a shoe bounced around the walls. The cells and the walls trapped everything; they seemed reluctant to let anything go. It was a lonely, plagued place.

After I said goodbye to the woman from Venus at the door, I walked out of the prison into the icy-blue yard where inmates used to exercise. A prison stagecoach, painted black with heavy bars on its windows, faced the main door. It was forlorn-looking without its horse. Its hidden interior was shrouded in black shadows. A tree swayed slowly and creaked near the stockade fence. Shrivelled-up leaves rattled across the surface of the ground, scattered by the wind that periodically whirled them round in circles like a mini-twister. The yard felt empty and haunted. The huge wooden gates which faced me, studded with iron nails like a medieval castle, were wide open. The bleached wooden watchtowers on each corner of the high, sharp fence were deserted and lifeless. In the distance the hills looked ulcer-grey and barren. Even though I'd only been a visitor briefly passing through the state penitentiary I was glad to leave it. A solitary, windswept and blown figure, my mind numbed with the cold and wind, I tried to figure out why the place seemed familiar. For several minutes I couldn't figure it out. I stopped in my tracks remembering the ill-fitting striped uniforms, the tin cups in the mess-hall, the staring, under-fed faces and the pleading eyes. Then I got it. It reminded me of images from Nazi concentration camps.

A tidy little gift-shop was in business next to the prison. They had Butch Cassidy's image on T-shirts and mugs. A sign on the door said 'K.I.L.T.S. Please Help!'. I asked the girl behind the counter what this stood for.

'Oh, it means Kids-In-Laramie-To-Scotland,' she chirped. 'We have a local theatre group for kids and we're hoping to send them to Scotland for the Edinburgh Arts Festival next year.'

I dropped a donation in the can and nosed around the store for a few minutes. I picked up a cheap little book of local writing and paid for it.

Moments later I sat in my truck as it swayed from side to side in the strong wind. I switched the radio on and tuned into the local weather forecast. A man with a high-pitched nasal voice said the winds were 60 miles per hour in Laramie. A cheap, tinny musical jingle followed the information – the news programme and the weather forecast had been sponsored by a local company which made snowblowers.

Just before I drove off I read a little poem someone had printed in the booklet I'd bought. It said:

> *And the wind crept by*
> *Alone, unkempt, unsatisfied,*
> *The wind cried and cried –*

I pulled out on to the long, empty highway and drove north. Over the next ten minutes I periodically looked in my rear-view mirror as the prison sank further and further into the grey distance. Then quite suddenly it was gone.

To the west the flat landscape eventually gave way to the high

Rocky Mountains which stood guard like awesome, gigantic waves frozen in a black, angry sea. In front of me was the longest and straightest and bleakest highway I'd ever seen in my life. All I had for company during the long drive ahead were my thoughts.

And the incessant Wyoming wind.

7. The Cowboy Years

I remembered the last time I played Cowboys and Indians.

I was ten years old and a group of us used to play in the shadow of what was Europe's largest steelworks, the Ravenscraig, near Motherwell in Lanarkshire. During our school summer holidays we would go on long walks into the woods near the village of Cleland where we all lived. My friend Patrick's uncle usually accompanied us.

The lush trees in the woods were an escape from the grey industrialisation which surrounded us. We ran in and out of the dark caves formed by the branches, whooping and clapping our mouths like the Hollywood Indians we'd all seen on TV. All the other boys were bigger than me, so I always managed to draw the short straw which meant I had to be the Indian. This was not very good from my point of view. The cowboys always won the battles so I had to suffer the indignity of constantly being beaten up for most of the afternoon. I made an incredibly miserable Indian as a result.

As we played our games Patrick's uncle sat watching us

quietly. He rarely spoke except to answer the odd daft question from us. The rest of the time he simply rested on a rock, smoking his pipe and contemplating life.

All the young cowboys fought over who was to be John Wayne. In our part of Scotland John Wayne had taken on increasingly mythic proportions. Our fathers were categorised into who could and who couldn't beat John Wayne in a straight one-to-one fist-fight. Such discussions often petered out simply because at least two of my friends weren't entirely sure who their fathers were.

Then there was the John Wayne-Irn Bru legend. Someone had heard a rumour that John Wayne enjoyed drinking Scotland's favourite soft drink whilst on dusty movie-sets. Naturally, we were stunned into silence when we heard this. At ten years of age such information was truly life-affirming. We could hardly believe our hero, the star of countless western movies, actually consumed the same sticky sweet rusty orange-coloured drink that us kids bought from the local newsagent's. The world, for the first time, suddenly seemed a lot smaller to me.

Of course the rumour grew until it was said John Wayne didn't drink just one bottle of Irn Bru between takes on a desert film-shoot. No, we somehow convinced ourselves, he drank three whole bottles – each about a pint and a half – in one go.

So, the night before what turned out to be our last game of Cowboys and Indians, we clubbed together all our pocket-money, wages from paper rounds and takings from milk-delivery jobs to buy several bottles of Irn Bru. We were going to sort out once and for all the question of who was the real John Wayne amongst us.

One of my pals dropped out before the contest even began. He had asthma and almost choked to death straight after the priest gave him his first Holy Communion. Some took this as a sign that he was a devil-worshipper and that he'd go straight to Hell. But we knew he'd just forgotten to take a puff on his inhaler. Therefore he magnanimously decided not to take part in the John Wayne-Irn Bru contest on the grounds that there was a good chance he would die.

I quickly fell by the wayside after drinking a quarter of a bottle. I knew I was defeated when the fizzy drink started coming out of my nostrils. Two or three other boys also gave up before long. The biggest amongst us went last. He was truly determined to prove he was Cleland's John Wayne. Before he began he took the whole John Wayne Irn Bru rumour one stage further when he said: 'Of course John Wayne smashes the bottom of one bottle and inserts the second straight into it so he can drink the two at the same time. That way he doesn't even need to take a breath between bottles!'

Again we were speechless.

He then proceeded to gulp for all he was worth. And he gulped. And gulped. And kept on gulping. He gulped his way through two and a half bottles. When he finished there was silence. Our little group was bewildered and impressed beyond words with this truly awe-inspiring display of John Waynism. He smiled, raised his arms in victory, turned around grinning and promptly puked up all over me. My world turned a rusty shade of red. It was an Irn Bru shower. Three hours of shampooing couldn't get it all out of my hair.

When the next day dawned I found my head glued to the pillow with Irn Bru. The gut-wrenching display of the previous night had put a pall over things and we weren't our usual selves when we went to play Cowboys and Indians later.

I wonder now if we knew then that it would be our last time ever.

As usual we ended the afternoon's proceedings by sitting in a ring on the grass and discussing the merits and deficiencies of our favourite Hollywood outlaws. We only picked serious cowboy films; *Billy the Kid vs. Dracula* and its follow-up *Jesse James Meets Frankenstein's Daughter* didn't make the grade with us. (We did once spend about an hour talking about Abbott and Costello in a film called *Ride 'em Cowboy* which I think some of us secretly liked.) We stuck to the real thing that told the 'true' stories of 'real' outlaws. So somebody took Jesse James as a hero, a couple backed Billy the Kid and at least one liked Wild Bill Hickock. One of my friends and I chose Butch Cassidy and the Sundance Kid. I liked them because they were funny. And we all really liked Butch in the scene when he sneakily kicked a big brawny guy right in the balls! Unbelievable!

We all talked about that scene and screwed up our faces imagining the pain. We rolled about on the grass clutching our crotches tightly. Balls are very tender and very vulnerable – even at ten we knew this. Girls didn't have a clue. What did they know of the agony of jumping on your bike to deliver news-papers, only to slip and crush your balls on the crossbar in a split-second? How could they understand how our young lives pass before our eyes when this happens? Butch must have known, though. He knew where to kick a big guy wielding a knife all right, didn't he?

My pal said he liked the Sundance Kid because he was the fastest gun in the West and that he liked the bit in the film where he shot a guy's belt off, then fired more bullets at it, causing it to whip across the saloon floor like a slithering snake. As we talked about outlaws we mentioned the places they came from: Chey-enne, Deadwood, Boothill. But we couldn't agree on whether Bonanza was a TV series' name or a real place, so we gave up. I think we liked hearing ourselves say these places out loud in our Scottish accents. It made them seem more real and perhaps a bit nearer.

But our conversation that day, like our earlier exploits, died out earlier than usual. And now, looking back, I believe, each one of us in our own way knew the reason why.

The arrival of a visitor to the village had affected our lives. This visitor was a couple of years older than us and had, for

The 1969 movie *Butch Cassidy and the Sundance Kid* featured Paul Newman as Butch Cassidy, Robert Redford as the Sundance Kid and Katherine Ross as Etta Place (courtesy 20th Century Fox)

TOP: Butch's Scottish grandfather; his father, Maximilian Parker; and his mother, Annie Gillies Parker (courtesy Bill Betenson); BOTTOM: Robert LeRoy Parker alias Butch Cassidy. This photograph was taken when Cassidy was in jail in 1894. He always claimed it was a bad likeness because it made his eyes look too small; RIGHT: Harry A. Longabaugh alias the Sundance Kid with Etta Place (both courtesy Dan Buck and Anne Meadows)

LEFT: Harvey Logan alias Kid Curry, the most feared, brutal and unhinged member of the Wild Bunch, with his girlfriend, probably a prostitute named Annie Rogers; RIGHT: William Ellsworth 'Elzy' Lay, the quiet, well-read and thoughtful friend of Butch Cassidy (both courtesy Bill Betenson)

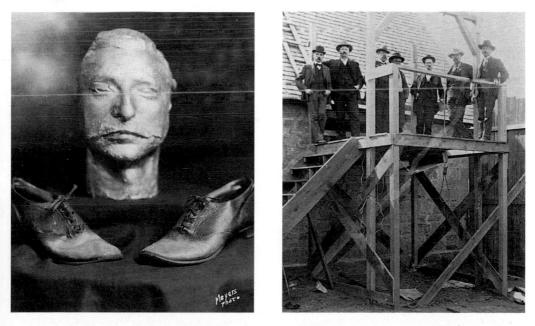

LEFT: the death mask of Big Nose George Parrot and the pair of shoes made from his skin (courtesy Wyoming State Archives); RIGHT: frontier-justice: this particular set of gallows was erected for the hanging of Charles F. Woodard in Casper in March 1902, but it's representative of countless others used during the same period (courtesy Casper College Archives)

Joe LeFors and the complicated and deadly Tom Horn. They were both part of a new breed of lawmen at the turn of the century who were every bit as ruthless, fast and egocentric as the men they tracked (courtesy Bill Betenson, left, and Wyoming State Archives, right); a train carriage blown up by the Wild Bunch at Wilcox (courtesy Wyoming State Archives)

TOP: the original Hole-in-the-Wall cabin in Wyoming. Used by countless outlaws, this area was a virtual no-go area for the law (courtesy Casper College Archives); BOTTOM: the Wild Bunch caught letting their guard down for one brief moment in 1900. This photograph was a gift for detectives all over the USA. Seated from left to right: Harry 'Sundance Kid' Longabaugh, Ben 'Tall Texan' Kilpatrick and Robert LeRoy 'Butch Cassidy' Parker; standing: Bill 'News' Carver and Harvey 'Kid Curry' Logan (courtesy Dan Buck and Anne Meadows)

Chicago & North Western Depot.
Casper, Wyoming.

Opposite page: TOP: Oscar Hiestand's Harness shop, Casper, in the 1890s, a typical scene from a frontier town in the West; MIDDLE: the train station in Casper – it was from here that the armed posse headed for Johnson County in 1892 (both courtesy Casper College Archives); BOTTOM: cowboys at the CY ranch in Wyoming about 1890. The trumpet hanging on the wall indicates the entertainment that these cowboys enjoyed in this rather bleak-looking cabin. Some believe that the man second from the right might be Tom Horn (Collection of Emilie Demorest Mosher; Frances Seely Webb Collection, Casper College Library)

This page: TOP: having managed to evade North American justice, Sundance, Etta and Butch relax in front of their cabin at Cholila in the Chubut territory of Argentina around 1903 (courtesy Paul D. Ernst); BOTTOM: a posse, not exactly chomping at the bit, readying itself to chase the Wild Bunch following the Tipton train robbery in August 1900 (courtesy Wyoming State Archives)

TOP: nothing remarkable in this photograph of a railroad crew around 1910 – except one thing: is the man fifth from the left an older, very much alive Butch Cassidy? Did he assume another identity and settle down after his alleged death in Bolivia? BOTTOM LEFT: an enlargement of the above picture; compare to the photo of Butch on page 2 – is it the same man? (courtesy Bill Betenson); BOTTOM RIGHT: William T. Philips – a resident of Spokane, Washington. Many people claimed this man was Butch Cassidy who'd returned from South America to settle down to respectable married life (courtesy Dan Buck and Anne Meadows)

some reason we couldn't understand, managed to encroach on all our waking thoughts. Perhaps a few sleeping dreams were also invaded by the visitor's presence – mine certainly were. None of us admitted this to the others, though. I suppose we didn't even know what we were feeling. All we knew, in our confused silence, was that we felt different. At some times of the day we even looked different. We woke up in the morning with bulges in our underwear after strange dreams. We'd all been changed for ever by this visitor; the stranger whose name was Marlyn, who was from England, who was blonde, who was beautiful, who had blossoming breasts and who we all wanted to kiss.

And who, as far as we knew, didn't fancy boys who played Cowboys and Indians with somebody's pipe-smoking uncle looking on.

Consequently, even though it was a bright sunny day in the woods, we all were happy enough to leave early and head back home less bloodied from our gunfighter battles than usual.

In the distance the huge Ravenscraig steelworks made its usual clanking and banging. The deep grumbling from the furnaces went on night and day. Often in the middle of the night there would be an unearthly bang from deep in its iron bowels. We'd jolt awake, know instantly what it was and fall straight back into a deep sleep. Somewhere in the very back of our minds, maybe because of dinner-table talk from our parents, we knew that as long as that place kept making odd noises and nocturnal farts we'd have food on the table and presents at Christmas and on birthdays.

As we trooped home in the late-afternoon light the atmosphere amongst us was flat and tense. We were growing up by the second and a whole chapter of our lives, the cowboys years, has just been closed permanently. We promised ourselves that we'd go back and play the next day, the next week and the following summer holidays. But we never did. Our imaginary guns, chaps, hats, holsters and horses were locked away somewhere and forgotten about. Very soon we'd be embarrassed to admit we had even enjoyed them once.

Patrick's uncle walked ahead of us pondering the scenery and puffing on his pipe as usual. I studied him and watched the faraway look in his eyes. He fascinated me more than he did the other boys because I knew he'd travelled the world as a merchant seaman. While we ran around in circles shooting one another and dying amid the Texas tumbleweed that often blew through our imaginations during the short West of Scotland summers, I would look up and see him gazing into space. In my mind I imagined him thinking about white sand shimmering on a foreign shore, lit by the last golden rays of a deep red sunset. There was a dark-skinned woman sitting on the shore waiting for him and in my imagination she was always incredibly beautiful.

I once plucked up the courage to ask him what it was he was thinking about in his deep daydreams. Was it the sea? Was it the ocean? Or was it a sandy beach with a stunning woman waiting for him?

'No,' he answered, refilling his pipe, 'I'm thinking about my football pools coupon actually.'

I never quite believed this answer. I knew he'd been about and I'm certain his mind must have returned to the places he'd seen during his travels.

He once brought his nephew Patrick a straw hat that had a band around the brim that said 'Haiti' on it. I thought it looked deeply exotic. From that moment on I imagined all natives of Haiti being short like me, brown-skinned and wearing little straw hats on their heads that said 'Haiti' in red lettering.

Shortly afterwards he gave Patrick a box of little Action Men that he'd acquired on his travels in the Far East. None of us even owned one doll, so to see three or four together was breathtaking. There was even one that talked. We all sat in silence as

Patrick dressed the little plastic man in a frogsuit that had a hole in the back so you could hear him talking when you pulled a string that dangled between his shoulder-blades. After he'd finished dressing the figure in the rubber suit he plunged him into the bathtub and pulled the string. The man said something but none of us knew what it was. Patrick pulled him out and dried him off with a towel. Then he pulled the string again carefully. 'Mushi, Mushi . . . garble, garble, garble,' said the little figure.

I'd seen badly dubbed kung-fu films and I had half an idea the Action Man was speaking a language from the Far East. Whatever the case, it certainly wasn't English. My pal was stony-faced and confused. I think he had his suspicions about the ethnic origins of his Action Man as well. No one wanted to say anything since he was bigger than every one of us. He was our John Wayne and liable to clobber us if we laughed at him.

His face suddenly brightened when I took the plastic man from him and pulled its string, saying just as the tinny-sounding gibberish started: 'Listen, he's talking in top-secret military code!'

My pal smiled; I'd given him an escape route and saved his face. Everyone breathed a sigh of relief and we promptly set about drowning the Japanese Action Man in the bath. Out of the corner of my eye I caught my pal's gaze. He owed me and he knew it.

The price I exacted was the loan of the Haiti hat and an American Action Man which had a cowboy outfit. For hours I looked at the straw hat and the word 'Haiti' in red writing on it's little white band. I closed my eyes and imagined the sun, the sea and coconuts and the woman on the beach.

And then there was the cowboy Action Man. This one didn't talk, he just stood there with an unlikely looking crew-cut and a determined expression on his face. He had real leather chaps, a plastic stetson and a shiny little gun. I played with him for two whole days whilst wearing Patrick's Haitian straw hat. My ten-year-old mind happily wandered off on an exotic voyage looking for cowboys.

A day or two later I handed back the hat and the cowboy Action Man to my pal as agreed. He grabbed the little plastic man off me and casually threw him on to the bedroom floor. He announced he had new toys to play with. I still liked the old ones. His uncle had bought him a pair of red and yellow leather boxing gloves. He seemed as keen on these as he was on the other gifts when he was first given them. Because he only had one pair of gloves I didn't think we could hold a proper match. But he had a suggestion. We put on one glove each, put the spare hand behind our backs and knocked hell out of each other for hours. We ended up sweaty and itchy, with bright red faces.

As I was leaving he accidentally sat on the straw hat. Laughing loudly, he pulled it out from under him, scrunched it up violently and then threw it into the bin.

I stormed off in the huff, leaving him confused. The forlorn cowboy Action Man figure lay at his feet as he stood at the bedroom door watching me go. He genuinely couldn't understand why I was so annoyed. 'It was only a stupid hat!' he called after me.

I ran home crying, feeling angry and sorry for myself.

8. Hole-in-the-Ceiling, Hole-in-the-Wall

Sheets of thin snow scudded across the Wyoming highway. I pulled off Interstate 25 at a fuel station. Around me the increasingly hilly landscape looked shrouded and grey. A solitary customer stood at the gas station pumping fuel into his red truck. He wore a thick woolly hat pulled down over his ears and was totally oblivious to my presence.

The place I was in was called Chugwater – a name not easily forgotten. I squinted around. The area looked like it sounded.

Inside the gas station a few old locals sat around wearing hats and heavy layers of dark woollen clothing. Steam had condensed on the window near where they sat. They were stiff, fat old characters with bulbous noses and baseball caps tipped back on their heads at a jaunty angle. One chewed on a matchstick and wore a bright, very conspicuous camouflage hunting jacket. Its cuffs and elbows were shaded a dark coffee colour with layers of shiny grease. All the old guys had thick and powerful hands.

None of them spoke to each other, they were all just sitting there staring into space. Then, quite unexpectedly, one of them began to fart. The sound was loud and seemed to last for a long time. The others didn't react.

The farter looked up at me from under his cap and blinked his watery eyes. 'Hell of a day.' The others all coughed in agreement.

Then he put a full stop to his pronouncement by sounding off a very short – though in terms of its decibel level, remarkably dramatic – second fart. Just as he did this one of the other men beside him suddenly checked his wristwatch. It made me wonder if he set his watch by the activities of the other guy's bowels.

After the farting stopped they all stared into space again. One slowly closed his eyes and began to fall asleep. His old lips flapped like wet sheets on a washing line as he snored.

No one said a word.

The men reminded me of old miners back home in Scotland that I'd known when I was a newspaper delivery boy. The old men used to wake up every morning at five o'clock and troop down to the only shop in the village that was open at that early hour – the newsagent's – where they would congregate and pass the time. For decades they'd risen at that time in the morning for their early shift in the mines and even when they retired they couldn't get out of the habit.

A sign in the Chugwater gas station said: 'Try Our World-Famous Chilli'. The woman behind the desk taking my money smiled and thanked me in a chirpy sort of way. Country and Western music played in the background. I bought a little postcard of the town and went back to my truck to continue my journey north.

The old guys stared out of the window at me as I drove off.

❈

On a whim I decided to look around the town so I ignored the signs for the highway and drove by some dilapidated buildings looking for Chugwater. I drove for ten minutes without seeing a thing. The snow was billowing around the truck and the light was starting to fail. I pulled over and referred to the postcard in an effort to get a fix on the town. The image on the card was ancient, maybe from the 1920s, and it showed an old car driving through a vast landscape with a couple of houses in the background which I assumed was Chugwater in its early days. I looked up and squinted out of my window. In the distance I saw low hills, more hills and then off on the western horizon, mountains. Near the gas station I'd just left were a few clapped-out old buildings. I glanced back at the postcard. It showed the same scene seventy years previously. Even the buildings looked unchanged. That's when it dawned on me. The town of Chugwater consisted of these half-dozen dilapidated old houses. I examined the postcard again. I was wrong; things *had* changed. The sepia-coloured postcard showed six or seven houses – now I counted only four. Above one old wooden house there was a faded sign; like the one in the gas station, it announced: 'Chugwater's World-Famous Chilli'. A strong gust of wind whipped under it and whacked it backwards and forwards against the faded red paintwork. The clapping sound echoed across the road and into the grey-and-green distance. I wondered who had made the chilli world famous as I retraced my short journey back to gas station where I joined the main interstate highway again.

My route took me northwards towards a large town called Casper in northern Wyoming. The railway line ran alongside the road for long stretches. Thin trees poking out of the rocky landscape were bent over by the wind. My truck wobbled from side to side as I sped along the grey highway.

In the previous few days I'd become addicted to the Weather Channel on TV. It was sad. Hour after hour I'd sit with my mouth open watching the presenters yack on about how warm it was in places like Miami or Dallas. Then they'd grimace and say, 'Now we'll look at the picture out west,' before starting to talk about where I was. Their reports said Wyoming was the worst place to be. In the north-western states the storms were mostly heavy rain but by the time they'd crossed the Rocky Mountains to where I was they'd turned into blizzards. To begin with I'd scoffed at the idea of a twenty-four-hour weather channel. Who had such a pathetic life that they needed to see what the weather was going to be like all the time? Well, me for one. After a couple of days I'd even begun to get to know the presenters. One guy reminded me of a university lecturer I once had. He looked sad and permanently hungover. Even his suits looked as if they had headaches. My viewing had refined itself to the point where I made sure I was watching when my favourite presenter appeared. She was a black woman who always seemed on the verge of laughing when she talked about bad weather.

About fifty miles south of Casper the weather changed for the worse. The forecast said the road would be 'slick in parts'. I thought this meant some ice here and there. In actual fact the road had turned into a very long white ice-rink. Cars drove bumper to bumper. Then the wind got up again. I switched on the radio to pass the time. The weather reporter told me the coldest place in America was due south of Casper. He also said 'ground blizzards' were making driving particularly hazardous. I turned the radio off in a foul temper.

No one had warned me what a 'ground blizzard' was. I'm glad, because within minutes I found myself in the middle of one.

A ground blizzard is a complete white-out caused by the wind blowing the dry snow lying on the ground across vast stretches of unprotected land. This means that you can't see your hand in front of your face despite the fact that seconds before the sky was blue and the sun was shining. It's one of those odd games that nature likes to play every so often to show you who's the boss. A ground blizzard appears on the horizon like a white ghost. You drive into a cloud of snow. The sky can still be seen through the windscreen but then it goes dark grey all over. Suddenly you are in the middle of a blizzard. You pass cars tipped over on their sides, while the car in front is visible only by its brake lights. You lose your sense of distance. The road vanishes completely, vehicles on the other side of the road are gone too and quite suddenly you're trapped in this odd world where sound is dramatically dampened. Everything outside your car looks the colour of thick milk.

Then, as if by magic, you drive out of it like an aeroplane emerging from a cloud. And the blue sky is back, the sun is shining and the road looks normal. But your hands are white from gripping the wheel and you've sweated buckets from sheer naked fear.

I drove thirty miles through regular stretches of ground blizzards. I was soaked in sweat by the time I reached Casper. I felt stupid for feeling so worn out from driving through weather conditions the locals probably dealt with on a daily basis.

Casper looked to be recovering from one massive blizzard and preparing for the next. Huge snowdrifts lined the roads and cars splashed through knee-high slush that the ploughs hadn't touched. I pulled into a motel and checked in for the night.

'Hey! We got a customer!' The manager was an Asian guy with a bright smile. 'Everyone else is leaving but you're arriving.'

'Why are they leaving?' I noticed a steaming swimming-pool behind the reception looked very empty.

'Now is the winter of our discontent.' He swiped my Visa Card and smiled. I didn't react. My mind was still thirty miles down the highway in a ground blizzard.

'Shit weather is coming in, man – try channel nineteen for

the weather news.' He shrugged as if to say 'not my fault'.

I headed for my room. Fat kids and their equally obese parents passed me carrying tartan travelling blankets and large wedges of pizza that drooped at the edges. The hallway reeked of burning fat.

❁

My stopover point of Casper in northern Wyoming was a relatively short drive from a place called Kaycee. This had once been the site of the KC ranch, a well-known landmark a hundred years ago. If you'd been an outlaw in this area a century ago you wouldn't have stayed in Casper too long because that's where the big businessmen and their friends the sheriffs were. Instead you'd have mounted your horse and ridden northwards towards the KC ranch. Once there you'd have headed about thirty miles west into the high red hills until you found a stream and some other landmarks which told you you were near Hole-in-the-Wall. Many outlaws had hidden themselves here at one time or another.

Nowadays Hole-in-the-Wall is on private land, part of a large group of seemingly impenetrable sandstone hills that rise in a dramatic, almost vertical sweep from the thin grass fields. The so-called 'wall' starts off at ground level as a series of large boulders and ends as a huge red cliff-face. You can't imagine ever finding a way through it, over it or around it. It seems to stop you dead in your tracks. From a distance it looks nothing special. That's where its secret lies. There is a slight, hardly visible crack in its exterior which allows you, if you know where the gap is, to pass through the wall to the other side. That's where the outlaws set up their headquarters. Like many historical places it sounds far more romantic than it really is.

I'd come to this area because of its rich outlaw history and because of its direct connection with the Wild Bunch. Some said that Butch Cassidy liked Hole-in-the-Wall because he believed one man could hold off an entire posse with just one rifle. Others dismissed it as nothing more than a few low-slung wooden cabins where louse-ridden outlaws liked to hibernate during long winters. Either way it was a handy, well-used place which the law rarely, if ever, entered. Although it was one of Butch's favourite haunts, it was not his main one. Like all outlaws, he moved around. He had to.

Hole-in-the-Wall was used during the Wild West's real heyday, from 1875 till 1895. Frank and Jesse James had gone there after fleeing from trouble in Deadwood, South Dakota. The Sundance Kid had also used the hideout after trying to rob a train in Malta, Montana, in 1892. He'd managed to steal only nineteen dollars and twenty cents (not exactly something to brag about around the campfire), and get himself arrested and locked up in the process. The only successful part of the botched job was Sundance's subsequent jail-break which saw him flee to Hole-in-the-Wall.

Other outlaws, such as the Logan brothers, had used Hole-in-the-Wall as a base from which to run their cattle and horse-rustling enterprises. The area's dangerous reputation meant nosy law officers rarely poked their beaks in to see whose brands were on the livestock that grazed behind Hole-in-the-Wall's red sandstone. Locals in nearby settlements paid little or no attention to the outlaws – some turned a blind eye while others lived in fear. The occasional businessman in nearby Casper gladly traded with the thieves living in the Hole, who in turn happily turned a fast buck selling stolen livestock fattened on winter grazing near the outlaws' cabins. From Casper the cattle and horses were quickly taken by rail to other, more profitable, markets.

For a while places like Hole-in-the-Wall flourished quietly. Inevitably, however, the changes taking place in the rest of the west began to affect even the worst of the worst outlaws living there. The 'frontier' both as an idea and a reality was slowly disappearing. The explorers, miners, railroad workers, hookers, gamblers, gunslingers, thieves and outlaws were in many ways already turning into caricatures of themselves. The railroad had opened up almost everywhere for examination. People from the east, 'dudes' in fancy suits and delicate lace-up shoes, were appearing with alarming regularity and in greater numbers. At first they were made fun of and sent home with their pants around their ankles, but towards the mid-1890s there was a definite whiff of change in the air in Wyoming, Utah, Colorado and indeed throughout the rest of the Old West. The whole of western America was slowly becoming 'civilised'. That meant businessmen were starting to hound politicians to clean things up and politicians in turn began badgering sheriffs to clamp down on local lawlessness. The outlaws were, to all intents and purposes, starting to get in the way. They stirred the imagination of the settlers too much. People were required to conform and pay taxes. They were required to respect the rights and property of the larger landowners. And so places like Hole-in-the-Wall began to take on more significance than they probably deserved. Once a vague stopping-off point for outlaws moving between states, it now became a haven for such men to live the life they imagined they were entitled to. All the rotten eggs began to drift towards the same destination. They had no choice. It was one of the few places left where outlaws could still be outlaws without anyone complaining. They met there in greater numbers than ever before and lived in fear of the local sheriff or landowners who might, just might, get brave and decide it was time to flush them out once and for all.

After he was released from Laramie Penitentiary in 1896 Butch Cassidy headed straight back into a life of crime. His first port of call was Robbers' Roost in south-east Utah, another lawless area where few sheriffs ever set foot. For the most part the faces he'd met in Brown's Hole before he'd been sent to jail were still there, as were the regulars at Hole-in-the-Wall. And they all still tended to look towards Cassidy as their leader. He was always full of madcap ideas which kept deranged minds occupied.

In the winter of 1896–97 he had a crazy scheme which involved tents – big canvas tents that measured twelve by sixteen feet. His plan was for Elzy Lay and his new wife to stay in one and for Sundance and his girlfriend Etta Place to stay in another. Butch persuaded them to do exactly that – for the entire winter. They would have afforded little or no protection from the high winds and blizzards which brought huge snowdrifts to the mountains. Spirits were kept high with booze, other women and card playing, however. Gambling was enjoyed by all and plans were hatched for raids and robberies the following spring.

The area was very sparsely populated, but the few who did live near Robbers' Roost knew full well who occupied the large, conspicuous tents bought with stolen loot. The best known of the locals was an Englishman called J.B. Buhr – known as Wheezin' Buhr because he suffered from bad asthma. He kept his head down most of the time and minded his own business. A local newspaper in the area, however, went out of its way to draw attention to the gang in April 1897:

> Something must be done to break up the gang of robbers and murderers now ensconced in the San Rafael mountains, and the state will have to do it . . . For many years it has been known that if a desperado reached the mountain fastnesses in that region he had entered the 'City of Refuge'. No officers have ever gone there, for the reason that for a small company of officers to do so would simply be to go into a trap where death would be as certain and swift as if they plunged into the mouth of a volcano . . .

This, of course, was exactly what the outlaws in Robbers' Roost wanted people to think. The reality was probably a little less dangerous. The public's perception of reality, however, meant that volunteers to go into the area were few and far between. That didn't stop the odd sheriff from trying from time to time to raise a posse to raid the area and arrest the outlaws. Reputations were enhanced when efforts, no matter how half-hearted or vague, were made to at least enter the Roost.

Butch Cassidy's presence in the area was certainly not the only reason why sheriffs were, in theory at least, keen to venture into Robbers' Roost if they got a chance. While he'd languished in the State Penitentiary for eighteen months his fellow outlaws, including the Sundance Kid, had got on with robbing as many people as possible. That, after all, was their livelihood.

When he returned to his outlaw friends, Cassidy took things easy for a while, probably gently easing himself back into the position of leader, while letting the other thieves and rogues do their own thing. One of the first documented hold-ups he participated in after his release was the Montpelier Robbery in Idaho on 13 August 1896. He took seven thousand dollars that day – enough to hire a lawyer for his friend Matt Warner who was cooling his heels in prison awaiting trial. Butch's personal lawyer, Douglas A. Preston from Rock Springs (where Cassidy had served his time as a butcher), was hired to get Warner off. The fat fee and the fancy clothes bought for the accused man failed to work their magic, however; Warner was sent down for five years. Butch was furious and offered to ride into town to help Warner in a jail-break. The wily older man told Butch to cool it, though, and said he'd serve his time without causing any trouble. Butch slunk off, angry and annoyed that his stolen money hadn't done the trick for his friend. There was a day when bribes, fancy hats and the threat of a gang of outlaws hitting town to aid a fellow ne'er-do-well would have been

enough to scare any judge into letting an accused man accidentally slip through his fingers. Not any more. Those days were
going fast. Pressure was now being regularly applied from the
state governors to secure convictions. It could be Butch's turn
next. Times were changing.

Cassidy's next outing was to the town of Castle Gate in his
home state of Utah. Riding a horse which one writer claims
was given to him by a man named Neibaur (the only surviving
messmate of the Austrian Grand Duke Rudolph, a royal who
was involved in a very tragic love affair resulting in his rather
messy suicide which his family subsequently covered up by
executing all his friends who'd witnessed the deed, with the sole
exception of Neibaur who escaped to America), Butch rode
into town and quietly cased the place for a few days. On
Wednesday, 21 April 1897, he and some accomplices robbed the
guard on an incoming train of eight thousand dollars – their
spring salary in their eyes – stopping only to cut telegraph wires
as they sped out of town. Their getaway was helped by an
unusually inept local sheriff who, as one chronicler commented,
'ran around in circles, lost several hours and, when he at last got
under way, started off in the wrong direction'.

The sheer audacity of the robbery and the coolness with
which it was executed cemented Butch Cassidy's reputation
amongst law-abiding and law-breaking people alike. He was the
public's outlaw and the outlaws' outlaw. And, like the celebrity
he was, he decided to party in style.

The outlaws' knees-up was held on 29 July 1897 in a town
near Robbers' Roost called Baggs. It was high summer,
although the days were muggy and thick, the nights were cool
and clear. When there was a full moon some of Butch's gang,
especially characters like the fevered Harvey Logan, were
known to 'go a bit funny in the head'. Butch was well aware of
this. By throwing some of his Castle Gate loot at the gang,
buying them drinks and fine clothes, he was in a sense buying

time and goodwill. Through the warm haze of heavy beer and rough whiskey several itchy trigger-fingers calmed down somewhat, and many glazed eyes looked towards Butch as a loyal leader and friend rather than as a competitor and show-off.

When it came to women and booze, Butch was known, for the most part, for his moral rectitude and physical restraint. On this occasion in July 1897, however, he hit the saloons in Baggs with as much relish as any of his boys. Within an hour twenty-five bullet holes were put in the ceiling of one establishment in Baggs. Butch smiled patiently and paid for the damage with a silver dollar piece for each hole. So impressed was one local aspirant with this display of conspicuous consumption that when he found himself short of cash he bolted out of the bar to rob and shoot dead a passing Mexican shepherd. He joyfully returned some time later with $480 with which he promptly bought everyone a drink. At Cassidy's insistence a minute's silence was held for the dead shepherd. Then everyone got legless.

So much money was spent in Baggs that night that it is said the local barman vanished with his takings the next day only to reappear months later as the proud proprietor of the finest saloon in the larger town of Rawlins. It was a night that passed into legend before the outlaws had even finished their first drinks.

At the end of the celebrations, those still conscious raised a glass to absent friends, especially the Sundance Kid who was on the run after an abortive attempt to rob a bank in Belle Fourche, South Dakota, a few weeks earlier. Rumours had reached Butch and the rest of the gang in Baggs that Sundance was hiding out with another man in Hole-in-the-Wall.

Sundance's troubles began when he and four accomplices – Walt Punteney, Tom O'Day, 'Flatnose' George Currie and Harvey Logan's brother, Lonnie – failed to thrash out the exact course of action each would take when the robbery got under way. Consequently, the whole thing turned to farce. O'Day was drunk when the robbery began, courtesy of two early-morning visits to a nearby saloon; he turned up late and failed to tie up his horse outside properly. Inside the bank Sundance and the others started shouting, waving their guns about and demanding cash. When a bystander's gun misfired inside the bank, the owner of the hardware store opposite ran out to see what was going on. O'Day tried to salvage the situation by shooting at him and chasing him back inside his shop. The robbers inside the bank panicked, grabbed ninety-seven dollars from a customer and fled for their lives.

The drunken O'Day didn't know what was happening and in the ensuing getaway he was left behind. Even his horse, its reins left lying loose by its inebriated owner, casually wandered off down a side street. Despite this, O'Day was determined not to be thwarted in his attempt to escape. Spying a likely-looking mule which didn't seem to have an owner he hopped on its back and gave it a good whack.

The mule didn't move.

He tried kicking it: it still didn't budge. He tried slapping it: no joy there either. The mule wasn't playing ball.

The drunken, staggering, cursing O'Day fell off the beast and weaved his way over to an outhouse where he thought he could hide until the fuss died down. It also gave a him a chance to take a few extra 'curers' – gulps to steady his nerves – from the pint of whiskey he had in his pocket. The owner of the outhouse, however, soon noticed something was wrong; even by western standards, the little structure stank more than usual. Several other people, with twitching noses, also began to focus their attention on the outhouse. As the owner would later testify in open court to the amusement of everyone except the judge, O'Day apparently 'smelled like a skunk'. The residents of Belle Fourche were just discovering what Butch and the boys had known for years – Tom O'Day hadn't seen a bath in his adult life and rarely washed even the body parts which stuck out from his clothes. He was duly arrested and imprisoned. And later, with the aid of a long-handled brush, he was forcibly washed.

The other robbers fled in different directions – Logan and Flatnose headed for Baggs and Butch Cassidy's gang for solace; Sundance and the fifteen year-old Punteney rode like the clappers for Hole-in-the-Wall in Wyoming. A posse of a hundred men tried to keep up with them. For weeks on end the outlaws held their own. Along the way Sundance and the teenage boy hooked up with Harvey Logan and decided to ride to Montana. Eventually all three were ambushed by the determined posse. Logan was shot in the wrist during the gun battle. Once again, the hapless Sundance Kid was in custody – it was his third time as an outlaw he'd found himself inside a cell. By late September he and the teenager were identified as the robbers from Belle Fourche, South Dakota. They played for time and claimed the law had arrested the wrong men. The sheriffs were sceptical and moved them to Deadwood Jail to await trial. On 31 October 1897, however, they were involved in a spectacular jail-break. Although O'Day and Punteney would subsequently be arrested, Sundance and Logan managed to gain their freedom. By any standards they were lucky men.

Another face missing from the Baggs party in July 1897 was Butch's pal Bob Meeks. Heads were shaken whenever Meeks' name was mentioned. The thick-jowled Bob, one of Butch's co-robbers from the slick Castle Gate job, was languishing in jail for attempting to rob a saloon in the town of Fort Bridger. The month before the Baggs party he'd been arrested along with two other characters who were known by their aliases of Dick Thompson and Waterhole Charlie. It was the start of a terrible run of luck for Meeks who would end up, in his own way, as legless as any of his drunken outlaw friends propping up the bar in Baggs.

Meeks was sentenced to thirty-two years, the maximum in

Idaho, for his crime. Shortly after entering the state penitentiary the desperate, claustrophobic criminal decided to make a bid for liberty by eating soap at regular intervals. A fellow thief had whispered to him during exercise that this produced symptoms similar to those displayed by TB sufferers. After a few weeks of eating carbolic soap, the wheezing, pasty-faced, shivering Meeks was huckled out of prison to a hospital. A few days later he climbed the wall and jumped to what he hoped would be freedom. Instead, he landed so badly that he smashed his right hip to pieces. Surgeons in the hospital had to amputate the whole leg. The authorities took pity on the one-legged outlaw and released him after he'd been discharged from hospital.

Thereafter the lonely Bob Meeks suffered from paranoia and alcohol abuse. He regularly shot bullets at his missing leg in an attempt to quell the ferocious itch he felt in the phantom limb the moment he drifted off to sleep.

Meeks died wearing a straitjacket in a Wyoming insane asylum in 1912, telling staff until the bitter end that his friend Butch Cassidy would one day come riding out of the hills to whisk his friend off to the old life of high adventure and mayhem.

These absences from the Baggs gathering in July 1897 illustrate how fluid and loose an organisation the Wild Bunch really was. While Butch and his friends were drinking Baggs dry and shooting up the saloons, prominent outlaws like the Sundance Kid, Harvey and Lonnie Logan and Bob Meeks were all off elsewhere carrying out their own half-baked jobs. Most would be caught at one time or another and the financial returns were rarely very high. Apart from his eighteen-month incarceration for horse-stealing, Butch Cassidy managed to stay free and rich. By common outlaw standards of the time, that was a very unusual achievement.

It's also worth remembering that these same outlaws were, more often than not, more than a little unhinged; they were dangerous characters who were very choosy about who they allowed to buy them drinks and lead them into robberies. The fact that Cassidy was consistently liked, trusted and respected by these men means that it's fair to suggest he was something special.

❀

I drove through the snow-covered streets of Casper towards the local archives which were kept in a nearby college. The place felt like a frontier town. The streets were wide and open; someone later told me they were broad enough to allow a ten-horse carriage to turn around in a full circle.

The college sat above the town in an incongruously modern building. Elegant old gingerbread houses surrounded it, their snow-covered lawns spacious and generously proportioned. Beautiful oaks lined the streets. Warm copper-coloured lights glowed through fine lace curtains.

The archives for the area were packed into a few rooms above the hushed, thickly carpeted college library. One of the archivists, Kevin, quietly showed me to a desk and began pulling out boxes for me. He spoke in low tones but soon warmed to telling me about the area. I told him I'd driven through Chugwater.

'Did you try the chilli?'

'No, but I saw the signs for it. Why's it world famous?'

'Because it's easy to cook and they serve gallons of the stuff to anyone who arrives there during the winter blizzards. I'll bet there's one person in every country in the world who's eaten the stuff. Hundreds of drivers get stuck there for days on end when the big snows come in. Your penance is they serve you Chugwater chilli . . . which you have to pay for. It's the only town for hundreds of miles. You should be glad you didn't get stuck there. I did – once. Never again. My guts couldn't withstand the shock twice in the same lifetime.'

I could tell he wasn't kidding. He smiled and went back to the archives. I watched him leaf carefully through piles of old documents.

'Of course you know all about the KC ranch, Hole-in-the-Wall and how Butch Cassidy and the Wild Bunch used it as a hideout?' he said.

I related to him the extent of my knowledge. He nodded and looked through some more papers. He stopped at one page in particular and tapped it with his finger. Then his face slowly broke into a smile.

'What about Big Nose George? Hole-in-the-Wall was one of his favourite haunts.'

'Who?'

'Big Nose George Parrot. An outlaw. One of the first to use Hole-in-the-Wall when he was on the run. He predated Butch and Sundance by a few years but I'll bet they knew his story.' He seemed enthusiastic and I was intrigued if only by the name.

'Hold on,' he said. He disappeared into a back room. Seconds later he reappeared waving an old photograph.

'That's our man – Big Nose George in all his glory!' He clapped down the picture for me to examine.

I looked at the mugshot. George did indeed have a nose of Cyrano proportions. It was gloriously big, a facial feature of truly legendary dimensions. It almost stretched to his chin. Even a huge bushy moustache shrank in its presence. His eyes peered off into the distance and his hair was slicked back. He looked every inch the frustrated outlaw. Frustrated because, I'd learn later, he couldn't disguise his big schnozzle. Even with a cotton pillowcase over his head, train guards were known to shout: 'Did you see that fellar's profile when he turned side on? I'd know Big Nose George anywhere!' That nose haunted George all his life.

'He was ruthless,' said Kevin. 'He used to rob innocent

people on the Oregon Trail – people who had little or nothing to begin with. When stagecoaches died out he moved on to trains. Around here was his territory. His last robbery was in August 1878 – it was botched by George and his two accomplices, one of whom was called Dutch Charlie. In the process of trying to rob the train they also killed two local sheriffs – that's what got everybody's blood up at the time. George's two fellow outlaws were arrested and brought back to Rawlins to be hung. At his hanging, when Dutch Charlie was asked if he had any last words, the widow of one of the slain sheriffs stepped forward and said: "No, the sonofabitch ain't got nothin' to say!" Then she kicked the barrel from underneath him.

'After that disastrous 1878 job Big Nose George went on the run. When he heard what they'd done to Dutch Charlie he knew he could be next. He eventually surfaced in Montana two years later where his big mouth and his big nose made him stand out in a crowd. He was arrested and sentenced to be hung in Rawlins in March 1881. He subsequently tried to break out of jail but was hauled before a lynch mob whereupon he begged forgiveness and confessed to the crime. Unusually, they let him go and the sheriff put him back in prison. Later he tried to break out again, this time using a small penknife to saw through his heavy ankle and hand chains. He would have succeeded if it hadn't been for a quick-thinking sheriff's wife who grabbed a gun when she heard a commotion in the cell where Big Nose George was being held. He'd taken her husband hostage. The woman locked George and her husband in the cell together and called for help. When assistance arrived it turned out that George had attacked the sheriff, fracturing the other man's skull in three places. At that point the local lynch mob turned up and hauled George off to the nearest telegraph pole to be hung. As he was dragged out of the cell he apologised to the blood-covered sheriff and claimed he'd "got religion".'

'Did they hang him?' I asked staring at George's snapshot.

'Yeah, eventually,' said Kevin, 'on the fourth attempt. He wouldn't die and the rope and gallows were badly prepared. Wait a minute, I have a contemporary account of it in a book around here somewhere.' He disappeared back into the small ante-room again. I looked out of the windows. It was pitch dark and the wind was howling. Moments later he sat down and began to read. His voice filled the empty room.

'Here we are . . . It's from a newspaper report dated 22 March 1881. It's headline says, "Gone Up Higher! The Penitent Sick Man Recovers and Attempts the Life of the Jailer. An Indignant People Assist Him on His Way up the Golden Stair. Big Nose George Forcibly Taken from the Jail and Hung to a Telegraph Pole".' He went on: "At about the hour of 10.30 p.m. that night, a number of the citizens of Rawlins – I would say the best citizens of Rawlins – appeared at the county jail and requested a personal interview with one George Parrot, otherwise known as Big Nose George . . . They proceeded with him to a telegraph pole in front of J.W. Hugus and Company's store (on Front Street between Third and Fourth). About seventy-five people were assembled there. All those concerned with the hanging were masked. They procured a rope and fastened it to the pole. When a barrel was brought and George was placed upon it, another man in a white mask fastened the rope around his neck and said, 'All right.' Then someone said, 'Kick the barrel,' and the barrel was kicked away from under him. He, however, fell to the ground, either from the rope being too long or slipping, and someone said, 'Hang him over and make a good job of it this time.' A ladder was then brought and placed against the pole. Two or three men assisted George to mount the ladder, the man with the white mask again adjusting the rope. George said, 'It is a shame to take a man's life in this way,' and 'Give me time and I will climb the ladder myself and when I get high enough, I will jump off.' The ladder was pulled out from under him as soon as the noose was adjusted and he fell, his hands becoming untied. He climbed six or seven feet up and cried, 'For God's sake shoot me, boys, you wouldn't do this to a mangy mongrel dog! Do not let me choke to death!' He slipped down several feet and then climbed up again a little ways when he slid down again and finally hung with his arms about the pole for some time. Finally his arms fell to his side. Someone touched S.T. Lewis on the shoulder and said, 'Doctor, see if that man is dead yet.' Lewis went and felt his heart and could feel no beat, so he pronounced him dead. Another doctor, however, felt his pulse and said, 'He is not dead yet!' The crowd by this time had increased from 150 to 200. W. Daley, the undertaker, cut the body down at about 12 o'clock by the order of the coroner.'"

Kevin sat back in his chair after he finished talking. 'What do you think of that?'

'Gruesome.' I looked down at the photo of Big Nose George and imagined him swinging from a telegraph pole.

'It gets worse.' Kevin leaned over the book he was reading from and cleared his throat.

'"Another local doctor, named John Osborne, exhumed Big Nose George's body shortly after it was stuck in a pauper's grave. He wrote in his notes: 'I was permitted to make a plaster of Paris death-mask and also to remove the skin from the breast of the body, which was tanned and from it a pair of dress shoes was made. I instructed the shoemaker to keep the nipples on the skin to prove the skin was human. But he did not follow my instructions —'"'

'Good God! They skinned Big Nose George!' I cried. His image in the picture before me now took on a pathetic air.

'Hang on, I'm not finished yet. The doctor's assistant also kept a piece of George for posterity as well. Listen: "To his assistant Dr Lillian Heath he presented the top of the outlaw's skull. She shined it up a bit and used it as a door stop, the first thing a caller would see. When she received the skull cap it was still bloody with a piece of hair on it. There was a bullet mark on the skull. It was thick, only thin in one place. It indicated very small mentality. The sutures were grown together and the grey matter could not expand."'

'So much for the "civilised" doctors, eh?' I shook my head. 'Did no one give a damn about him?'

'I think there's something in here which answers that. Let's try this pile,' said Kevin.

We both leafed through some old documents and clippings until we came across one which mentioned that George's widow had requested his death certificate be sent back to her – in France. A letter from the French Consulate in New York to the Wyoming Acting Governor in August 1881 said:

> Sir: I have the honor to ask respectfully for a transcript or certificate of death relating to the late George Parrot, alias George Au-Gros-Nez, who was lynched in the beginning of last March at Rawlins Carbon County, Wyoming. The aforesaid certificate of death is required by the widow of this convict. Therefore I will be very much obliged to you if you have the kindness to give the necessary orders for sending this document to my office.
>
> I remain, sir, Respectfully Yours.
>
> A. Lefaiore.
>
> Consul General of France.

'So what happened to Big Nose George's ransacked corpse – did it eventually find a resting place?'

Kevin smiled. He leaned back in his chair and took his glasses off and rubbed his eyes. 'Well, there's one final twist. In 1950 a gang of construction workers were digging the foundations of an old store in Rawlins when they came across a tightly lidded whiskey barrel. They opened it to discover the still-intact skeleton of Big Nose George jammed inside.'

We sat in silence for a moment or two.

'Hey, I've got something I want you to read for me.' Kevin walked quietly across the room and pulled out a small tartan book that looked ancient and valuable.

'What's that?'

He seemed awkward and a bit embarrassed. 'It's Robert Burns. With your accent and all I was wondering if . . . The pages are marked. Would you mind?'

I took the tightly bound little book from him, smiled, opened it at the page-marker and began to read 'Tam o' Shanter'.

❁

The town of Casper, I discovered from further research in the college archives, had also been the major hub of activity during the so-called 'Johnson County War' which had taken place in the early 1890s. The term 'war' made the whole episode sound far more important than it actually was. But in symbolic terms, at least, it was very significant. It also confirmed the changing atmosphere in the West at that time.

The war was precipitated by the lynching of one Cattle Kate Watson, a rustler and prostitute who had 'the largest bosom for miles around', and her sometime husband and pimp, James Averill. Both were hated by the large ranch-owners since Cattle Kate and Averill blatantly robbed and rustled anything they could lay their hands on. The couple were lynched by a posse paid for by the area's cattle-owners in late 1889. Their deaths were brutal and painful. They were hung from a split cotton-wood tree which formed makeshift gallows. The *Casper Mail* newspaper reported that 'the kicking and wailing of those people was awful to witness'. It took about half an hour for the two rustlers to die. A ranch belonging to the couple was later auctioned off. It was bought for fourteen dollars and nineteen cents by one of the men who'd lynched them.

The cold-blooded murders of Watson and Averill underlined

the power of the Wyoming Stock Growers' Association. All the main cattle barons in the state belonged to this organisation and they all had a vested interest in cracking down on rustling. With strong – though underhand – political, economic and legal backing they had literally erased Watson's and Averill's very existence. Residents in the Johnson County and Hole-in-the-Wall areas were horrified. Many apparently honest cattle breeders and livestock dealers had dirtied their hands on more than one occasion by doing business with well-known rustlers. Both they and the district's lesser homesteaders were suddenly seized with the notion that a heavily armed posse could ride into their lives at any moment and seize both them and their stock. A sinister atmosphere of paranoia descended upon everyone who lived north of the town of Casper.

These fears were borne out by developments in 1892. The main protagonist in the whole affair was a man named Nathan Champion who lived in the Kaycee area. He was involved in rustling in the late 1880s to such an extent that he was known as the 'King of the Rustlers'. He believed he was above the law. This was bolstered by the fact that sheriffs in the area tended to turn a blind eye to such activities – by 1892, for example, out of a hundred arrests for rustling, only one single conviction was secured. The cattle barons who owned much of the land and the livestock on it were haemorrhaging profits; as far as they were concerned, desperate measures were called for. Champion – who wrote cheeky and abusive letters to the press deriding the cattle owners – had to be made an example of. They decided to hire some outsiders who had no emotional ties to the situation. Thus, on 5 April 1892, a posse of fifty-five men led by Major Frank E. Walcott left Denver and headed north out of Cheyenne for Casper on a special train which had been fitted out to their specifications. Two journalists from local newspapers were aboard the train acting as observers: public relations were all-important. The weather, however, was against them and a late spring blizzard slowed them down significantly. By the time the posse reached Johnson County most of the locals were waiting for them. But it didn't deter the gunmen from trying to nail the man they regarded as the ring-leader – Nathan Champion. A messy battle around his cabin followed, the outcome of which was that both Champion and his partner Nick Ray were killed. The posse had pumped twenty-eight bullets into Champion to make sure he was dead.

It was a short-lived victory for the hired guns. When news of the deaths reached the locals they took up arms and besieged the area around the Champion homestead. Cavalry from a nearby fort had to be sent for to rescue the invaders and escort them to safety. One writer commented on the impact of this incident: 'Through crafty propaganda, public sentiment had been moulded in favour of the cattle thieves, who posed as small cattlemen persecuted by big cattle barons.'

This was far from the case. But the very idea that the small 'underdog' settlers were being hounded to death by mercenaries paid for by the rich corporate cattle and ranch owners was enough to fill many outlaws with a sense of righteous indigna-tion. The subsequent newspaper publication of Champion's diary, kept up until the very minute of his death during the siege at his ranch by the hired posse, also exacted sympathy from many settlers and outlaws. The latter group were horrified that anyone would dare try and stop them doing what they did best – breaking the law. To them, breaking the law was an integral part of being a citizen of America and living in the West. If people were going to start killing them for stealing things and subverting the course of justice then they might as well pack up and go home to lead normal, law-abiding lives – a prospect which filled them all with utter dread.

News of the Johnson County War even reached the ears of Butch Cassidy who knew the Hole-in-the-Wall country and its residents intimately. His friend Matt Warner reported the situation in a style which conveys the outlaws' reaction:

> This move to exterminate cattle rustlers and put an end to cattle rustling seemed to us like a final blow to the Old West. We listened to Butch Cassidy's eloquent call to action, grabbed our Winchesters, and rode out to defend and preserve the Old West. Our peculiar way of defending the Old West was to get a good tough outfit of horses together and plenty of artillery, make a fast dash up into Johnson County country, take a big herd of cattle right from under the noses of the cattle kings, and show 'em they couldn't get away with their game of murdering and exterminating rustlers. 'If we let 'em get away with what they've started,' said Butch, 'this here won't be a free country any longer.'

Butch was, in essence, correct. After the Johnson County War, the rules of the game *had* changed. The West, for an outlaw of the 1890s, was not a 'free country' any more. But that didn't stop Butch, or the members of his Wild Bunch, from trying to live the law-breaking life they felt they were entitled to.

Somewhere at the back of their minds they may have suspected that they were the last of their kind.

❋

Before I left Casper, Kevin from the college archives suggested that I visit one of the town's oldest bars, the Bootleggers. He said that many of the most famous outlaws, including Butch and Sundance, Big Nose George, Harvey Logan and all the rest, had at one time or another passed through its swing doors. In more recent times, the likes of John Wayne, John Ford, Gary Cooper and Ernest Hemingway had sunk a few in there too. On my last night in town I headed for this famous watering-hole which, in its heyday, had been known as the Wunderbar. The new name Bootleggers, was a reference to the fact that Casper had been big on temperance during the days of prohibition. Some of the photos I'd spied in the archives had testified to this – old ladies with big overcoats, small round glasses and thick moustaches on their upper lips stood sternly overseeing barrels of booze being axed to pieces. The much sought-after liquid ran achingly into a nearby stream. You could almost hear the sound of grown men sobbing in the background as the matrons of Casper had their moment of power and glory.

I had a meal in the bar and talked to Debby, the owner. In her early forties she was small and pretty in a high-school cheer-leader sort of way. Her towering husband, all smiles and geniality, was also introduced. Then he was dismissed; he was officially in disgrace for some unforgivable disaster he'd brought about in their married life. He slunk off, managing to look friendly and in the doghouse at the same time.

'Oh yeah, this place saw them all,' said Debby. 'Whoever passed through Casper usually passed through that front door and often passed out on that floor. The tiles are original incidentally.' Debby flicked her blonde hair and fixed me with her green eyes. I noticed she had muscles in her forearms and she didn't look as if she suffered fools gladly. 'How's the food?'

'Fantastic.' I wasn't joking. It was the best food I'd tasted since I'd arrived in America.

She looked at me in disbelief. She was clearly having trouble believing anything that came out of a man's mouth, no matter who he was.

'I hear you're haunted,' I said to her. Kevin at the college had told me this.

'Yeah.' She perked up a bit. Her husband was summoned back to the table. He looked happy to be wanted, however briefly. 'Tell him about the ghost thing,' she instructed him. He smiled and nodded like a big kid. 'Well, I was in here by myself one Sunday night. I looked over in the corner and saw what looked like smoke. That's it, I guess.' He smiled. He nodded. He shrugged. Then he was told he could leave again. So he left.

Debby watched him go. She looked sad for a second or two. Then she took a deep breath. 'So the food's good, huh?'

I said again that it was excellent. She nodded and looked around at other customers coming and going. Finally her eyes shifted back to me.

'Other people have noticed objects moving. You know – "leave a box here and it turns up there" – that sort of thing. One person was touched in the back. And someone else saw the form of a woman downstairs as well.'

'Have you any idea whose ghost this is?'

'Well, the establishment can be traced back to the nineteenth century – it was inhabited by a woman who'd had three children. Two of them died from meningitis. In fact, Casper was quarantined for a while – nobody came or went from the town. People say it's the woman and her dead infants that haunt the place.'

She propped her chin on her hands and looked at me. I returned the stare for a moment. She was pretty. Very sad and very pretty. She blinked.

'Then again, many an outlaw came in here and never left after a gunfight. It could be the ghost of an outlaw, I suppose. Who knows? C'mere, let me show you something.'

We walked over to the bar. A TV showing baseball played in the background. A couple of men and a woman sat in the corner, smoking and drinking. Every so often a laugh erupted from their conversation.

Debby pointed to the ceiling. 'You'll have to take my word for it but underneath that ceiling is the real one. It's made of pure brass and it's pockmarked with bullet holes that were put there during gunfights at this very spot last century. And see that brass railing behind you? Well, that's where the women stood. They weren't allowed to cross that.'

The walls of the bar were covered with old photos of cowboys and what Debby referred to as 'western collectibles': leather and sheepskin chaps, holsters, spurs, boots, belts, waistcoats. One picture actually taken in the bar showed a group of men standing together having a drink. They all wore battered, sweat-stained cowboy hats and expressions of boredom or tiredness. In the middle of the group was a huge horse which was lapping up beer from a large jug sitting on the bar. No one looked in the least bit surprised or impressed by its presence. I looked at the photo closely. One of the men beside the horse had his flies undone. Another conspicuously hid his face. Maybe he was a wanted man who didn't want his picture taken. To a man they looked worn out and rough. Most had thick hands and burly shoulders. More than one looked sourly straight into the camera lens. The photographer had been a brave man to disturb them while they were drinking.

'That's my grandfather.' Debby pointed to a handsome man in another old picture. I squinted at the image. He looked proud and tough. Behind his head a sign hanging on the wall read: 'Don't Ask For No Darn Fool Dude Drinks!'.

It was time for me to leave. I thanked Debby for showing me around and for talking to me. I waved to her sheepish-looking husband who was serving people at the bar. He smiled a big wide-open handsome smile and waved me off. Debby looked away as I bade him farewell.

'The next time you're here, if there's less snow, I'll take you up to my ranch to so some horseriding.' I believed her. She seemed straightforward and open and I'd enjoyed chatting to her. I thanked her and kissed her goodbye.

'Watch yourself driving. There's another blizzard due in.' She genuinely sounded concerned. I said I would be careful. In the half-light of the doorway I noticed her distracted expression. She looked lost in her thoughts, as if something serious had suddenly occurred to her.

'I forgot to tell you something else,' she said.

'What?'

'My family are the largest breeders of Welsh corgis in America.'

9. Another Smiling Dog

I got up at five thirty the next morning. I looked out of the window. Casper was blanketed in snow. It was still pitch dark. I groaned and closed the curtains. I looked at the blank, lifeless TV and left it that way. I couldn't face the Weather Channel.

In the hotel foyer dozens of people milled around. Most wore cowboy hats and heavy boots. And that was just the women.

The receptionist seemed cheerful despite the early hour. I asked him about the weather. 'Big one's about to blow in over the mountains,' he told me. 'Folks here are hauling out I guess.' He smiled and offered me a complimentary lollipop after I'd paid my bill.

I ate breakfast in a nearby diner. It was only quarter past six yet the place was packed to capacity. Old ladies with lots of make-up and dyed woolly hair hobbled in wearing nylon trousers. Thermal long-johns sinking beneath the bottom of the trousers collapsed around their thin ankles. Crumbling men in baseball caps and padded jackets picked their way out to ancient old cars that resembled spaceships with their high fins and whitewall tyres. Truck drivers with order-forms sticking out of the top pockets of their dirty overalls and young girls wearing large, college sweatshirts, the cuffs pulled down over their cold hands, all queued up for service.

The diner smelled of smoke and grease and coffee and warm plastic. The waitresses were middle-aged women in white uniforms, outfits which made them look like tired nurses. They wore too much rouge on their cheeks, regulation thin white training shoes on their feet and thick white tights on their legs. They zipped in and out of the tables serving customers like anxious fireflies.

I ate breakfast and drank lots of coffee. I was dressed for cold weather and eating hot food made pools of sweat run down my back. I left the imprint of my overheated backside on the orange plastic seat when I stood up to leave.

As I drove out of Casper the dark brown of the pre-dawn light was giving way to a murky pewter sky. Clouds were banked along the black mountains. The snow was still falling but at least the light was slowly lifting. A long line of cars was heading out of town ahead of the impending winter storm.

I drove on to the highway and headed south. Within minutes I was in a ferocious ground blizzard. I drove for miles trying to keep an eye on the barely visible lights of a truck in front of me. Then it pulled over into the inside lane and I decided to overtake it. I put my foot down on the accelerator and gripped the wheel. I couldn't see more than five feet in front of me. The heavy snow had slowed time and dampened sounds as it did during previous blizzards. My hands shook from gripping the wheel and the muscles in my arms throbbed although I'd been on the road for only a short time. Then it happened.

There was a flash of light.

I was out of the other side of the blizzard. The snow had suddenly ceased. The sky had instantly cleared. The sun was shining brightly.

I looked over my shoulder. The curtain of white was behind me. It stretched across the highway, across the fields and across the hills on either side of the road as far as the eye could see. I watched it for a few seconds glad to see the back of it, safely locked in the frame of my rear-view mirror. Then I looked straight ahead out of the windscreen as the wipers did their work. I could see for miles clear across the plains, the hills and into the mountains. Nothing obstructed my view. There wasn't even a wispy cloud in the sky in front of me. It was breathtaking.

Okay, it wasn't really *that* breathtaking. There were ugly oil wells in the way – field after field of them in fact – pecking at the ground like aliens from a 1950s B-movie. If I had a mind to I could have let them spoil the view. Instead I chose to overlook their existence. I was too busy looking at the landscape behind them. It was nature at her awesome, comically-epic best. As far as I was concerned, everything else paled in comparison.

In any case, when I stopped to take some photographs I saw a number of deer wander down to one nearby drilling well. The cranking and clanging oil drill didn't seem to cramp their style too much. They seemed used to it. Hesitating, they nervously chewed on the scrubby grass near the platform. Their huge eyes blinked at me barely thirty feet away. Then, unexpectedly, they bolted off toward the hills in the distance. A screeching generator near the drilling platform had noisily spluttered into life, frightening them into a breathless, stricken panic in the process. A small dog suddenly appeared from a nearby field and barked first at the deer and then at me. I stood for a moment watching the mutt which stood motionless watching me. I was angry at the clanking generator which had spoiled my opportunity to snap the deer and the scenery. I began to see the drills for what they were – a series of ugly mechanical stains on the land. Then, quite unexpectedly, the little dog wandered over to the well and cocked its leg. It peed on the contraption for all it was worth. It was as if it had read my thoughts.

When it was finished, it shivered all over, shook itself and rubbed all four paws on the ground. Then, I swear to God, it showed its teeth and grinned at me. I thought I was seeing things. Maybe it was something I'd drank in Bootleggers the previous night. Before I could react the dog shot back off towards the field it had came from.

Now, strange as it may seem, that wasn't the first time I'd known such a dog. One of my uncles had a dog that used to do the same thing. It was a stray which had rescued him one night when, in a drunken stupor, he'd fallen head-first into a deep rubbish tip on his way home. If the dog hadn't dragged him out Lassie-fashion he'd have died when the next load of garbage was dumped on top him the next morning. My uncle survived the incident and kept the dog. In fact, it outlived him. He once sat me down and called the crazy animal over to the couch where we were sitting. He asked the dog how it was keeping. No response. It gave the regulation stupid-dog look.

He asked the dog if it liked its food. Still no response. Still the regulation stupid-dog look.

'Give us a big smile!' he said suddenly.

The dog smiled at us.

Honestly. Not a dog-bearing-its-teeth smile but a real, human, great-to-be-alive smile.

It was a genuine, in the flesh, fully-performing, smiling dog.

Now *that* was breathtaking.

❋

A century ago, life in the ragged, unforgiving northern states of the west had worn down Butch Cassidy. Too much bad weather, too much bad luck going around, too much so-called progress and too many dudes in the way, spoiling the view. Time for a change of plan. Time for some serious sunshine. So, after the successful Castle Gate hold-up in April 1897 and the shenanigans in Baggs which followed, Butch headed south to drop out of sight for a while. He holed up in a ranch in Alma in New Mexico, calling himself by an alias. His likeable personality and his ability to carry out a hard day's work meant he was good at this part of the outlaw's life. He was good at vanishing when his sixth sense told him the law might be on his tail.

A month before the celebrations in Baggs, the local law officers had made one of their rare forays into the outlaws' stronghold of Robbers' Roost. They carefully avoided hounding any big names like Cassidy, the Sundance Kid or the murderous Harvey Logan, but they did nail two characters, John Griffiths (known as Blue John or the Cockeyed Rustler) and his partner in crime, James 'Silver Tip' Howells. Both were long-time residents of the Roost area and both were on nodding terms with Butch and his Wild Bunch.

Cockeye was described in his arrest sheet as being: 'Thirty-five years old, with sandy hair. His left eye was blue, his right eye was brown and cocked, giving him a perpetual squint. He was dressed in disreputable clothes, always wore his shirt open all the way down the front and spoke with a cockney accent.'

Silver Tip Howells was known as such because of his long bushy beard which had gone prematurely silvery-grey at its ends. Both he and Blue John were questioned at length by the officers not only about their own activities but also, crucially, about the whereabouts and movements of Butch Cassidy and the Wild Bunch. Wisely they claimed to know nothing about any other outlaws in the Robbers' Roost area. Blue John swore to the sheriffs that he'd ridden all over the Roost country without seeing any such outlaws as are supposed to infest that region.

Without a shadow of a doubt, Butch would have gotten wind of the law's interest in him after they'd arrested these two minor outlaws. That alone would have encouraged him to head south after the party in Baggs in the high summer of 1897. The fact that associates like Harvey Logan, Bob Meeks, Sundance and others were all on the run in other parts of the west probably encouraged him to disappear for a while as well. He knew that his fellow outlaws, if they were still free men, would surface sooner or later.

And they did. In ones and twos Harvey Logan, Elzy Lay, the Sundance Kid and others arrived at Butch's new place of work in New Mexico. He quietly made sure they all obtained employment. The owner of the ranch, an Irishman from Salthill near Galway who suffered from what we now call athlete's foot and who had the unlikely name of Captain William French, was impressed by this new bunch of cowboys who all knew the recently employed cowhand. They worked hard and no rustling ever took place when they were on the job.

Like Captain French, Sundance and the other outlaws soon began to get itchy feet. Back-breaking ranchwork didn't suit them for long. They'd gotten lazy. After spending the winter of 1897 in New Mexico they decided to head for Nevada in the following summer. Along with Harvey Logan and George 'Flatnose' Currie, Sundance held up and robbed a train near Humboldt, Nevada. They stole some trinkets and about $450 in cash. After the heist Sundance hightailed it back to New Mexico to Butch and the ranch. A few hundred dollars wasn't much to show for a lot of riding and a sore ass from the saddle. But at least it had broken the monotony for a while.

The winter of 1898 was again spent in New Mexico doing hard ranchwork and by March Sundance's feet were itching once more. Again he hooked up with Flatnose and Harvey Logan. It was time for another trip to Nevada. The town was Elko and the target was a saloon. They only managed to rip off $550. By any standards they weren't exactly hitting the big time.

Butch, as usual, was one step ahead. When the Wild Bunch next met Cassidy it was to discuss their biggest job to date. Butch had already made all the plans. All they had to do was carry out his orders. Butch had his beady eye on a new, moving target – a train packed with money and other valuables. He planned to rob it at a remote location called Wilcox in Wyoming. For the 'Wild Bunch' now read 'The Train Robbers' Syndicate'. Different title, same gang. The faces were more or less interchangeable. Either way, Butch ran the show.

The year was 1899.

10. Hold-ups, Stick-ups, Hangings and Tumbleweed

I drove to Wilcox, Wyoming, the place where Cassidy and his gang carried out one of their most famous heists. Actually, I should have said In-the-Middle-of-Nowhere, Wyoming. That's what it felt like. A town called Wilcox, or at least half a dozen houses which formed part of a settlement, were once located in that general vicinity. That was a hundred years ago. Now it's just an empty landscape. Low hills, flat grassland and the biting wind are its only residents.

The drive there took me along a deserted road for dozens of miles. On the way I met only one other vehicle, a huge truck battering along in the opposite direction. Occasionally I passed what looked like huge wooden goalposts just off the road. Creaking signs suspended by a swaying chain hung from most of them. These were usually rough planks of wood with a name carved into them. They were the entrances to Wyoming's Red Desert country's many ranches. The actual ranch buildings were located miles and miles into the surrounding hills. A rough, cinder track led visitors to the ranchers' front doors. Their land consisted of thousands upon thousands of acres. And it all had to be worked every month of the year, year in, year out.

After much examining of my maps, constant referring to old books, clippings and texts, and several changes of direction, I eventually located the place where Butch Cassidy and his gang robbed the Union Pacific Overland Flyer Number 3. The identity of the robbers, whose crime took place in the early hours of the morning of 2 June 1899, is not known for certain. According to eye-witnesses there were six men, and most historians of the period agree that Elzy Lay, Harvey 'Kid Curry' Logan, the Sundance Kid, George 'Flatnose' Currie, William 'News' Carver and Ben 'The Tall Texan' Kilpatrick were most likely to be the perpetrators. Butch's planning of the whole operation is not in doubt. His physical presence is, however, in question. As a condition of his pardon three and a half years earlier he'd promised the governor of Laramie Penitentiary that he'd never commit a crime in Wyoming again. He may well have kept this promise by doing everything to make the 1899 Wilcox robbery happen, *except* taking part in it. On the other hand, the whole robbery was carried out under the cover of darkness and there's every possibility Butch could have been there without being identified.

I tramped across wide-open fields towards the exact spot where the train was flagged down by one of the outlaws who carried a red emergency flare. I could see why Cassidy chose this place. It was hell and gone from anywhere, perfect for a pitch-dark ambush. Gunshots and explosions could rip through the night without any light sleepers hearing even the faintest sound. The track stretched for miles and miles in either direction. The swords of rails cut through the yellow and white winter landscape until they vanished over the horizon. Wooden snowbreaks designed to prevent drifting in wintertime were the only other man-made features on the landscape. They stood like weathered ships, their beleaguered skeletons forlornly cracking at the edges when the wind snapped against their joints.

When I reached the place where the robbery had taken place I stood for a few moments trying to get my bearings. The wind nipped my ears under my thick woolly hat. A light, almost transparent, veil of snow started to fall. I felt exposed and vulnerable despite my expensive outdoor clothing. Wrapped up in a feather jacket, with its state-of-the-art windproof shell, my hands protected by Gore-Tex gloves and with my legs shielded with fleece-lined trousers which I was assured would outlast their owner, I marvelled at the people who had lived, worked and robbed in this vast area of the United States. They must have been very tough. It was a mystery to me how they managed to survive when the cold set in. No wonder records referred to people going mad in the long, Arctic winters. The summers brought their own problems, too – usually plagues and diseases. Crops often failed. Livestock perished. The settlers and ranchers had worn clothes that were basic and functional but frequently inadequate. Swaddled in my twentieth-century creations I couldn't help wondering how I'd have fared on the frontier a century ago. Badly, no doubt. I should have felt safe and secure in my gear. But I didn't – I felt like an inadequate visitor.

❋

The robbery at Wilcox was carried out quickly and with an impressive degree of precision. Two outlaws flagged the train down. When it stopped, they boarded it and ordered the engineers to drive it down the tracks. One of the robbers apparently had a 'foul mouth' and was 'very profane' – this was probably Harvey Logan, who was always eager to thump, bully or shoot anyone who annoyed him. Four other outlaws joined the train when it reached the designated spot. They used dynamite to blow the mail-car doors open when one of the guards refused to co-operate. Then they headed for the express car. Charles E. Woodcock was the messenger in charge of this part of the train. He refused point-blank to do what the outlaws asked. They cursed him and decided to blow the doors instead. That they did: they blew the whole thing sky-high. Woodcock, black-faced and suffering from instant amnesia, was duly helped out of the ruins of the carriage. He was lucky to be alive. One report suggested Harvey Logan was all for killing the stubborn guard and that Woodcock was only saved when Butch Cassidy, present in this account, stepped in and said he deserved to live because 'he had nerve'. The outlaws then helped themselves to unsigned banknotes and various other valuables.

According to eye-witnesses (the train had a number of passenger carriages, too), the outlaws apparently recoiled when they noticed in the darkness that many of the banknotes were covered in blood. From the fragments of hurried conversations that were overheard, it was suggested the injured Woodcock may have bled on to the money but it was soon agreed he was bleeding too lightly for this to have been the case. A few minutes passed while the men stood around, sniffing and rubbing the blood between their fingers. Then one of them tasted it. The 'blood' turned out to be from a consignment of raspberries which had been blown up along with everything else in the express car.

One strange thing about this robbery was that Butch Cassidy's lawyer, Douglas Preston from Rock Springs, was spotted by one of the gawkers who eyeballed the goings-on from the safety of their seats in the passenger section of the train. When confronted later, Preston panicked and squawked loudly about having an 'alibi'. This bizarre reaction is the surest sign that Butch was the mastermind, if not the leading participant, of the robbery at Wilcox.

After the heist the gang let off a few rounds of gunfire before fleeing into the black hills with their loot. Witnesses noted that as they were starting on their getaway, the outlaws were 'laughing their heads off'.

They'd just robbed the Union Pacific Railroad of anything between thirty and sixty thousand dollars. No one, to this day, knows for sure exactly how much they got.

After the robbery the gang split up. Three went in one direction, three in another. Posses of various sizes, strengths and degrees of competence were soon organised after the train had limped into the station at Medicine Bow, then Laramie. Photographs taken at the time show just how much damage the thieves had caused. The express car was in pieces and the sturdy metal safe had an enormous hole blown in it. Locals are standing around gazing into the camera lens with a mixture of shock, bewilderment and amazement. At least two of the posses were well organised and well financed. Specially outfitted trains carrying men and horses hit the trail from Medicine Bow. Other posses came from Laramie and Casper. The days were almost over when railroad officials, cattle barons, sheriffs, politicians and even local people allowed these incidents to happen. That's not to say that a cash inducement wasn't necessary to grease the wheels a little bit:

> The Union Pacific Railroad Company and the Pacific
> Express Company have jointly offered two thousand
> dollars per head, dead or alive, for each of these men and
> the United States Government has also offered a reward
> of one thousand dollars each making three thousand
> dollars per head for each of these men.

A total of eighteen thousand dollars sat on the table. The money seems to have served to narrow the gap significantly between good intentions and outright action. The events which followed were neatly summarised in a message sent by the Union Pacific Railroad several days later:

> Three members of the robbers went north mounted and were followed eight hours later by a posse. The robbers crossed the Platte River at Casper about three o'clock Sunday morning and were followed from Casper by another posse from that point who overtook them about four o'clock in the afternoon twenty-eight miles north-west of Casper where a running fight occurred, the robbers shooting three of the horses of the pursuing party and escaping to a point about fifteen miles further on where they were again overtaken the following Monday morning by both posses, at which time Sheriff [Josiah] Hazen, of Converse County, was shot and killed from ambush. In the confusion which followed the robbers eluded the posses and are supposed now to be somewhere in Johnson or Big Horn Counties and are being closely followed by the pursuing parties.

The 'pursuing parties' didn't have any luck. Butch and Sundance got clean away after the Wilcox job. Along with Elzy Lay and Ben Kilpatrick they seem to have taken the wise decision to head south towards familiar ground. Other contradictory reports suggest Sundance may have headed north with Harvey Logan, Flatnose Currie, William Carver and Elzy Lay, who is also credited with having headed in two directions at the same time. We'll never know for sure who went where and with whom. All we know for certain is that one group headed south while another group headed for Hole-in-the-Wall. A local newspaper commented:

> If the robbers succeed in reaching Hole-in-the-Wall they will find friends who will fight for them and stores

of food and ammunition. The region is so wild that
nothing less than a systematic attack by a large number
of men will drive out the bandits.

Both groups evaded capture. The posses didn't catch any
ringleaders. Tempers flared amongst the pursuers and frustration
reigned. In the future they'd employ different tactics. And
different men.

❁

For Elzy Lay the Wilcox job was almost the end of the line.
Bright, thoughtful and quiet, he had been Butch's closest friend
and most trusted companion. In later years Sundance would
step into these shoes, but before the turn of the century Butch's
confidant had been Lay. After the Wilcox robbery he probably
headed north with Logan and Currie. Then, for some
unknown reason, he joined up with Thomas 'Black Jack'
Ketchum, his brother Sam who sometimes went by the same
alias, and one G.W. Franks, who may or may not have been
another better-known Wild Bunch member using an alias.

This move was a colossal blunder. Or, if you take the long
view and if the outcome of the whole thing is considered, it was
maybe the best thing that Lay ever did.

Thomas Ketchum was, to put it mildly, as mad as a hatter. For
years he had been a nervous wreck because of his precarious
love-life. Years before he met Lay fresh from the Wilcox job in
the summer of 1899, he'd been jilted by a young woman named
Cora who had two-timed him. Then, in a devastating 'Dear
John' letter which succeeded in mentally unhinging Ketchum
for the rest of his life, she humiliated him by revealing all about
her erotic entanglements with other, more virile men. One of
the symptoms of his madness was his inability to stop himself
from robbing the same stagecoach or train at exactly the same

spot, at exactly the same time, over and over again. He was the West's most predictable robber – not a title to be proud of. Once he fixated on something he just couldn't stop himself. He would count his money over and over again. He would check his ammunition endlessly. And he would fly off the handle at the slightest provocation. Why the normally astute Elzy Lay took up with such a lowlife non-starter and his equally stupid brother Sam after working with Cassidy's élite Wild Bunch is anyone's guess. Maybe he was just desperate.

The four outlaws – the Ketchum brothers, Franks and Lay – held up a Colorado Southern train on 11 July 1899 in New Mexico. This was just five weeks after the Wilcox robbery in which Lay had participated. The gang swiped a cool thirty thousand dollars.

Tom Ketchum split up from the rest after the heist and made a dash for the plains by himself. But Ketchum had bad luck written all over him – other outlaws considered him a jinx. On one occasion the owner of a gambling joint even offered him a glass of milk *before* he started playing cards, on the grounds that he was such a loser the milk would be all he'd be able to afford once the game was over. Tom Ketchum's liberty and apparent good luck always had a time limit.

The other three outlaws were surrounded at Turkey Creek Canyon by a well-armed posse just twenty-four hours after robbing the train. Lay and Sam Ketchum were both badly injured but they managed, along with Franks, to scramble out of the canyon to safety. Sam didn't get far, however. His shoulder injury meant he was forced to hole up in a cabin for a few days to evade capture. His mind was spinning. He heard voices, saw ghosts and began talking to himself. Then there was the terrible smell. What was it? It was the gangrene emanating from the hole in his shoulder. A willing rancher who owned the cabin and a young tearful ranch-hand held him down and hacked off the outlaw's arm from the shoulder. Sam Ketchum died a few days later from a combination of severe shock and heavy blood loss. To the bitter end he'd refused to answer questions from unsympathetic law officers about the whereabouts of his mad brother Tom 'Black Jack' Ketchum.

A month later Tom, by this time completely off his head, tried and almost succeeded in single-handedly holding up a train near Folsom in Arizona. A short gun-battle had taken place between him and a brave guard protecting the train. Ketchum was injured with buckshot and managed to drag himself under the train and escape into nearby bushes. He lay there out of sight for a while but was discovered and arrested the following day. At the time of his arrest he was propped up on one leg against a tree talking to himself whilst trying to pick out with his bare, bloody hands the buckshot pellets which were buried deep in the pectoral muscles on his chest.

Black Jack was cleaned up and hauled off to face the law in Santa Fé, where he was duly tried and convicted of train robbery. The judge sentenced him to death in Clayton, New Mexico. Practically frothing at the mouth, Ketchum waved and smiled from behind the prison bars as he watched the daily progress of the gallows being built for his execution. He objected with loud hysterical shouts when a stockade fence was erected to stop gawkers from watching the hanging. On the day of the execution he refused to see a minister saying he'd die as he lived 'and he ain't gonna change me in a few minutes'. Waving and smiling at newspapermen who couldn't believe his bravado, Ketchum bounded up to the gallows and proclaimed, 'I'll be in Hell before you've had your breakfast, boys!' A black cotton sack was placed over the outlaw's head, then the noose was fixed around his neck by the hangman. A heavy silence fell over the crowd. The hangman gripped the heavy handle which would open the large trap-door that Ketchum stood on. No one said a word.

'Let her rip!' Ketchum's voice roared out maniacally from beneath the black sack.

The trap-door opened and he shot through the hole.

His last words were prophetic to say the least.

Ketchum was decapitated.

The long drop ripped his head clean off his shoulders. Like a football, the outlaw's head rolled out of the sack towards the confused and still-silent spectators. Ketchum's eyes were wide open and his trademark thick black moustache glistened in the morning light. The rest of the corpse flopped over, landed sideways and began spraying blood from the neck all over the front row of reporters. Mass hysteria broke out. People fainted. Some ran like hell. Others threw up on the spot.

As the bedlam continued, a deaf violin player high on the gallows played an Irish jig. Hidden from sight and unaware of the panic going on beneath him, he closed his eyes and heard his own music in his head. He wasn't being tasteless, he was merely carrying out the executed man's last wishes – 'Have someone play a fiddle when I swing off,' he'd demanded.

The Ketchum brothers' erstwhile companion in crime Elzy Lay was later captured and given a long stretch in the New Mexico Territorial Prison. His good nature prevailed during a later prison riot, however, when he used his reputation to quell the disturbances amongst fellow inmates. He was subsequently pardoned and released. A reformed man, he educated himself as an engineer and almost struck it big in the western oil fields. He ended up working as a water master for the Imperial Valley Irrigation System and died at home on Los Angeles in 1934 without ever having broken the law again.

❄

I left the site of the Wilcox train robbery and headed east. Heavy lumps of grey clouds filled the sky on the horizon. My eyes were distracted by the swirling snakes of snow that slithered a few inches above the road surface. They hypnotised me as I watched their tails slide off the road into the fields where millions of them waited. I blinked and pulled over for gas into an ancient fuel station. I was glad for the break.

The man inside the building eyed me suspiciously when I wrote him a cheque for the fuel. 'Don't see a lot of these around here.' He stared at my chequebook and rubbed his stubble-covered chin. 'In fact, the last one was from a lady who turned out to have done something she shouldn't have.'

I eyed him back.

He smiled and showed some cracked, stained teeth. 'No sense in jumpin' to conclusions though.' He sounded insincere. A radio in the background was playing Bing Crosby singing 'Danny Boy'. Out of the corner of my eye I saw a shadowy figure moving around behind me. I turned around.

'Hey, Mister, that's a nice rig you got there.' A thick-set man in his thirties stood near a sheet of cardboard that held some bootlaces. He pared his thumbnail with a penknife and jerked his head back to flick a greasy lock of hair out of his eyes.

'Where ya from anyways?' His nose twitched and he automatically used the blunt end of the knife to scratch it.

'Scotland.' I began gathering up my wallet and a can of soda I'd bought.

'Robert Louis Stevenson.' He ran his thumb along the blade to test its sharpness.

'That's right, he was from Edinburgh.' I thought my voice sounded nervous.

'I know. I can read.'

'Lives in books. Can't get enough of them.' The guy who had served me suddenly wheezed back into life.

'Yeah, but they gone and closed the free lending library down here so no more books. That's why I'm here. Magazines.' The man pointed towards the top shelf of the rack. It was lined with pornographic magazines.

'He's sailed the world – probably been to your neck of the

woods too.' The man behind the counter was now leaning on his elbows.

'I've been everywhere. And I know one thing – a man gotta take any port in a storm.' The guy with the knife looked completely blank and I was unable to read him.

'Yessir.' The man leaning on his elbows got up, winced with pain in his shoulders and began to rearrange some lighters that were on display in the small window.

'That's true.' I started to move away towards the door. The man with the greasy hair snapped shut his knife, wiped his hand on his orange overalls and extended it to me. I shook it firmly. His hand felt strong.

'Name's Dave. I'm an engineer. Pleasure to make yer acquaintance.'

I walked towards the door.

'Hey, watch out for the tumbleweed!' Dave flicked his hair away again nervously. He stood in funereal half-shadows next to a small display of ladies' tights.

'I haven't seen any,' I said.

'You know what they say about that stuff!' Without prompting he suddenly told me the story of the tumbleweed. This is the gist of what he said.

According to Dave, cowboys used to find pieces of tumbleweed blowing around out on the range when they were out working miles from anywhere. Nothing unusual there – except that all these special pieces of tumbleweed had notes tied to them. The notes were from a lonely widow, said Dave, who was desperate for a strong cowboy to make her feel like a woman again. In precise copperplate handwriting she gave every detail of her requirements in the notes and described in intimate terms how the cowboy could fulfil them. The only thing the note didn't say was where she lived. Apparently cowboys were known to walk off the job and go looking for her when they came across one of these pleading notes. Some disappeared never to be seen again. Others tried to search for her every so often and ended up dying old, embittered men, convinced 'they'd just missed her' or that her home was 'just over the next hill'.

'Some of the ranchers and cowpunchers and rustlers ended up in saloons in town here bragging they'd bagged themselves that widow – but they boys was jest full of sheet!' Dave smiled and wobbled and flicked his hair with a jerk of his head when he laughed. I noticed his fat nose had lots of blackheads on it. They looked like pinprick-sized ink-stains on a scarred and abused wooden school-desk.

'Nobody ever found that lady. Cowboys around here went mad from desire because of them notes on tumbleweed. Ha! Ha!' He turned the penknife over in his hands. I could make out a four-leaf clover emblem on it.

'Did she exist?' I leaned on the frame of the door. The paint felt oily.

'Well, there's them that say a hunchback from this here town who them cowboys laughed at when they came into drink the place up on a Saturday night dreamt the whole scheme up just to get his revenge! The ugly sonofabitch wrote all the notes himself!'

I shook my head.

'Isn't that the best goddamn story you ever did hear?' Dave clapped his hands and howled with laughter. The guy behind the counter smiled and showed his bad teeth again. He looked like he was eating a mouthful of potatoes.

I left them laughing together. As I opened the door, the icy wind hit me full in the face. I walked over to my truck and climbed in. The interior smelled like new paint. My eyes had trouble adjusting to the bright winter landscape after the gloomy darkness of the gas-station shop.

Dave and the guy who'd served me stared out the window as I drove off. I thought I saw one of them saluting me like a soldier. For some reason I didn't wave back at them.

Within seconds I felt bad and I wished I had.

11. We Like Our Guns in Cheyenne

'Jim Lowe was a stocky man of medium build, fair complexioned. He had a habit of grinning and showing a row of small, even teeth when he talked.'

This passage was written by the Irishman Captain William French in a battered manuscript entitled *Reminiscences of a Western Ranchman*. His memories of running a ranch in Alma, New Mexico, are, if nothing else, an interesting slice of history dealing with life in the West at the turn of the century. What makes them really intriguing, however, are his references to one of his former cowhands called Jim Lowe who was last employed at the ranch in 1899.

Jim Lowe was Butch Cassidy.

After the Wilcox train robbery Cassidy had disappeared as usual for a while, leaving the wilds of Wyoming and riding south to the comforting anonymity of New Mexico. Captain French hobbled out to meet him on his bad feet and immediately welcomed the cowboy back to his old job like a prodigal son. Butch started work on the ranch the next morning. He was careful not to spend any of the stolen money from the Wilcox job here. He simply kept his head down and got on with his work.

The Union Pacific Railroad had different priorities. They were willing to put up big money to buy the manpower and the resources to catch the thieves who had robbed their train. Meetings were held, voices were raised and fat fists were thumped on tables. It was time to hire the big guns, the famous names, the outlaw-trackers every bit as well known and calculating as the robbers and rogues they hunted.

They hired Joe LeFors, a livestock inspector, deputy US Marshal, sometime lawman-at-large for the Montana and Wyoming cattle and sheep industries and freelance private detective. LeFors, of medium height, thin-faced with a pinched nosed and piercing eyes, was an incredibly vain and ambitious man who knew the value of publicity and who went out of his way to cultivate the image of a relentless lawman and pursuer of wrongdoers. In a manuscript which came to light only recently, he recounted how he became involved in the hunt for Butch Cassidy and his Wild Bunch:

> I had no more than sat down to dinner when a Western Union messenger came and handed me a message from J.R. Fielding, who asked if I would join the U.P.R.R. posse on Teapot Creek and represent the Burlington R.R. The U.P. train Number 3 had been held up at Wilcox station west of Laramie. The robbery had taken place at 2.15 a.m. on June 2, 1899 . . .

As it turned out, LeFors would have only limited success in tracking down the Wild Bunch after Wilcox, but he *was* persistent. His breed of lawman posed a real danger to the outlaws. The old image of the fat, corrupt sheriff hoisting himself into his saddle after a good lunch before setting off in the wrong direction on a half-hearted attempt to apprehend outlaws he dearly hoped he'd never run into, was beginning to become a thing of the past. LeFors rode hard and fast, and his fastidious appearance – starched white shirt, fancy hat and neat bow-tie – betrayed the meticulous, severe inner workings of the man. He considered himself every bit as hard and ruthless as his quarry and he could not abide being slowed down by ponderous local sheriffs who, when they should have been chasing outlaws, used time-wasting, heavy baggage and overplanning as a disguise for their fear. He describes the post-robbery scene with thinly veiled contempt:

> About 8.00 p.m. I rode into the Tisdale Ranch and there found the entire U.P.R.R. posse and U.S. Marshal Frank A. Hadsell. The posse had put in a hard day but had accomplished little . . . They had something like forty men plus a grub wagon and cook – far too many for fast movement. I looked them over, and could see some members of the posse would not get very far. Wheeler [the Union Pacific chief special agent in charge of the posse] and I talked things over, and I advised him to send our grub wagon back and discharge all but twelve or fourteen of his men. I said I thought we should get some bread and baloney, and be prepared for a fast, hard chase.

The legendary Pinkerton Detective Agency also got a piece of the action when the railroads brought in one of their operatives, Charles A. Siringo, to chase the Wilcox robbers. The agency were almost universally hated in the West after its abortive attempt to kill Jesse James in January 1875. A bomb thrown by the agents through the window of a farm owned by Jesse's family, killed the outlaw's eight-year-old brother Archie and blew the arm clean off the shoulders of Jesse's mother. The agency's Scottish founder, Allan Pinkerton, insisted repeatedly that his operatives had done nothing wrong, but his denials fell on deaf ears. The incident was condemned as an 'inexcusable and cowardly deed' by the press, and Pinkerton's reputation was badly tarnished. By the turn of the century the agency's main operative on the Wilcox robbers was Siringo, who trailed the outlaws for thousands of miles and through several states. Even the widely respected Siringo found that the outlaw trail eventually went cold, however, and he reluctantly had to throw the towel in.

Many believe that there was one other lawman who was hired after the Wilcox robbery to hunt down Cassidy and the Wild Bunch. Intense, dogged, scheming, charming, resourceful and, above all, utterly cold-blooded, he was cut from the same cloth as LeFors and Siringo, and was feared and hated by many who lived near or on the wrong side of the law. By the late summer of 1899 he was already a legend and the mere mention of his name struck naked panic into the hearts of even the most brutal outlaws. He was known as Tom Horn.

None of these three famous manhunters nor the legions of lesser-known lawmen who chased the outlaws following the general clampdown after the Wilcox robbery ever actually caught Butch Cassidy and the Sundance Kid or the Wild Bunch. But they did, individually and collectively, have a significant impact upon their lifestyle in general and their life of crime in particular.

❋

My next port of call was Cheyenne, the state capital of Wyoming. If I had a dollar for every outlaw known to have passed through this city at one time or another, I could have retired and bought a ranch there. Butch, Sundance and all the other members of the Wild Bunch had quietly visited this place on numerous occasions. Butch's brother Dan Parker made a more public excursion to Cheyenne when he was escorted there by sheriffs to stand trial and be convicted for robbing a stagecoach in December 1889.

I also wanted to visit Cheyenne because it was the town from which most of the famous detectives – especially LeFors and Horn – had operated. LeFors considered Butch and Sundance his two principal targets, especially after they'd successfully avoided capture by the posses led by him following the Wilcox train robbery.

Cheyenne had boomed on the back of big railroad money and through the profits of the cattle barons. It was the place where the politicians did their deals, where detectives were hired and fired, where the posses invariably set out from. It also epitomised the changing face of the West. At one time Cheyenne had been a lawless haven for characters like Poker Dan to drink and gamble in its many saloons. Other well-known gamblers who called Cheyenne home included Whiffle-tree Jim, Squirrel Tooth, the Coon Can Kid and Timberline. A Scots gambler called Duck McKenna earned his nickname in the area because he'd a nervous tendency to duck down and flee the premises any time he heard a loud noise. Some think he may have been on the run after committing a crime. Or just plain mad.

Wild Bill Hickock also spent many a night gambling in Cheyenne as well as tasting some of its more illicit pleasures. He left the town towards the end of his life to become part of Buffalo Bill Cody's travelling Wild West shows. His participation in the shows flopped, though, because he was completely drunk most of the time. He got so bad that he even began shooting live bullets at fellow Indian performers so he could 'see 'em dance!'. After Wild Bill was shot in the back of the head in Deadwood, Dakota, on 1 August 1876, his short, cross-eyed killer, Jack 'Broken Nose' McCall, fled the area having already been acquitted of another murder. McCall's freedom didn't last long; he was chased through Cheyenne into nearby Laramie where he was re-arrested, re-tried and hung for shooting the famous Wild Bill Hickock. When he was executed on 1 March 1877, after wetting himself on the gallows, McCall's final words were 'Oh God!'.

Another regular visitor to Cheyenne was Martha Jane Cannary, better known as Calamity Jane. The various colourful tales and dime-store novels about this strapping buckskin-clad character pretty much hid the reality. Far from being a frontier beauty she was in fact extremely ugly, foul-smelling and violent as well as bordering on the illiterate. Rarely did any of this reach print – only a few brave souls ventured to tell the truth about her. It's not hard to see why. The editor of the *Cheyenne Daily* suffered the consequences after printing some rude tales about Jane in his newspaper. He returned to his office after lunch one day to find the place wrecked – Calamity Jane, whip and nine-inch Bowie knife in hand, had paid a visit looking for the hapless journalist. Not only had she demolished the place, she'd also successfully terrified several burly male reporters who scuttled out of the way when she'd entered. A note was left for the editor which demanded:

> Print in the paper that Calamity Jane, the child of the
> regiment and pioneer white woman of the Black Hills,
> is in Cheyenne or I'll scalp you, skin you alive and hang
> you to a telegraph pole. You hear me and don't you
> forget it.
> CALAMITY JANE.

Jane loved to hear of her supposed exploits and thoroughly enjoyed adding to her own fabricated legend. Her full-time occupations were prostitution and self-publicity. She managed to worm her way into an introduction to Wild Bill Hickock whom she claimed thereafter to be her lover. She died in 1903, working as a prostitute to the end, though by this time a broken-down alcoholic. Her final words on her deathbed were 'Wild Bill! Wild Bill!'. She was laid to rest beside her fictional lover, thus achieving in death what she probably never did in life – the chance to sleep with Wild Bill Hickock.

By the turn of the century some of Cheyenne's rougher edges had been smoothed off. The fat-cat politicians were determined to see things change. They saw to it, using fair means and foul, that Cheyenne became a more 'civilised' town, and didn't pay too much attention to the blood spilled in the process.

❀

It was near twilight when I pulled off the highway into town. The bright blue sky behind me was shaded indigo at one edge and deep red at the other. The remaining rays from the dying sun on the horizon eventually blinked out, leaving me in the gloaming.

The town itself was deserted. The shops looked faded and washed out and everything seemed to have seen better days. There didn't appear to be a single person on Main Street. A sign for the Indian Motel blinked on and off in a futile attempt to rustle up business from the non-existent passers-by. Tinsel decorations hung forlornly from street-lamps. They swung in deep, ship-rigging dips, creaking and whining in the wind. Behind the main thoroughfare railtracks ran parallel to the town. Every so often, dinosaurs of carriages punched into one another, the metal couplings hooking and clawing and squeal-ing, metal on metal.

Downtown Cheyenne was windswept. The classic, timeless image of the cowboy was used to sell everything: boots, shirts, jackets, hats, belts, booze, chewing tobacco. One store across from an Italian barbershop was fronted by a neon sign showing an electronic cowboy on a rodeo horse. Both the horse and rider bucked in slow motion, the greasy noise from the mechanism squeaking when the horse's legs came close together. The paint on the cowboy was flaked and dried out. The whole sign jerked and strained in the wind. It looked as if it might crash to the ground at any minute.

Things clearly hadn't changed much since 1885 when a young British visitor by the name of John Fox had arrived in Cheyenne determined to see the Wild West for himself. Having got some funny looks upon his arrival off the train at Cheyenne station, Fox deduced that his attire – traditional English leggings, tweed jacket, derby hat and breeches – wasn't exactly inconspicuous. Some local cowboys had already poked fun at him and splashed him with mud as he walked down Main Street. Sharper than most English visitors who usually ended up being run out of town half-naked and robbed, Fox ducked into a western outfitter's store and re-emerged half an hour later wearing a cowboy hat, leather boots, stiff jeans and a blue flannel shirt. Dressed like all the locals, no one gave him a second glance and he headed off on his way quite safely.

Over a century later, wearing an akubra hat from Australia and a pair of Wrangler jeans I'd bought in Scotland, I drove out of town towards a hotel I'd spotted on my way in. A bank of red lights halted me at a level-crossing. A long, seemingly endless freight train rolled by. Mine was the only vehicle waiting to cross the tracks.

Out to my right a figure caught my eye. Just yards from where I sat in my truck I spotted a man wearing a very bashed and dirty cowboy hat squatting at the kerb. He must have been in his early sixties and was wearing a threadbare yellow jacket that had a filthy fake sheepskin collar which he'd turned up for protection against the freezing wind. His lined face was swarthy and unshaven, his features pinched and sharp. With great difficulty he slowly extracted from his pocket a brown paper bag containing a bottle of booze. With his face twisted into a mask of concentration, he held up the bottle to the street-lamp to see how much liquid it contained. Satisfied, he took the cap off and held the bottle to his mouth. With his eyes closed and his lips clamped around the neck of the bottle, he drained every last drop of its contents. The train rattled and thumped on its way behind him. He appeared not even to notice its presence. When he'd finished drinking he carefully screwed the cap back on and, slowly bending over, sat it down on the pavement. Taking an eternity, he unfolded himself and stood up. Then, arching over at a painful angle, he groped at the bottle until he finally plucked it up. Then he staggered over to a nearby trashcan. Holding the rim of the container for support, he dropped the bottle into the black depths. A moment passed. He hoisted his jeans up and peered into the bin to double-check the bottle was safely and properly disposed of in a responsible manner, then he lurched off. He weaved away a few paces, before suddenly remembering the crumpled-up brown paper bag in his pocket. He shuffled back to the bin. As he dropped the bag into it a gust of wind whipped the paper up over his head in a defiant and dramatic arc. The man looked suspiciously from side to side as if he regarded the sudden slap of wind as a terrible omen from the gods. He appeared scared and frightened of unseen demons. He stopped for a moment and looked round. The grubby simulated-sheepskin collar was hauled up around his ears. He waved one arm angrily. Then he spotted me still sitting in the truck at the lights as the last few freight-cars rumbled by. He waved to me and smiled a wolfish grin in my direction. Then, carefully picking his steps, he paced off down the street.

The train finally cleared the tracks and the signals changed. I looked over my shoulder at the drunken old cowboy as he shuffled off into the shadows. He appeared to be singing at the top of his voice.

❀

The lamp in my hotel bedroom looked like a cowboy. When you turned it on, the cowboy's hat lit up.

I was hungry and cold. The Weather Channel woman said that Cheyenne had the lowest wind-chill (it was -14°C) in the USA. Winds had hit 75mph at one point. I left the hotel and went to a diner. I chose a dish called 'prairie stew' – it tasted just like Irish stew – and I ordered two platefuls.

'I used to work on a car production-line in Oxford.' Mary was my waitress. She was in her sixties, a native of England, and had arrived in Cheyenne three decades before. Now she worked in a diner serving locals and people like me who were passing through. I asked her how she'd ended up in Wyoming.

'The old story, I'm afraid.' She looked over her shoulder and settled in beside me. I noticed she was holding her tray like a crusader's shield in case anyone questioned her lack of activity. 'I fell for a man in uniform, an American.'

I could hear a large clock ticking on the wall. I was the only customer in the whole establishment. 'Where did you meet him?'

'Oxford. Well, near Oxford. He was in the Air Force. I was young, he was young – need I go on?'

I smiled and looked down at my empty bowl of stew. I was already regretting the second plateful. It sat in the deeper, darker recesses of my stomach like a load of cement.

'Anyway, I washed up over here. I married him, gave him a family and divorced him. Now he's gone and I'm here. Stuck. I need two jobs just to make ends meet.'

She stared out the window, thinking. She seemed eager to confide in me or anyone who might know what her former life in Britain had been like. She carelessly fingered her uniform, which was meant to look like an outfit worn by a western cow-girl. A lariat hung limply around her neck and her blouse had some cheap fake rhinestones sewn into it. The get-up looked like a hasty effort for a small-time, small-town amateur production of *Oklahoma!*.

'I miss the English culture – the galleries, the tea-shops, the clothes, Marks & Spencer's even – no one around here has a decent sense of humour. And there's nothing to do. Don't get me wrong; it's okay if you're an outdoor freak – climbing or riding, that sort of thing – but I do neither. And as for the *men*!'

Another waitress wandered past prompting Mary to stand up and begin wiping my table-top.

'The men . . . Oh dear! Cowboys? Ughh! Please, don't start me about cowboys! I'm a lady and I like to be treated like one.'

I thought of the old guy I'd seen on the street earlier with the bashed cowboy hat and the bottle. Mary moved off towards the cash register. I picked up the bill she'd left and followed her.

'Listen, don't stay in this country too long. I've been here thirty years and I'll tell you what bothers me the most – health care. It'll break you in the end! This country never takes care of its own people. It's shameful, terrible!'

I smiled and paid the bill. Just as she was taking the money from me, Mary leaned over and touched my hand. I leaned forward so she could whisper into my ear.

'Still, it's an okay country to make a big pile of money in if you can!'

I could still hear her giggling as I stepped out into the freezing night air.

❀

After the 1899 Wilcox train robbery just west of Cheyenne, Butch Cassidy didn't allow his big pile of money to burn too much of a hole in his pocket. He was always very good at keeping his ill-gotten gains safely stashed away somewhere. But

In Colorado Springs with the retired rodeo-rider turned western-wear salesman who told me he longed for the golf course in St Andrews, Scotland (S. O'Neill)

Four views of Laramie State Penitentiary, the only jail ever to hold Butch Cassidy; OPPOSITE: Butch's cell and the watchtower; ABOVE: a view of the interior of the prison (E. O'Neill)

TOP: not recommended – I'm about to drive into a Wyoming ground-blizzard. The blue sky and the cars, including mine, will soon disappear. I'll survive and at least I'm inside a warm truck. What must it have been like for outlaws like Cassidy on a horse? (S. O'Neill); BOTTOM: the deserted plains of Wyoming. Butch and his gang fled into the hills in the distance after the Wilcox train robbery (E. O'Neill)

TOP: trains roll along the same track as they did a hundred years ago in Wyoming – only now Butch Cassidy isn't there to hold them up (S. O'Neill); BOTTOM: looking westwards down the line at the site of the Wilcox train robbery (it's colder than it looks in this photograph – there were 70mph winds and a -18° wind-chill factor) (E. O'Neill)

TOP: looking eastwards over the Utah mountains, near Butch Cassidy's home in Circleville;
BOTTOM: a deserted silver-mine in Utah. The dreams and the hopes and the ghosts of the miners
still linger in the air (E. O'Neill)

TOP: Butch's old home where he lived with his family until he fell under the influence of a likeable local rustler named Mike Cassidy. It was the start of something big (S. O'Neill); BOTTOM: Bill Betenson, great-great-nephew of Butch Cassidy, standing next to the poplar trees planted a century ago by his famous relative (E. O'Neill)

The movie-set of *Butch Cassidy and the Sundance Kid* in the ghost-town of Grafton in Utah. It's hard to tell the real buildings from those used in the Hollywood film (E. O'Neill)

the same couldn't be said about some of his friends and accomplices who could never resist the temptation to dip into their loot. By October 1899, a few months after the heist, a small amount of the stolen cash turned up close to where Butch was working on the WS ranch in Alma. The trail soon led to the ranch itself. Fortuitously Cassidy, still masquerading as Jim Lowe, wasn't around when a couple of Pinkerton detectives came calling. When he was later confronted by Captain French about his identity he came clean and admitted he was the famous outlaw. French didn't fire him but he did pass him over for promotion on the ranch. Cassidy left shortly afterwards.

Butch was running out of options. The Wild Bunch was starting to fragment; his best friend Elzy Lay was behind bars and George 'Flatnose' Curry would be killed within a matter of months. He had no doubt also heard that Joe LeFors, Charles Siringo and the dreaded Tom Horn were all, directly and indirectly, on his case. He knew times were changing and that his time was limited. He needed to take some action.

It was at this point, acting alone or after talking things over, that Cassidy made a most unusual (although in the annals of outlaw history not without some precedent) move to secure a safe and free future for himself. Remembering the deal he'd struck with the prison governor years before on being released from Wyoming State Penitentiary, Butch decided to attempt something similar with the law and the authorities who were chasing him. He decided to try and get himself off the hook.

He made the attempt in his home state of Utah, where he knew his reputation was at its best and where his good Mormon bloodline might count for something. The man he went to was Judge Orlando W. Powers, a well-known and highly respected legal figure at the time. Cassidy probably knew him through the criminal grapevine and had almost certainly come into contact with Powers when he'd defended Butch's friend Matt Warner at his trial in 1896. The outlaw asked for amnesty from prosecution for all the old offences he'd committed in the past in exchange for a guarantee that he wouldn't commit any new crimes in the future.

With the benefit of hindsight, this attempt by the outlaw to straighten things out seems to confirm his legendary good character. On the other hand, however, it might be considered astonishingly arrogant and naïve. Butch Cassidy could never have settled down to a quiet life even if they'd let him – if only because there were plenty of other judges from plenty of other states who wanted to see him swinging from a rope. His past entanglements with characters like the infamous Harvey Logan would also have ensured that his house would have been under constant scrutiny from detectives, sheriffs and Pinkerton agents, all interested in the company the former outlaw might be keeping.

As it turned out, the judge in Utah couldn't help him. Cassidy pleaded his case again with enough sincerity to move the judge to appeal directly to the state governor. Again there was no deal. Judge Powers took matters into his own hands, however, and made contact with the Union Pacific Railroad company. Would they agree to leave Cassidy alone, to call off all their operatives and posses, if he agreed not to rob another U.P. train? In addition, Powers suggested, the U.P. might consider *employing* the famous outlaw as a train guard! After all, who would dare rob a train guarded by none other than Butch Cassidy?

The Union Pacific management treated the offer seriously. Chasing Cassidy and the Wild Bunch was costing them a fortune, especially since their heists were, by any standards, considerable. After slight hesitation they agreed to meet the outlaw and discuss terms. The contact between the U.P. and Cassidy was made through the outlaw's lawyer, Douglas A. Preston. Cassidy considered the offer of a meeting and responded positively. He told Preston to tell the U.P. to meet him at a remote spot called Lost Soldier Pass, about forty-five miles from Rock Springs, a place he knew would give him the best possible chance of making a dash for it should a trap be sprung by the railroad officials or any sheriffs who might have brave ideas.

If that meeting in October 1899 had gone ahead as scheduled it would have been a remarkable event. Contracts may have been thrashed out, headlines would have recorded the outcome, photos of Butch wearing a U.P. guard's uniform would have been published. In the event none of this happened. The meeting never took place. The hand of fate intervened in the form of a storm which delayed Cassidy's lawyer and the U.P. men. They arrived at Lost Soldier Pass a day late. Butch was nowhere to be seen. All they found was a scrawled note from the outlaw:

> Damn you Preston you have double-crossed me. I waited all day but you did not show up. Tell the U.P. to go to hell and you can go with them.

One subsequent attempt was made by the railroad to come to some amicable arrangement with Cassidy but that flopped as well despite the involvement of Butch's pal Matt Warner. Then, the following May, a couple of lawmen were gunned down; some outlaws on the fringes of the Wild Bunch were suspected. Given that Butch was the head of the gang, his role – however slight – in the killings came under scrutiny. And his chances of leaving his life of crime behind were becoming slimmer by the day.

Cassidy's belief that a personal effort to clean up his act was all that was necessary for him to retire and lead a 'normal' life (funded by his ill-gotten gains) testifies to the fundamental realities governing his life at that time: beneath the outward bravado he must have been a very desperate and very scared man.

At some point that summer Butch must have thrown caution

to the wind and decided upon another strategy. On 29 August 1900 he and his Wild Bunch were back in business, robbing trains with a vengeance. They stopped a Union Pacific train in the early hours of the morning near Tipton in Wyoming and robbed it of about $55,000 and some jewellery. The excessive amounts of dynamite used on the job certainly left an impression on the witnesses. The outlaws managed to blow the roof, the carriage walls and one end of the baggage car to pieces. And they demolished the carriage attached to it as well. By sheer coincidence, the guard on the train that night was none other than Mr Charles E. Woodcock, the very same man the robbers had almost killed a year before at Wilcox. Remembering the injuries he'd sustained on that occasion, Woodcock hesitated only briefly before giving himself up to Cassidy and the gang.

The thieves rode off into the night with their loot and it wasn't long before substantial, well-organised and well-financed posses gave chase. Joe LeFors, by now hired as a US Deputy Marshal, was one of the lawmen who set out after the outlaws. Though they must have been anxious to saddle up, the posse found enough time to pose for photographs. All holding rifles and sternly staring into the lens, most were wearing improbably formal-looking clothes for such an arduous task. It's chilling to consider that such photographs were often take in case the posse didn't come back in one piece.

LeFors' manuscript records the events as he gave chase to the Tipton robbers:

> The day was hot. The horses and men were suffering for water. The robbers had decided on this route, not that they cared for it, but just because they figured they could outride any posse. They had figured that by going past Soda Springs we would be set afoot, and perhaps some of us would perish. I had no doubt this was part of their game . . . We got to Little Snake River just at sundown.

I spotted the robbers going up a long slope on the other side of the river . . . They were climbing the hills for a night ride. The next morning we determined they had stopped about a mile down the river and had something to eat. They had readjusted the pack, and I believe, divided the money, as there was a big amount of paper torn off the express packages.

Joe LeFors and the posse gave up shortly after this point. The Wild Bunch had eluded their best efforts. A subsequent newspaper report explained what the robbers had done to finally throw the posse off their scent:

The bandits had resorted to the old trick of running into a bunch of range horses which they drove some distance and then allowed them to scatter, making it almost impossible to discern which was the trail left by the horses ridden by the robbers.

One outlaw missing from the Tipton robbery was Harry Longabaugh, the Sundance Kid. He was already on his way to Nevada working on a job of his own, and had sent word to Butch that he wouldn't make it to Tipton in time to rob the train. His own target was stationary – a bank, in a town called Winnemucca.

Sundance had only one thought in his mind – how to rob the bank and make a fast, clean getaway with as much money as possible. In on the raid with him were Harvey Logan and Bill 'News' Carver. They were a deadly, well-experienced trio. Curiously, they had four horses, which suggests that Butch Cassidy may have agreed to join them as soon as he'd cleared his feet from Tipton.

The three outlaws hung around the town of Winnemucca for a week in mid–September 1900. The sight of three cowboys camping out, minding their own business and tending to their horses was nothing new to the small town's residents. But, needless to say, they *weren't* minding their own business. They were stopping local children and bribing them with candy in return for details about bank hours, staffing arrangements and details of the fastest and shortest getaway routes. They kept up this routine for about ten days until they felt they'd gleaned as much information as possible about their target. Then they struck.

At noon on 19 September, the three men walked through the front door of the bank. Brandishing their weapons and with Harvey Logan holding a knife to the throat of one customer, the outlaws proceeded to rob the bank of everything of value. Official Pinkerton files estimated they got away with $32,640 – an enormous amount of money at the turn of the century. Local posses gave chase but they hadn't a hope of catching experienced bandits who'd outrun better and faster pursuers in the past.

Local legend in Winnemucca contends to this day that the robbery may have been an inside job. Some torn letters found by posses chasing the outlaws suggests this may well have been the case.

Another story says that one of the local children befriended by the outlaws was left a beautiful white horse by them as they fled the scene of the crime.

It's possible that Butch took part in this robbery. The six hundred-mile ride from the scene of the Tipton hold-up would have been back-breaking but not inconceivable for an experienced cowboy like him to do. The young boy who received the white horse certainly believed that the outlaw who'd given it to him was none other than the legendary Butch Cassidy. He sent several letters to Butch's sister in later years verifying the tale and enclosing a picture of him proudly riding the animal.

The Winnemucca robbery was one of the most daring and

successful jobs ever carried out by the Wild Bunch. Normally Butch would not have robbed both the train and the bank within such a short space of time. The heat from the law would have made life unbearable for him. But the changing situation demanded new and unusual measures.

The outlaws simply had to make as much money as possible in the shortest amount of time.

❁

The winter afternoon light in Cheyenne only lasted a few hours before everything was plunged back into darkness. In between blizzards and gales I took the opportunity to visit an old-fashioned general store on the outskirts of town. It was a one-stop catch-all store, the sort of place where, a hundred years ago, a cowboy could have bought a new outfit, a saddle, some booze, a length of rope, or anything else that took his fancy.

I walked in through the front door to the sound of Jim Reeves crooning 'Little Drummer Boy'. The place was deserted and gloomy. A cramped display of tents was set up in the middle of the shop. A cardboard cut-out attached to one of the canvas flaps showed a photograph of a very happy-looking family all posing in front of a similar tent with some white mountains in the background. The tent looked improbably small for such a large family.

Behind the tents was a special counter that seemed to double as a pawn shop. It was hidden from general view so customers could hawk their valuables without anyone noticing. Next to the camping display were rows upon rows of saddles and bridles. The thick, brand-new leather gave off its unmistakable odour, hanging like fresh sweat in the air. I ran my hand along one of the saddles; the smooth seat gave way to the heavily tooled decorative areas under the legs. Icy light from the street-lamps outside the windows illuminated the little metal diamond details on the buckles. The rows of shadowed, dark-brown leather saddles with their shining silver stirrups looked like expensive, gilded seats in the first-class carriage of a luxury train waiting for passengers.

Behind me stood an enormous mahogany glass-fronted case. The dark wood had a funereal air, all varnished and polished to perfection like a coffin lid. Its brass-fittings and red-velvet lining added to this impression. Whoever had made it had tried to suggest quality and reliability, but instead it gave off a shallow and assured feeling of unease that no amount of considered packaging could dilute.

I stood in silence in front of the case which towered over me. I felt overwhelmed by its sheer size when I looked up at it. A vague feeling of nausea washed through my guts. From floor to ceiling it was full of hundreds of guns.

'Nice merchandise, huh?' A tall, slightly stooping man came forward out of the shadows. I hadn't noticed him before and his sudden appearance gave me a fright.

'Interested?' His name was Lonnie. It said so on a bright blue name tag on his apron.

I shook my head and said I was just looking.

A moment or two passed. Jim Reeves was still singing over the loudspeakers. The front door opened, its noise breaking the awkward silence. A very attractive red-haired woman entered the store. Lonnie seemed to know her and they immediately entered into a huddle to discuss something. I hunkered down on my knees, pretending to scrutinise the 'merchandise'.

'Joe says it ain't right, Lonnie – whad'ya reckon?' She pulled out a handgun from her purse.

Lonnie held the weapon up to the light. He examined it and rubbed his bony hands across his mouth. 'Better leave it here. I'll have one of the boys check this sucker out. If that's all right with you – and Joe.'

'Sure thing, Lonnie – hey, that's nice . . .' The woman flicked her hair back and pointed to a rifle on the wall. It looked like hundreds of others as far as I could tell. Black and oily and dangerous-looking.

'Sure is! Ain't she just a beaut?' Lonnie fingered the butt of the gun and smiled.

The woman licked her lips and screwed up her eyes. 'Joe'd sure like that.'

'Yeah,' said Lonnie, his eyes twinkling, 'Maybe for Christmas, huh?'

The woman laughed and gathered her bag up to leave. Just before she got to the door she paused to check her make-up and to turn her mobile phone back on. Then she hurried out to her saloon car.

'You ain't from these parts, huh?' Lonnie was back behind the case after taking the woman's handgun into the back room.

I told him I was from Scotland. He eyed me up for a second or two then unexpectedly launched into a speech.

'Your government oppresses you. Strict gun laws are bad. But they won't try that here – no sir!' He spoke slowly but very deliberately. 'This here is the last outpost. They tax us and try and take away our freedom to buy these guns – if they do that we're finished! But we won't let them! We know if they take away our guns then they can make us do anything they want. We have the right in our constitution to bear arms. That means be free, free from government, free to fight!'

He leaned over the counter and wagged his finger at me. His halting delivery and genial nature reminded me of a dark, warped version of James Stewart.

'And I'll tell you something else. If they tried to take our guns away from us there'd be another American revolution – I should know 'cos I'm an ex-serviceman myself. We like our guns in Cheyenne and that's the way it's gonna stay!'

I nodded slowly. There was silence and I wasn't in the right frame of mind to respond to his comments. After a moment or two I gently began to move towards the door.

Lonnie took the hint. He pulled a rag from his pocket and started wiping the top of the counter. 'Any time now, y'here? You have yersel' a real good day.'

I looked back as I closed the door behind me. He stood against the red-velvet lining of the mahogany case, his head and body framed by row upon row of guns. He waved to me as Jim Reeves sang 'Distant Drums' in the background.

❈

Just over a month before Butch Cassidy and his Wild Bunch robbed the train at Tipton two terrible killings took place in one small area of the West, stunning local residents.

The first victim was Matt Rash. He lived in a remote part of Colorado and was a full-time rustler. He was killed on 8 July 1900 in or around his own cabin. Three bullets had been pumped into him. His valuables and money were still in the cabin when his body was discovered, so robbery had not been the motive.

Speculation about the killer's identity was rife. People had a rough idea who had shot Matt Rash, but no one seemed entirely sure what the killer looked like. From the scene of the crime it appeared that Rash may have known his murderer and even dined with him prior to his brutal slaying. The victim had been shot by an extraordinarily powerful and extremely accurate rifle. Whoever had pulled the trigger knew exactly what he was doing – it wasn't a murder as much as it was an assassination.

In the weeks that followed Rash's murder, many terrified cattle thieves in the Brown's Hole area – a well-known haunt of Cassidy, Sundance and all the other Wild Bunch members – awakened to find notices tacked to their cabin doors. These had mysteriously been pinned there during the night. The message was simple: the thieves were to stop their rustling and clear out. Or else face the consequences.

This scare tactic had been used earlier in various parts of Wyoming shortly before victims of the mysterious killer were found 'dry-gulched' – left for dead in the arid countryside. Rustlers knew it was the same man doing all the killing because he always left his calling-card at the scene of his crimes – a rock carefully placed under the head of his slain victims.

A few months later, in October 1900, just two weeks after Sundance, Carver, Logan and possibly Cassidy raided the bank in Winnemucca of tens of thousands of dollars, another outlaw was clinically murdered. This time it was the turn of Isom Dart, a black rustler who lived in Brown's Hole. One morning as Dart stepped out of his cabin a shot rang out. The fatal bullet was fired from a high-velocity Buffalo rifle – a .30-.30 – a weapon powerful enough to blow a man's head off if handled correctly and aimed accurately.

After the killing of Isom Dart there was a mass exodus from Brown's Hole by the rustlers and thieves who'd thrived in its lawless environment for years. Without any fanfare they simply packed up and left. Some wouldn't return to the area until several decades had passed.

In his 1938 book *The Outlaw Trail* local writer Charles Kelly noted:

> From that time on, Brown's Hole began to be civilised and law abiding. Rustling was not entirely abandoned, but the organisation broke up when its principal leaders were killed or left the country. Butch Cassidy used the Hole as a hideout during the next year . . . but the good old days were numbered, and the Hole never again saw the rip-roaring times of former years, when it was a rendezvous for all bandits on the Outlaw Trail.

The killer was Tom Horn.

Horn's terrifying reputation was known by many; the man himself, though, was known by only a few. A former western scout, tracker, Pinkerton agent and range detective, he was judged to be ideally suited for the job of quietly blowing the brains out of the rustlers and outlaws who had proved unstoppable by all other means. Horn himself was considered by some to be completely insane. Others claimed he was a moral and likeable fellow. None, however, disputed the fact that he was more than capable of killing other human beings in cold blood.

Legend has it that Horn's going rate was $500 a man. His methods were simple and effective: integrate and work with the outlaws; find out their working habits and the nature of their crimes; secure first-hand evidence of law-breaking; back off and wait for the right moment; kill the criminal from a safe distance with a hunting rifle; place a rock under the corpse's head; post notices of warning to others; flee the scene; collect his wages.

Serious-looking and made of solid, sinewy muscle, Horn was as hard a man as the West had ever seen. It was inevitable that someone like him would emerge sooner or later. Where soldiers, sheriffs and posses had failed, Horn succeeded. His chief employers in 1900 were the Wyoming Stockgrowers' Association, but they kept their connection with him very quiet. All arrangements were made through back-door dealings and under-the-table payments. Well-heeled members of the Association made contact with Horn and paid him to hunt down troublesome outlaws and rustlers. Horn seemed to have no conscience when it came to choosing how he made a buck. When someone in Cheyenne innocently asked Horn what he did for a living, the tight-lipped gunman replied, 'Killing men is my business.'

But by announcing his occupation in a part of the country where hearts, if not heads, tended to be on the side of the out-laws (who were still – rightly or wrongly – perceived as being

on the side of homesteaders and the underdogs in general),
Horn was digging his own grave.

This lonely, hated and complex man made his fatal mistake in
July 1901. In an area known as Powder River Road just north
of Cheyenne, a boy was shot dead by a bullet from a high-
velocity hunting rifle. He was a member of a local family which
was involved in a ranching dispute. The boy's father, Kels P.
Nickell, had been engaged in a long-running feud with cattle-
ranch owners who objected to his sheep farm. The victim that
misty summer morning, fourteen-year-old Willie Nickell, had
risen early to attend to his chores and, as he frequently did,
dressed in his father's coat and hat for warmth. The killer, locals
surmised, may have mistaken the boy for his father. Two shots,
the second to the head, had killed Willie Nickell outright.

The residents of Cheyenne were appalled. They immediately
assumed that the mysterious Tom Horn was to blame for the
tragedy. Their anger soon turned to fury – this cold-blooded
monster in their midst had gone too far this time. Blowing away
cattle rustlers and chasing train robbers was one thing but
slaying an innocent boy working the family farm was another.
What the hell was the country coming to? Were these ultra-
violent lawmen becoming as bad as the outlaws who justified
their existence?

Some locals believed that Horn had been paid by the cattle-
owners to rid them of the sheep-farm competition. No one was
entirely sure who the killer was, but gossip picked out Horn as
the most likely suspect. The evidence against him was scanty,
however. Apart from the manner in which the boy had been
killed and the fact that he'd been found with Horn's trademark
rock under his head, no one could really prove conclusively that
it had been him who'd killed young Willie Nickell.

Joe LeFors was called in to tie up the case against Horn. He
never had any great liking for the accused man, seeing him as
competition in the detective game. Several accounts say he was

determined to prove, by fair means or foul, that Horn had killed the teenage boy.

LeFors tracked down the suspect to a saloon in Cheyenne where he proceeded to get him drunk. With a crude listening device, some of the US Marshal's deputies overheard Horn giving (claimed LeFors at least) details concerning the Willie Nickell murder which only the true killer could have known.

Tom Horn was normally a very taciturn man but he had a well-known weakness for alcohol. By filling him full of strong whiskey LeFors was, metaphorically, giving Horn enough rope to hang himself.

After the drinking session and following his rambling claims, idle brags and almost incoherent revelations, Horn was arrested by Joe LeFors for the murder of Willie Nickells and was locked up in Cheyenne.

Although Horn was disliked by most of the rural Wyoming population and by those living in Cheyenne in particular, there was – and still is, nearly a hundred years later – doubt about his guilt over the murder. Many contested at the time that the vainglorious LeFors had set up Horn when he was drunk. The sullen Tom Horn simply claimed he didn't commit the murder.

After his arrest Horn made one attempt to escape but was captured not far from the outskirts of Cheyenne. He was tried by a local jury, found guilty and sentenced to hang. Joe LeFors gave evidence at the trial, mainly recounting how Horn had confessed to him during their drunken conversation. Many felt it reeked of Horn being framed:

> LEFORS: How far was the kid killed?
> HORN: . . . About 300 yards. It was the best shot that I ever made and the dirtiest trick I ever done.
> LEFORS: . . . Why did you put that rock under the kid's head after you killed him? That is one of your marks, isn't it?

HORN: Yes, that's the way I hang out my sign to collect the money for a job of this kind.

LEFORS: Have you got your money yet for the killing of Nickell?

HORN: I got that before I did the job.

LEFORS: You got $500 for that. Why did you cut your price?

HORN: I got $2,100.

LEFORS: How much is that a man?

HORN: That is for three dead men, and one man shot at five times. Killing men is my speciality. I look at it as a business proposition, and I think I have a corner on the market.

After his recapture, Horn resigned himself to his death and even wove his own noose. On the morning of 20 November 1903 he mounted the gallows. Calm and cool as always, he took the time to chat to lawmen on the way to his death – even asking one about his impending marriage. Then, after announcing that the gathering was 'the sorriest bunch of lawmen I've ever seen' and 'hurry it up, I've nothing more to say' – he was executed.

The corpse of the man who'd done more than anyone else to tame the last remnants of the Wild West swung in the Cheyenne winter light that morning, in full view of his former colleagues and paymasters. They'd used a killer to catch killers. Then, after bringing Joe LeFors in to set him up, they'd washed their hands of him.

But Tom Horn had left his mark.

❀

On my last night in Cheyenne I spent my time in the Wyoming State Archives. For hours I pored over old documents, clippings and photographs relating to the Tom Horn case. One photo-graph in particular caught my eye. It showed Horn staring straight into the camera lens awaiting his execution. He looked ordinary and unremarkable but the photograph had a quality which made it feel as if it could have been taken just a few years ago. Newspaper clippings dated as recently as 1991 revealed the continuing fascination that many amateur historians, outlaw aficionados and journalists still had for the case: 'Cheyenne Police say Horn bullets don't match'; 'Posthumous retrial scheduled for Tom Horn'; 'Cartridges dead end in Horn case'. These were just a few of the headlines that caught my eye. Nearly all of them leaned towards the conclusion that a miscarriage of justice had taken place when Horn was hung for the murder of Willie Nickell in 1903.

In the summer of 1900, over three years before these events took place, Tom Horn successfully scared the wits out of Butch Cassidy and the remaining members of his Wild Bunch. Horn was then at the peak of his bloody profession, regularly sneaking into outlaw haunts and picking off his victims. By the turn of the century, Butch Cassidy and the Sundance Kid were in their mid-thirties. They had had hard lives, covering thousands of miles in the saddle, mostly on the run, and their weather-beaten faces showed it. They were no longer crazy teenagers and Sundance was far from being a Kid. He also had Etta Place to think of, his quiet, strangely beautiful girlfriend who frequently accompanied him. Butch was the most shrewd of the Wild Bunch and he knew the threat that people like Tom Horn posed to his life. If such men could kill outlaws with tacit political and legal backing then it wouldn't have taken a great leap of the imagination for Butch to envisage himself one day lying with a bullet in his skull and a rock under his head.

Maybe that's what made Butch and Sundance and all the boys shed their outlaw skins, buy some fancy clothes and head south to Texas in the autumn of 1900 for a good time. They had plenty of cash after the heist at Tipton and the bank job in Winnemucca, and the thought of leaving the wild northern states of the West, full of its tenacious Joe LeFors and murderous Tom Horns, was probably very attractive. They also had the added incentive of knowing the railroad companies and banks had put $10,000 rewards on their heads.

I also planned to leave the spectres of Tom Horn, Joe LeFors and Cheyenne behind me and head westwards, straight across the Rocky Mountains. My goal was to reach the birthplace of Butch Cassidy in Utah – the little place called Circleville – to try and establish whether any of his descendants were still around.

I drove out of Cheyenne first thing in the morning. The pale light of dawn took ages to illuminate the landscape. The town looked as half-alive as it had been throughout my entire stay. Only a few cars passed me as I reached the outskirts. I departed watching the sky turn first white then grey as thick clouds banked up on the horizon.

A banshee wail of a freight-train sent me on my way, its scream echoing into the gloomy distance.

I should have guessed what I was in for.

Maybe my poking around in the Cheyenne archives had disturbed a few spirits. A massive unforgiving blizzard, powered by roaring 100mph winds, closed the highway and shut every minor road in the area for several days. My attempt to head west screeched to a sudden halt at a remote hotel near the town of Rawlins on Interstate 80. I'd already passed several huge trucks blown over on their sides. At least two of them had happened only seconds before I'd came upon them. The drivers stood around, flapping their arms like floundering fish and holding on to their hats in the wind.

I'd given up trying to drive through the storm when I'd spotted the grey, shrouded horizon moving towards me at a remarkably high speed. I knew I was in trouble when I realised mine was the only small vehicle on the road as far as the eye could see – which admittedly wasn't very far. But I knew the locals weren't easily put off getting about, so if I was travelling and they weren't then the chances were that they knew something I didn't. I had to bounce the truck across the deep snow in the middle of the highway and skid back on to the road in the opposite direction. Then I drove like hell to avoid the curtain of snow that swept along behind me. Needless to say it finally caught up with me. I stopped at Rawlins, the place where Big Nose George Parrot had been lynched. Maybe his spirit had been disturbed by my enquiries as well.

On seeing me stagger through the door of the local hotel looking like a snowman, the receptionist put her hands on her hips and said, 'Honey, you ain't goin' nowhere in that weather! Now sit down, take a load off and I'll get you some hot coffee.'

I did as I was told, dripping wet and freezing, and looked at the TV which was quietly flickering away in the corner. I was surrounded by empty tables and chairs. Magazines lay scattered over several couches. There wasn't another guest in sight. It was like a ghost ship – everyone had beaten a hasty path out the door away from the approaching blizzard. Everyone except me – who'd been driving straight into it. Not surprisingly the TV was tuned to the Weather Channel. This seemed to be standard practice in every place I'd stayed. The presenter smiled and chirped and pointed to a large band of snow working its way across the Rockies. Another band was following it. A sign saying 'Winter Storm Watch is in Effect' kept flashing at the bottom of the screen in bright day-glo lettering.

I felt like putting my snow-encrusted boot through the screen.

12. Welcome to Lost Wages

'Welcome to Lost Wages everybody! And ladies – do you have that credit card ready? Gentlemen – have you got your wives on a leash? Time to party! We're in the one, the only, yes – we're in *Laaaaassss Vegaaaasssss!*'

The Western Pacific flight was still at twenty thousand feet. It didn't seem to matter, though. The party had already begun.

I had given up trying to cross the Rockies in December. In retrospect it had been a foolhardy idea anyway. Instead I headed due south from Wyoming back into Colorado Springs, from where I caught a flight to Las Vegas. My plan was to drive north through the desert in Nevada, through a small part of Arizona, then into Butch Cassidy's home state of Utah.

I spotted several cowboys, young guys wearing starched jeans and shiny boots and buckles, boarding the plane for Vegas at Colorado Springs. They wore high hats and looked very clean. Even their nails were manicured.

The Western Pacific flight was sponsored by the Professional

Rodeo Cowboys Association. A huge lurid painting of a rodeo rider on top of a bucking horse was splashed across the side of the plane. It was an improvement on the illustration on the last flight I had taken. At least the cowboy looked nothing like Bart Simpson.

I stepped out of the front door of the airport. It was scorchingly hot. After Wyoming and its blizzards, Las Vegas felt like a furnace. I stood for a moment taking it in.

'Jeez, it's freezing!' An old lady lit a cigarette and coughed her way out the door. 'Hurry up and find my jacket, Stanley.'

Her husband winked at me as he fumbled with the suitcase zipper. 'Yes, dear.'

'It's really, really freezing.' The old woman hugged herself to keep warm and took another long, deep drag from her cigarette.

I passed through her cloud of smoke towards my rental car. I was already sweating.

❀

'Broke and Stranded in Las Vegas. If You Help Me, God Will Be Very Good To You.' A beggar held the sign. He was standing at the side of the road just outside the Strip. His hair was matted and his eyes were downcast. Another beggar stood about forty yards further down the road. He looked jealous of the other man's hand-painted sign and seemed to be shouting abuse at him. The beggar with the sign concentrated on the passing cars. He looked very calm under the circumstances.

I went for some lunch at a nearby hotel. It took me ten minutes to find the reception – everywhere was obscured by slot-machines. Cocktail waitresses wearing more on their heads than on their bodies walked in between the tables carrying drinks and snacks. Fat women with long white cigarettes sat at the machines. They looked half-dead and bored out of their minds. Every so often a machine made strange noises and its lights flashed on and off. People slowly looked around at the winner. But the winner didn't even smile. He or she just scooped the money up into their fat hands and started feeding it into the machine all over again.

Crowds of cowboys sat around crap-tables and poker games, their heads bowed, still wearing their hats, mumbling to each other and trying to look tough. I was too hungry to take it all in.

'What do you think of Las Vegas?' asked Tadeese, an Ethiopian waiter whose mother had once met Spencer Tracy.

I shrugged. 'What do *you* think of it?'

'When I go home I live in here.' He tapped my bread knife on his chest where his heart was.

'But when I'm in Las Vegas, I live on the outside. There's a big difference. I miss my mother – she manages to live in there and out here at the same time. A very special person.'

'Has she visited Las Vegas?' I asked Tadeese.

'Oh yes, she likes Engelbert Humperdinck.'

❀

I went to see the National Finals Rodeo, which was the reason all the cowboys were in town. They were paying out prize money in excess of four million dollars. The press room was located in the bowels of the building. I had to have my photograph taken for a pass.

'From the UK, eh?' said the old cowboy taking my photo. He walked slowly and his hands were twisted into arthritic knots. 'We had a guy from *The Economist* in here earlier today.'

'Oh, what was he here for?'

'The rodeo. But he didn't look like *you*. You're done, this'll be ready in a moment.' He started putting together a press pass for me.

'Why? What did *he* look like?'

'Well, he looked very *British*.' He handed me the card which he'd glued together. It was still hot. 'Yeah, he looked very British, English . . . *proper*, you know? Not like you.'

The rodeo began in the evening. Every night seventeen thousand spectators crammed into the Thomas and Mack arena to watch the saddle-bronc-riding, the bull-riding, the barrel-racing, the calf-roping, team-roping, steer-wrestling and bareback-riding. In between events fans walked up and down the long hallways drinking beer and eating hotdogs. Many looked like old-time gunfighters, with their frock-coats, handlebar moustaches and black ties. The women were all long legs and plastic grins. Everyone wore cowboy hats and jeans. Shiny rodeo buckles in gold and silver were on sale for three hundred dollars apiece. I saw a man buy two for his small children. He paid cash for the buckles which were half as big as his children's heads.

'Can you help me here, sir?' said a young rodeo cowboy who was competing. I noticed the further west I travelled the more times I was called 'sir'.

I nodded and piled his plate high with food. He had the use of only one arm and wasn't able to feed himself. He told me his name was Chance Dixon and that he was a saddle-bronc-rider – 'one of the top fifteen in the world'. When I reminded him the 'world' didn't include anywhere outside the USA, he laughed and punched my arm with his good hand. It hurt.

'Ah'm proud of my boy,' his father told me later. 'He gone give me this here ring after he won his last finals. God bless his lil heart . . .' He held up a huge tasteless-looking ring to my face. I dutifully inspected it.

Chance's father had been discharged from hospital in Las Vegas just twenty-four hours earlier. He'd had his second heart-attack. When I met him he looked strained but relieved to still be alive. He sat with the young man's dreamy-looking wife in the stands, watching as the rodeo cowboy tried to hold on to a bucking horse despite his bad shoulder injury.

'My entire life is riding on this – I got a new house, a new pick-up truck and a new wife.' The cowboy looked worried when we'd met earlier. Then he smiled a big hearty grin. Suddenly he looked off his head. 'Hey, I've just got to cowboy up and win, though!'

I had accompanied him into the medical centre which was sponsored by a company which manufactured cowboy boots. The place was like a small, busy field hospital. The man in charge of the place was ancient. He looked like Rumpole of the Bailey in a cowboy hat. He shuffled forward with a needle full of cortisone and plunged it into the messed-up shoulder of my new friend.

'This'll need surgery, it's dislocated,' said the old doctor. Then he smiled a wolfish grin, slapped Chance on the back and veered off across the room to treat someone else.

I sat with him and watched as another rodeo rider came in with a piece of bright white bone sticking out of his neck at a forty-five-degree angle. He couldn't breathe properly and the bone should have been attached to his collarbone.

'Why do you do this?' It was an obvious question but I had to ask it.

'I love it when you've just got off a 1,500-pound animal, you're standing in front of thirty thousand people, and they're screaming and clapping and yelling and going crazy. That's more of a thrill to me than money ever will be.'

Then we watched part of a pizza commercial that was flickering away on a screen in the corner of the room. Other cowboys lying around on treatment tables were watching monitors showing what was happening inside the arena.

'It must seem like some life to you, huh?' He looked sheepish for a moment.

I nodded in agreement and helped him down off the table. His arm was all bandaged up after taking his third consecutive fall. He had a large bag of ice and an electric muscle-stimulator attached to it under the wrapping. He grimaced in pain as I draped his shirt over his shoulders for him.

A few moments later we said our goodbyes and he shuffled off down the dark passageway towards the stadium, his heavily muscled back silhouetted against the bright lights of a local TV crew. I turned to walk away. Suddenly he called out my name.

'I'll win one for you tomorrow night!' he shouted. He smiled his broad grin, waved again and was swallowed up into the darkness.

I could hear the announcer's cheesy voice off in the distance somewhere whipping up the crowd into something less than a frenzy before the 'Tribute to a Horse' routine started.

I left early the next morning. The hotel breakfast-bar was full of excited Nigerians. Old ladies squinting through clouds of cigarette smoke played slot-machines while they queued for food.

On my way out of Las Vegas I passed signs for 'Little Darlings – Totally Nude Show' and 'Fitzgerald's Irish Bar – Come and See the 35-foot Leprechaun'.

The hotels, the neon, the buildings, houses and diners slowly receded. Gently, almost imperceptibly, I entered the Nevada desert. The bright sand dotted with bushes and solid, powerful Joshua trees became the view for hundreds of miles. It felt clean and pure after the grime and rush and noise and hustle of Vegas which lay to the south behind me.

❀

In the summer of 1900, after the Tipton train robbery and the Winnemucca bank hold-up, Butch and the boys headed south for a good time. While Tom Horn went on a politically sponsored killing spree, the Wild Bunch managed to stay one step ahead of things by riding to Fort Worth in Texas to spend their loot. Fort Worth was to Butch and the other outlaws what Las Vegas had been to the cowboys I'd just met. It was an ideal town in which to kick back, let off some steam and pair up with a few hookers – all of which came at a price, of course. A high old time was had by all. Beer was drunk, whiskey was downed and loose women were bedded. One of the outlaws, William, 'News' Carver, got so carried away that he proposed to a prostitute he'd fallen in love with called Lillie Davis. He'd met her in Fannie Porter's brothel in San Antonio, Texas. The wedding was duly held and attended by all the rogues and a wild, drunken reception followed.

At some point in the proceedings somebody suggested having their photograph taken. And so, in their smart suits and fancy derby hats, they all trooped off to 705 Main Street, Fort Worth, the studio of photographer John Swartz. He hustled the five outlaws into his little studio, positioned them in front of a fairly nondescript background and set about composing his picture.

Butch was plonked into a classical-looking, though very uncomfortable, chair at the front right of the group. Ben 'The Tall Texan' Kilpatrick was seated in the middle of the front row. The tall, quiet man with the moustache, Harry 'The Sundance Kid' Longabaugh, was placed on Kilpatrick's left in a comfortable wicker chair. The man who had just been married, slighter than the rest of the group, was asked to stand at the back behind the Sundance Kid. That just left the intense-looking character who managed to smile and scowl simultaneously. Swartz wisely left him to find his own place in the portrait – he was experienced enough to know better than to fuss around touchy clients. Anyway, the insane Harvey Logan didn't like taking orders from anyone.

Finally, after a couple of false starts, Swartz disappeared behind the black cloth and held up his flash in his right hand. 'Okay, hold that,' he said. Only Cassidy allowed a smile to play across his lips. The rest tried their best to look like everyday guys.

The bulb popped. The image was captured and the five men paid their money and left.

Swartz was so pleased with the result that he later placed a copy of the picture in the window of his studio. It was a good likeness of the men who'd bustled and joked their way in through his door and he was delighted with the portrait.

A few days later, after they'd picked up their own copies of the picture, Butch and the boys said their goodbyes and split up. None of them realised that the act of having their photograph taken together would seal their fates. Soon several of them would be dead and the others would have to go on the run. All because their faces appeared in that portrait. For most of the Wild Bunch, that day in Fort Worth was the last time they ever saw one another.

Harvey Logan and Ben Kilpatrick headed north to hold up a train near Wagner in Montana on 8 November 1901. Both managed to get away although the latter was caught for a subsequent robbery along with his girlfriend and sentenced to fifteen years. When he was arrested Kilpatrick had a suitcase full of banknotes – about seven thousand dollars worth – from the Wagner job. He was finally released from prison in Atlanta in 1911, and teamed up with a fellow-inmate known as Ole Beck. Sadly by then both had trouble riding their horses through the towns which they'd once haunted a decade before. Now new-fangled motor-cars were everywhere and Kilpatrick cursed them, swearing he'd never buy one. On the night of 13 March 1912 the two jailbirds held up a train, the *Sunset Flyer*, near Sanderson, Texas. Claiming to be a detective, Kilpatrick entered the baggage car and proceeded to try and rob the train along with his less-assured accomplice. But they hadn't counted on the initiative of a young employee named David Trousdale. When Kilpatrick hesitated for a second, Trousdale calmly split the outlaw's skull almost in half with a railway mallet, killing him instantly. Before the stunned Beck could react, Trousdale grabbed Kilpatrick's rifle and shot Beck at point-blank range. He too was killed on the spot. Trousdale waited until the next station before throwing the would-be robbers' bodies off the train. Both corpses were later pumped full of air with a bicycle pump and held up for the cameras. The brave young baggage steward commented to local press: 'I'm more concerned about how I'll spend the reward money and the vacation time I've been given by my generous employers than I am about killing those two.'

The mad Harvey Logan went into business for himself. It would be a short career. Accounts vary about what happened to him. Some say he shot a rancher to settle an old feud, but was himself shot and captured in the process. What is certain is that he ended up in jail. On 27 June 1903, however, he escaped after almost killing a guard with a home-made garrotte. Logan turned up a year later in Colorado, robbing a train near Parachute with two unknown accomplices. Finding only a pathetically small amount of money in the safe, Logan and the two outlaws fled the scene, pursued by a detective from the Pinkerton Agency. After a lengthy chase Logan found himself trapped like an animal, surrounded by twenty men from the posse, all of whom had their rifles aimed at the rock behind which he was hiding. It is said he shouted: 'I'm hit and I'm going to end it here!' Then he blew his brains out. Other reports say the messy, bloodied body found by the posse was wrongly identified as Logan, and that the outlaw managed to get away after Parachute.

William 'News' Carver, the man who got married in Fort Worth, stayed on in the warmer climes of the south and kept up the outlaw life by robbing banks and trains occasionally. The changing times and his face in the Fort Worth photograph eventually caught up with him, however, and he was shot and killed in 1901 during a bank robbery in Sonora, Texas.

His last words were reputedly, 'Die game, boys.'

The other two men in the Forth Worth picture, Butch

Cassidy and the Sundance Kid, had problems of their own to contend with. Firstly, they had to work out what their next move was; secondly, they had to deal with the fact that they were now easily identifiable nationally and internationally as outlaws. All because of the Fort Worth portrait.

An eagle-eyed detective from Wells, Fargo and Co had spotted the photo in Swartz's studio window shortly after it was taken and made enquiries inside. His instincts proved correct. It *was* the Wild Bunch, in all their finery. They'd been living it up in the town's red-light area. And for once they'd let their guard down. Now everyone knew what they looked like. No more third-rate descriptions − a picture was better than a thousand words. Here it was − a recent image, taken under perfect conditions in a studio. For the lawmen hunting the outlaws it was nothing less than a gift from the gods. For the outlaws it was a devastating blow.

Within a few days of it being spotted in the window of Swartz's studio, Pinkerton detectives had copies of the photo. The image was glued on to wanted posters for each of the men. Copies were sent as far afield as England and Tahiti.

It was used to hunt down Kilpatrick, Logan and Carver with great success, and it must have caused Butch and Sundance considerable worry. The slightly crazy idea which Butch had about heading south, *really* heading south, to Argentina no less − which some said resembled the Old West in it's lawless heyday − suddenly sounded more attractive than ever. Hell, at least it would give them time to straighten a few things out. They had the money to do the trip, didn't they? It wouldn't be for ever, just until the storm over the Fort Worth photo died down. It wasn't much of a plan but it would do for now.

Sundance decided to head home with Etta Place to see his family in Phoenixville, Pennsylvania. It was time to do some hasty explaining and to say goodbye to them for a while. It also gave him a chance to travel north to Buffalo in upstate New

York to get some treatment for an unknown medical problem (possibly a gunshot wound in his leg or for the old cowboy problem of VD) at a clinic run by a Dr Pierce which specialised in 'all chronic diseases – particularly those of a delicate, obscure, complicated or obstinate character'. After being discharged from the clinic, Sundance and Etta travelled via Niagara Falls to New York City where they met up with Butch Cassidy. By 1 February 1901 the trio were registered under the names Mr and Mrs Harry Place and James Ryan at a nice guest-house in the city. They stayed in New York long enough to enjoy themselves – they went to the funfair at Coney Island, ate in fancy restaurants and Butch bought a watch costing $40.10 for Etta at Tiffany's. Wearing the gift she posed with her lover Sundance for a photograph at De Young's Studio on Broadway. Like the 'Fort Worth Five' portrait, it would eventually end up on a Pinkerton's wanted poster.

Towards the end of February, tickets were purchased and final farewells to the old life were made and, one jump ahead of the law, Butch, Sundance and Etta boarded a ship in New York called the *Herminius* bound for Argentina. The date was 20 February 1901. It was time to get out while the going was good. It was time to disappear for a while. It was time to travel.

13. On Travelling

When I was growing up in Cleland I hardly knew anyone who'd ever travelled. Apart from my friend Joe's uncle, the one who'd been in the merchant navy and who'd gone to Haiti for the straw hat, I'd never met anyone who had really *been* anywhere. Those that had 'gone away' had very rarely come back. That worried me, since I always thought that one of the main reasons for travelling was to come back in one piece, with the obligatory tall tale intact.

Travelling was never really talked about in my family. Not in any meaningful sense, anyway. Veiled references were made during adult conversations to 'him next door that went away abroad that time' or 'her brother-in-law that never came back after that thing happened'. This all made travelling sound really dangerous. Even when someone from the area did go away and make their whereabouts known through a letter or a telephone call it still sounded fraught with danger and riddled with pitfalls. But the absence and distance did lend the travellers an added (if not completely warranted) sense of bravery and worldliness.

My mother and father never went very far apart from the odd trip back to Ireland where my mother came from and where my paternal grandfather had left as a young man. Apart from Ireland the farthest we went was Ayr, a seaside town on the west coast of Scotland. Even going to Ayr for the day was a massive undertaking. It was all flasks, teabags, tartan rugs and, horror of horrors, our own dinner plates. Most people travelled to seek out new experiences. Not us. We took Cleland with us in the form of our rose-patterned china. 'People pay pounds for this, don't you be so particular,' Mam would say, passing out ham rolls, 'so eat up and get that look off your face.'

Our destination wasn't very original. Every summer the entire village of Cleland decamped to Ayr. Everyone went as part of the local Miners' Welfare Club free trip. We would usually set off at about half nine in the morning in a scene that was like a cross between *The Grapes of Wrath* and *The Great Escape*. I always thoroughly enjoyed myself and for a lot of people it was the highlight of their entire year. On arrival at Ayr the officious little men organising the outing would unfold long wooden tables, produce meat pies with grease hardened to a white frost on top and proceed to feed the multitudes. The wind gusting in from the Irish Sea always made things interesting and I recall seeing at least one cheap toupee take flight on to the roof of a nearby public toilet.

My last Miners' Welfare trip was the most memorable. It was a couple of years before I went to university and I was already secretly aware that I was more of an observer than a participant. While everyone played with the kids, went on rides at the funfair or, as most of the men seemed to do, got legless in pubs named after Robert Burns's poems, I walked alone for miles along the beach staring westwards. At the end of the day, when we all piled back onto our allotted buses, someone noticed that one of the party, an old man, was missing. We waited for a while. He didn't show up. A vote was taken and it was decided to head back to Cleland without him. Ten miles outside Ayr, however, he was spotted walking along the motorway. Cars zoomed by, honking their horns at him, but he plodded on regardless. Like a homing pigeon he was making for the only place he knew, Cleland. Our bus stopped, he got on, doffed his hat and sat down. A loud cheer went up. Everyone was well aware he'd been released from a local mental hospital just a few days before the trip and that he had trouble remembering his name never mind where he was or where he was going to. He'd wandered out of the house that morning, confused and uncertain, when he'd seen everyone heading towards the parked buses. Somewhere in his head, his brain still clawing and thrashing after ECT, a flicker of recognition had encouraged him to seek the company of others. He hadn't a penny on him when he'd turned up for the annual outing wearing his old double-breasted suit over a complete set of striped hospital pyjamas. His trouser cuffs were frayed and stained with mud and his left hand shook uncontrollably. My last image from that day is of him fast asleep with a smile on his face after everyone on the bus had chipped in to buy him a fish supper. He looked like a contented child in the glow of the orange streetlights when the bus finally returned to the village.

❀

My father never managed to master a map. This made any forays out of the village somewhat longer and more interesting than we'd planned. Our family possessed only one map. Dad had got it free along with a couple of glass tumblers in 1958 after buying two gallons of petrol in one go. He always took it with him on our rare 'jaunts', as he liked to call them, to the seaside near Edinburgh. He'd bring the map because the east coast of Scotland might as well have been the jungles of Costa Rica – our instinct always lured us to Ayr and the west coast because

Ireland lay in that direction. The east represented respectability, Presbyterianism and old ladies who wore tweed all year round. Hence we needed a map to find our way through the maze that was supposedly our own country. Dad couldn't actually read the map but I noticed he'd often unfold it, like he'd seen people do in films, when he had to frequently hang out the window and ask strangers for directions. After they'd told him how to get on to the right road he'd fold the map back up carefully and stick it in the glove compartment where it would stay until the next wrong turning. We would all be sitting silent and tense in the back of the car whenever this happened. I think he was secretly ashamed of his lack of skill but no one ever brought the subject up. Occasionally, when he actually found the right road, we'd all cheer in triumph. We felt like we'd pulled a fast one on the natives without being caught.

Dad was a semi-professional singer when I was younger. He got one step nearer a break on TV when he was invited to audition in Glasgow for a Scottish music show that used to be on in the evenings. He took my uncle with him for moral support and to help with directions when they drove to the city – which was only about fifteen miles from our village. He had his trusty map with him but it was no use. He had tried to read the thing, turning it this way and that in his hands as the clock ticked, but to no avail. They got lost and never made it to the audition. They gave up and came home with the excuse that 'somebody must have moved the River Clyde'.

Only 'well-to-do' people really travelled, said Mam. The 'likes of us' are too busy 'getting on with it'. She'd fall silent. Then she'd add: 'Maybe once you've been through school and college and university, once you're educated you can . . . you know . . . see things.'

Educated. I knew a lot of people who believed everything changed once you were educated. Mam frequently used the word when she was talking about travelling. Once I was educated I'd travel and see things for myself. That was the deal on offer. *See things.* I lay awake at night wondering what those things were and how the hell I'd ever get to see them. They seemed an awful long way off. Whatever they were.

The one and only time my father travelled on his own was when he set out on an unlikely excursion to see the Scottish Highlands. Always a theatrical dresser, he'd decided to wear a kilt for this backpacking trip. I think he thought that looking the part might somehow magically make him really *be* the part. On that occasion the clothes, to put it lightly, did not maketh the man. He'd ended up marooned on the *Waverley* the world's last sea-going paddle-steamer. It had half sunk off a miserable, rain-soaked island somewhere not far down the Clyde. TV crews in helicopters hovered overhead filming smiling passengers stuck on the upper deck waving at the camera. My father, with a couple of days' growth on his chin was spotted, kilt and all, waving forlornly on the early-evening news.

Initially my mother was ashamed and deeply embarrassed. What would the neighbours think? That Cleland wasn't good enough for us? Jesus, Mary and Joseph! He'd been caught, red-handed, trying to travel! It bore out her worst fears about people 'trying to be something they're not'. And if we did try and travel, 'sure, who would take us serious?'.

Dad was forgiven when he returned. 'There's plenty that don't even try,' said Mam. She stuck up for him because, I think, she thought he'd lost face in front of me and my sisters.

I, however, was secretly very proud of him for attempting his version of *Mission: Impossible*. It hinted at a hidden desire to travel, which I knew I'd inherited. He talked about that abortive trip for years and referred knowingly to places in the Scottish Highlands I knew he'd never seen. He made it sound like a big, well-financed expedition to the Himalayas to find the Yeti.

❁

One of the few people we knew who'd travelled was a neighbour who'd gone to Lisbon in 1967 to see Celtic play Inter Milan in the final of the European Cup. About seventeen years old at the time, Tommy was employed by the local Co-op supermarket as a delivery boy and was in the process of saving up money to get married to a local beauty. Apparently he took a brainstorm one day after seeing crowds of Celtic fans heading for Portugal on the TV. He decided he'd had enough of delivering pork links and pan bread around the village, went straight home, grabbed his Celtic scarf and passport, cashed in his savings account at the bank and stole the Co op van. His plan was to drive to Portugal and see the game. On his way out of the village he picked up an acquaintance to help him navigate and read the map. This man was an ex-army officer who, it was alleged, had travelled.

The trip turned into a total disaster. The soldier was mentally unstable after a strange incident in the Congo and so he spent the entire journey drinking heavily to forget something he'd done. Tommy also contributed somewhat to the débâcle by panicking when he realised Lisbon was not, as he'd thought, 'just south of Scotland'.

Things turned very sour when his paranoid companion refused to stop for toilet breaks – he believed they were being followed. This increased the tension in the claustrophobic van to breaking point. At Dover, fortunately, the soldier was refused permission to board the ferry to France since he'd forgotten to bring his passport with him, so Tommy had to proceed alone.

Once in France, as he put it, he simply 'got my head down and arse up', driving south to Spain then west to Portugal. By now his money and supplies were running out to say nothing of time. Then something terrible happened. He got a flat tyre. Stranded in the middle of nowhere on a burning hot Portuguese afternoon, he tied a spare shirt around his head and set off on foot to look for help. Later, when he staggered back after walking for miles without finding anyone, he found to his horror that the flat tyre had melted and stuck to the surface of the road. He sat down and wept.

A day and a half later, after abandoning the van and most of his belongings, he reached Lisbon on the morning of the match. Fortuitously, the one thing he hadn't lost were his tickets for the game, so his plan was to get into the stadium, meet up with other Celtic fans from Scotland and persuade someone to help him out of his awful predicament.

The match flew by in a heat- and hunger-induced blur. Footage from that memorable day shows Tommy, clearly in considerable distress (which could be mistaken for euphoria), to be the very first fan to invade to pitch after Celtic won the game. Thousands of fans followed his example, unaware that he needed medical and possibly psychiatric care.

While on the pitch, and by a complete million-to-one shot, he met the only other person from Cleland that had made it to the game. He actually bumped right into this guy in the middle of the jubilant crowd. This friendly face promptly turned around, shook Tommy's hand warmly as if he'd just met him at the local chip shop on a Saturday night, then disappeared back into the thronging masses. Tommy went to pieces. By the time Celtic's captain, Billy McNeill, hoisted the trophy above his head the poor fellow was wandering out of the city in despair. He says he spent the night in the gutter.

The next day, on a shimmering, sun-baked Portuguese high-way he stood with his two-week-old beard, thumbing a lift. In the distance he spotted a bus − or was it a hunger-induced mirage − on the horizon. He swayed and staggered as the bus drove nearer through the mirrored surface of the flat desert road. Finally he made out the green-and-white Celtic scarves and the British number-plate. He almost flung himself underneath the bus to get it to stop for him. Eventually the door opened. The burly driver leaned over towards him. Most of the passengers were sleeping off the previous night's celebrations as Tommy croaked out his request for a lift home.

'Where are you from?' asked the Glaswegian driver.

'Cleland, fifteen miles from Glasgow . . .' said Tommy in barely audible tones.

'Sorry pal, we're from the south side of the city – that's miles away, nowhere near Cleland,' replied the driver.

The door was shut a split-second later. The engine was revved and the bus drove off in a cloud of blue petrol fumes. Tommy, his hand still outstretched, buckled at the knees. He'd been abandoned. His life, because of adventure and travel, was in ruins.

The story of how he did eventually manage to get home was equally sad and just as scary. It was told in bedtime-story form to children in the village to serve as a warning about the dangers of travelling to foreign countries. Tommy told me recently that he was thirty-seven before he finally paid off the stolen Co-op van at the rate of a pound a month.

❀

Another football fan from Cleland followed the Celtic abroad, this time to Rome. She had a wonderful time on the trip and never once felt homesick or scared. She even managed to gatecrash a huge party which the world-famous actor Richard Burton had thrown for his new wife, Elizabeth Taylor. They were on location in Italy filming *Cleopatra* at the time. A newspaper photographer and a reporter from Glasgow took a photo of this woman as she stood between the two Hollywood superstars and the picture duly appeared in the following day's edition of the *Daily Record* back in Scotland. When some friends showed the paper to the woman's husband in Cleland he smiled and clapped his hands.

'Now would you credit it? In Italy, eh?' He lifted up the

newspaper and stared at the picture. His wife's image smiled straight at the camera between the two tanned film stars who looked confused, uncertain and caught off guard.

'What do you think of that?' asked a relative.

'Great!' said the woman's husband. 'Our Kathy looks fantastic. But who the hell are the other two beside her?'

She'd travelled all right but he'd hardly left Cleland in his life.

❄

My parents tried their best when I was young to convince me that I wasn't what Dad called a 'good traveller'. 'He'll be back,' Dad would say when he saw me pulling on a rucksack, or 'Oh, will you look at the stay-at-home traveller,' if he caught me reading a guidebook. I think they were both afraid I'd go away and not come back.

In later years Mam and Dad did break out and travel to Spain with me to visit one of my sisters who was teaching in Madrid. Dad got brave one day and took me with him when he ventured out to the bank to change some money. When the cashier spoke to him in Spanish, Dad nearly had a fit. It was exactly like the scene out of *Butch Cassidy and the Sundance Kid* when Paul Newman enters a bank to rob it, only to find to his horror everyone speaking Spanish. While I grinned stupidly, Dad went white, shifted in his seat and for a moment thought about leaving quickly. Instead, possibly because I was at his side, he touched the brim of his trilby and said 'No comprehende, Senior.' The man somehow understood him and began to speak in broken English while the transaction was completed. My father was delighted and almost ran back to the flat to tell my mother of his breakthrough.

'How did you know what to say?' asked Mam admiringly.

'Oh, I heard Humphrey Bogart saying it in *The Treasure of the Sierra Madre*,' he said, beaming with pride.

Therein lay Dad's big secret. He had travelled, at least as he saw it, in his mind through films. He'd been to New York with the gangsters, he'd been through the wars with Audie Murphy, he'd walked in the Holy Land with various Hollywood Jesuses, he'd even been up to the Scottish Highlands with an American actor running around on a set made up to look like Brigadoon. And he'd single-handedly won the West with every cowboy actor you could think of. My father had travelled extensively throughout the world all right, it was just that he hadn't actually been anywhere, that's all.

My mother was slightly embarrassed by his devotion to films. For her they were frivolous and not true to life. I often thought she didn't have much of an imagination – or that if she did have once that somewhere along the line life had got so hard and intrusive that it had obliterated her creative abilities. She simply couldn't suspend her disbelief when a film came on. It had to be 'true to life', she'd say, for her to be engaged. Otherwise it was 'all made-up oul rubbish' with 'them oul rubber guns and terrible language'. Dad took her to the pictures once to see something, buying her a box of chocolates as well. Afterwards he told us with disgust how she'd fallen asleep within twenty minutes of the film starting.

Mam's first love was books. Mostly she read authors who wrote 'good reads', as she put it. Nearly all of them reflected her own tough upbringing and lack of family to take care of things. The main character was always a woman from a working-class background who made it against terrible odds to eventually triumph over adversity. I think she read these books to give her a sneak preview of the victory that was hopefully just around her own corner. I admired her guarded optimism. Meanwhile, as she laid the book down on her bedside cabinet, blessing herself with the sign of the cross, she'd say it was 'the old dog for the hard road, nothing else for it'.

Travelling, I think, represented something dangerous and,

perhaps, wasteful to my mother. When Dad got a job with the railways we got free travel anywhere we wanted. That more or less changed everything. It was also the first time I realised that most people couldn't travel simply because they didn't have the money to spare. The free travel we were allowed meant Mam and Dad went all over Britain and really enjoyed themselves. We even went as far as Scarborough on holiday one year, which was a real adventure for us. We stayed in a modest guest-house run by a man with very long hair and dirty fingernails. I wore a cowboy hat and took photos of my parents outside big expensive hotels on the sea-front – I think they thought about pretending we'd stayed there.

I think my mother secretly wanted to travel abroad. She had two penpals in America for years – one of them lived in Colorado and the other in upstate New York. She had got their addresses from an Irish radio programme decades ago. She wrote to both for over thirty years.

My father, although treading many a mile of the hard road, would have given his right arm for a flight to Hollywood and the soft road. He loved James Cagney. Our house had several photographs of Cagney on the walls when I was a boy. For a time I thought everyone had pictures of Hollywood idols up next to John F. Kennedy, the Pope of the day and the Sacred Heart of Jesus.

I inherited my love of the cinema from my father. I'd no choice really. Travelling, though, I had to discover for myself. In later years, because I'd watched so many films as a child, I had to undertake a mad scramble to catch up with my missed reading. If someone had asked me when I was ten who created *Oliver Twist*, I'd have been unsure whether it was Charles Dickens or David Lean. To this day, despite having a degree in history, I still think of Bonnie Prince Charlie as really being David Niven in a skirt and a wig.

But my father and I always preferred westerns. When I was

young I never really asked him why he liked them so much, and I simply enjoyed them because they were full of adventure and mayhem. The fact that the weather always looked good helped as well. We didn't get much sunshine in Scotland.

Westerns were also the only type of films that excited my Dad enough to make tea and toast for us while we watched them. Normally I did the cooking. 'A Cowboy and Indian film is due on. It's a bad day when you're too old to enjoy one – remember that.' Then he'd wink and disappear into the kitchen to switch the kettle on.

We watched them all. The list is too long to remember. The seconds, minutes and hours of my childhood were marked by a steady procession of cowboy films. He'd let me stay up late to watch them and sometimes he'd write me a dodgy school note for the teacher if I slept in the following morning.

When I was older I asked my mother if Dad had always liked cowboy films. She laughed and blushed. 'On one of the first dates I had with your father he turned up wearing a fringed cowboy shirt. He said he'd seen Alan Ladd wearing one like it in a western movie.'

One day I asked him about this and he laughed at the memory. 'She's half-right – I did own a fringed shirt, but it was Errol Flynn that wore one like it.' He paused then added: 'I also liked cowboy films for another reason, though.'

'What's that?'

'The Indians – you see I always liked their moccasins and I wasn't happy until I wrote away to an American company and got a pair. I had to stitch them together by hand. They were the most comfortable things I'd ever worn in my life. I'd rather wear a pair of those than totter about in high-heeled cowboy boots any time.'

He was telling the truth. As far back as I could remember, my father was the only man in Scotland I ever knew who, come rain or shine, always wore Indian moccasins on his feet.

It suddenly dawned on me that throughout all those western movies we'd viewed together we'd actually been looking at two different things. While I'd watched the cowboys, my father had sat silently beside me watching the Indians. And he'd worn their moccasin footwear and a Hollywood cowboy's fringed shirt as a substitute for travelling.

❀

These were the stories and experiences of travelling I grew up with. They weren't very inspiring. I decided to start travelling when I was about fifteen. Because of Dad's job on the railway I qualified for free travel on the British Rail network. For my first trip alone I decided to go to London for a couple of weeks to visit a relative who lived there. In the days preceding my trip I spent most of my time reading guidebooks. I was nervous and couldn't sleep at night with excitement. I felt like I was undertaking a journey which was bound to end with me falling off the edge of the world.

During that trip I recall sitting under a tree in Hyde Park chatting to a Japanese girl who liked Hemingway. I nodded a lot and tried not to make it too obvious that I'd noticed she wasn't wearing a bra under her thin red T-shirt. We sat for hours until the sun went down and my bum went numb from the cold grass. She told me she always wanted to go to Scotland to see the Loch Ness Monster. She kissed me when we parted. 'Promise me you'll see the gardens in Kyoto some day,' she said to me. I agreed and thought briefly about returning the sentiment by mentioning Loch Ness but changed my mind. After she'd walked off I realised she hadn't told me her name. I felt too awkward to run after her so I stood there watching her stroll off towards Buckingham Palace swinging her leather satchel and running her hands through her long dark hair. I was glad I'd made the journey if only for that conversation. And the kiss.

If I hadn't travelled I'd have gone mad. Most of my peers spent the entire summer holidays hanging around outside the chip shop watching the world go by. They were the same guys I'd played Cowboys and Indians with years before. When a bus passed through the village they'd all stand opposite the bus stop scanning the windows to see if there were any attractive girls on board. If there weren't any females to ogle they'd make do with gesturing in a rude and aggressive way at any single males around the same age who happened to be on the bus.

'Why are you doing that?' I asked one of my pals. Seconds before he'd been making silent slashing gestures across his throat at a young uncomfortable-looking guy on the bus which was passing through Cleland.

'He's a wanker, that's why.'

'How do you know he's a wanker?'

'Because he's not from here so he must be . . . anyway, he's on that bus going somewhere else so that makes him a wanker, all right?'

The bus moved off. The group stood in silence, eating fish and chips and drinking a bottle of Irn Bru that was being passed around. It might as well have been a decade before, seeing who was John Wayne amongst us. Hardly anything had changed.

'So what are we doing now?' I asked one of them.

A collective shrug went around the group. Finally one of them answered. 'We're waiting on the next bus.'

That's when I knew it was time for me to travel.

14. Hey, These Things Happen

After their travels Butch Cassidy, the Sundance Kid and Etta Place arrived in Argentina in 1901 the way they'd planned it – anonymously.

They stayed in a fancy hotel, deposited some cash (about £2,000 in English notes) in the London & River Platte Bank in Buenos Aires and settled down to finding the best place for them to stay permanently.

Months passed.

They surfaced in the Chubut Territory. This was a desolate although not entirely charmless district – Indians, hardy pioneers, farmers and some immigrants accounted for most of the population in the area. The 1905 census of the Chubut region states that 12,417 people lived there. The residents were dwarfed by the livestock they kept, though – 1.36 million sheep, 225,000 cattle and 55,000 horses. It wasn't an easy journey from Buenos Aires to Chubut: a couple of sweaty trips on steamboats upriver, followed by a muscle-numbing trek on horseback or mule across open country.

After they'd settled, they made contact with some of the other inhabitants of Chubut, introducing themselves as James 'Santiago' Ryan (Butch), and Mr and Mrs Harry 'Enrique' Place (Sundance and Etta). A letter written by Butch to the mother-in-law of his old pal Elzy Lay (Lay was locked up at the time) a relatively short time after they'd established a home in Argentina gives us a good indication of the lives they were leading:

Cholila Chubut
Argentine Republic, S.Am.
August 10, 1902.

Mrs Davis.
Ashley, Utah.

My dear friend,
I suppose you have thought long before this that I had forgotten you (or was dead) but my dear friend I am still alive, and when I think of my old friends you are always the first to come to my mind. It will probably surprise you to hear from me away down in this country, but the U.S. was too small for me. The last two years I was there, I was restless. I wanted to see more of the world. I had seen all of the U.S. that I thought was good, and a few months after I sent A ———— over to see you, and get the photo of the rope jumping of which I have got here and often look at and wish I could see the originals, and I think I could liven some of the characters up a little, for Maudie looks very sad to me. Another of my uncles died and left $30,000, Thirty Thousand, to our little family of 3, so I took my $10,000 and started to see a little more of the world. I visited the best cities and best parts of the countries of South A. till I got here, and this part of the country looked so good that I locate, and I think for

good, for I like the place better every day. I have 300 cattle, 1500 sheep, and 28 good saddle-horses, 2 men do my work, also a good 4-room house, warehouse, stable, chicken house and some chickens. The only thing lacking is a cook, for I am living in Single Cussedness and I sometimes feel very lonely, for I am alone all day and my neighbours don't amount to anything, besides, the only language spoken in this country is Spanish, and I don't speak it well enough yet to converse on the latest scandals so dear to the hearts of all nations, and without which conversations are very stale, but the country is first class. The only industry at present is stock raising (that is in this part) and it can't be beat for that purpose, for I have never seen finer grass country, and lots of it hundreds and hundreds of miles that is unsettled and rural country. All kind of small grain and vegetables grow without Irrigation, but I am at the foot of the Andes Mountains, and all the land east of here is prairie and deserts, very good for stock, but for farming it would have to be irrigated, but there is plenty of good land along the mountains for all the people that will be here for the next hundred years, for I am a long way from civilisation. It is 16 hundred miles to Buenos Aires, the capital of the Argentine, and over 400 miles to the nearest rail road or sea port in the Argentine Republic, but only 150 miles to the Pacific Coast Chile, but to get there we have to cross the mountains, which was thought impossible till last summer, when it was found that the Chilean Govt. had cut a road almost across, so that next summer we will be able to go to Port. Mont, Chile, in about 4 days, where it used to take 2 months around the old trail, and it will be a great benefit to us for Chile is our Beef market and we can get our cattle there in 1/10 the time and have them fat. And we can also get supplies in Chile for one third what they cost here. The climate here is a great deal milder than Ashley Valley. The summers are beautiful, never as warm as there. And grass knee high everywhere and lots of good cold mountain water, but the winters are very wet and disagreeable, for it rains most of the time, but sometimes we have lots of snow, but it don't last long, for it never gets cold enough to freeze much. I have never seen ice one inch thick . . .

The $30,000 dollars mentioned didn't come from any dead uncle's will − it came, reluctantly, from the vaults of the Winnemucca bank.

The trio quietly settled down in Argentina, began home-steading and raising livestock, doing their damnedest to appear respectable and trustworthy. All their neighbours liked them. Even the territorial governor, Julio Lezana, who visited the area early in 1904, trusted them enough to spend the night in their well-furnished and relatively comfortable four-roomed cabin. On that memorable occasion he danced with Etta while Sun-dance played the Spanish guitar. They seemed rich, well mannered and, to some visitors, even a touch cultured.

One visitor who passed through their lives in 1904 was Primo Capraro, an Italian immigrant:

> The house was simply furnished and exhibited a certain painstaking tidiness, a geometric arrangement of things, pictures with cane frames, wallpaper made of clippings from North American magazines and many beautiful weapons and lassos braided from horsehair. The men were tall, slender, laconic, and nervous, with intense gazes. The lady who was reading, was well dressed . . . Later I learned that they were famous robbers of trains and banks in North America . . .

Other reports suggested that the outlaws had a secret room built into the floor of the cabin and had one of the very first telephones installed in the area. Just in case.

Butch became friendly with a Welshman named Daniel Gibbons who had emigrated to the area in the 1890s. Gibbons wasn't a rogue like Butch and Sundance but he would, if he thought the occasion merited it, turn a blind eye to certain events as a favour to his friends. Butch certainly liked him. A letter from the outlaw to Gibbons in February 1904 is revealing:

> Dear friend,
>
> I have been laid up with a bad dose of the Town Disease and I don't know when I will be able to ride, but as soon as I am able I will be down. And I will want to buy some rams, so please keep your ears open for we don't know where to look for them. If you hear of anyone that wants to sell please tell them about us. I have not been to Ñorquinco yet, so don't know what we will do there.
>
> Kindest regards to your wife and family,
>
> Yours most truly,
>
> J.P. Ryan.
>
> Look out for my horse.
>
> P.S. Place [Sundance] starts for the lake tomorrow to buy bulls.

'A bad dose of the Town Disease' probably means only one thing – Butch Cassidy was suffering from a grippingly painful bout of venereal disease.

A nearby Scottish neighbour, John Gardiner, also became friends with Butch – although not with Sundance. Apparently the Scot fell in love with Etta Place the moment he clapped his eyes on her and they seemed to have shared a scholarly interest in books and current affairs. Gardiner once told a friend that

Etta Place was the 'first and only love of his life'. He thought Sundance was a 'mean, low cur' and gladly avoided him. Originally from Glasgow, he later settled in Ireland, in Cong, Co. Mayo, where he married a local woman and lived to a ripe old age in a house designed and built by Oscar Wilde. He became friendly with a Co. Mayo native called Frank O'Grady and told him stories about loot buried near the outlaws' cabin in Cholila. By the end of the 1940s O'Grady was still trying to put together enough money to organise a treasure hunt. He died in 1980 without ever realising his obsession.

Sundance and Etta made a trip back to the States in 1902, just a year after they arrived in Argentina. Perhaps they were homesick. They arrived in New York on 3 April on board the SS *Soldier Prince*. They stayed in a rooming-house in the city, visited the sights, went to see Sundance's family in Pennsylvania again and even visited his brother Harvey in Atlantic City, New Jersey. Pinkerton detectives weren't exactly on their tails but they did file subsequent reports to the effect that Sundance had returned with Etta to the States, mentioning that he might have sought medical attention in Chicago for an unspecified problem. The pair left for South America again on 10 July. They'd make another trip to the States soon – they were certainly at the St Louis World Fair in 1904 and sent a postcard from there to Sundance's sister Samanna.

Although, as in his letter to Elzy Lay's mother-in-law, Butch griped about being alone at the times when Sundance and Etta were off on their excursions, he seems to have been more or less happy to settle down in Argentina.

All went well for a couple of years. The three seemed to have successfully built themselves a crime-free life. Even those who'd guessed at their dark past left them alone. Until the Pinkertons started poking around again.

In March 1903 a Pinkerton agent by the name of Frank Dimaio visited Buenos Aires following up on a tip that Butch and Sundance were lying low there. Although he didn't make it as far as Chubut Territory, Dimaio did leave behind a poster giving information about the outlaws, newly translated in Spanish, which was duly pasted up for everyone to see.

Nothing happened immediately, but the seed of disaster sown in Fort Worth by the group photograph was now replanted in Argentina and right across South America. It was only a matter of time before it bore fruit and someone somewhere blew the whistle on Butch and Sundance.

As it turned out, in fact, they were in many ways the architects of their own downfall.

On St Valentine's Day 1905, they allegedly (doubts still persist to this day) robbed a bank in Rio Gallegos, about seven hundred miles south of Cholila. The thieves were reported as being English-speakers and the prime suspects, rightly or wrongly, were Butch and Sundance.

Returning to a life of crime in South America wasn't exactly the same as robbing a bank in Wyoming. The three gringos stood out like sore thumbs. Their Spanish wasn't perfect and they often brought Etta along too. They weren't what you could call inconspicuous.

A friendly and sympathetic lawman, who may have been enamoured with Etta, tipped them off that the authorities were after them for the robbery. The trio packed up and fled to Chile. They had never actually owned the land at Cholila – they'd just settled it. But leaving their cabin and the land they'd worked must have been frustrating. But they hadn't quite finished with Argentina.

On 19 December 1905 the three of them – Etta dressed in men's clothes – and an unidentified fourth man (some suspect this was Harvey Logan who may have survived his alleged suicide and headed south, although it's highly unlikely), stole 12,000 pesos from the Banco de la Nación in Villa Mercedes, some four hundred miles west of Buenos Aires.

A few months later Etta Place returned to the United States and never went back to South America again. Her reasons for doing this are not clear. Etta was the most mysterious of the three outlaws who lived in Patagonia. Her eyes, level and steady, gaze out of the portrait she and Sundance had taken at De Young's studio in 1901. Her thick hair is fixed up on her head. Her small, delicate hands and straight back suggest a good upbringing where a young lady's posture was considered vital. Beyond this there is tantalisingly little real evidence to go on. Her 1906 Pinkerton's card states she was called 'Mrs Harry Longabaugh, alias Mrs Harry A. Place, alias Mrs Ethel Place'. She was 27 to 28 years old, between five foot four and five foot five inches tall, weighed 110 to 115 pounds, was of medium build, and had medium dark hair, which she wore 'high on top of her head in a rool from forehead' and she had a 'medium dark complexion'. The agents thought Etta may have come from Texas originally, perhaps even from Fort Worth, but they weren't sure. Even her name was uncertain – she probably took her surname from Sundance's alias 'Place' simply because he'd called himself after his mother's maiden name. Other theories suggest she was the illegitimate daughter of Emily Jane Place, who was related to Sundance's mother, and one George Capel, also known as George Ingerfield, the son of the sixth Earl of Sussex. Always referred to as 'Etta' by the Pinkertons, she signed herself 'Ethel' when she stayed in a New York hotel. She may have left South America because of grumbling appendix or an unwanted pregnancy – who knows? Some said she was a high-class prostitute whom Sundance met on one of his romps through the brothels of Fort Worth. That seems unlikely if only because of her graceful, fresh beauty – most 'soiled doves' in the West looked as if they had seen better days; even at a young age they appeared worn and old. If Etta was a working woman then she was an exceptional one. From her photographs she looked more like the demure schoolteacher some said she really was. A woman called Eunice Gray was suspected as being the real Etta but the years she claimed to be in South America don't tally with the known movements of Butch and Sundance.

Richard Llewellyn, the author of the well-known Welsh mining saga *How Green Was My Valley*, lived in Argentina in the late 1940s. He heard a tale that suggested Etta had left there bound for Paraguay where she eventually married a well-heeled civil servant and settled down to raise a family.

But all that is speculation. No one really knows what happened to Etta Place, the silent, beautiful lover of the deadly, taciturn Sundance Kid. Some say that after Harry Longabaugh left Etta in the hospital in Denver he proceeded to shoot up the boarding-house he was staying in. Then he fled in a huff and nursing a brutal hangover back to his old haunts in South America. He was never to see her again.

It was just him and Butch again. Two not-so-young outlaws on the run.

❀

Before travelling thousands of miles to the western states of America, I'd taken a quick trip to Washington DC for research purposes. There I met two part-time outlaw historians, Dan Buck and his wife Anne Meadows, and asked them about Butch and Sundance's time in South America. They had both travelled widely in Patagonia and Argentina, Bolivia and Chile, combining their love of that region with a fascination with Butch and Sundance.

Dan has had an ongoing romance with Patagonia, Chile and other areas of South America since the 1960s, when he spent a two-year stretch as a Peace Corps volunteer in Peru. His wife Anne was no less fond of these Hispanic countries and their house was filled with artefacts, ancient books and several venerable maps – all acquired during numerous expeditions.

Both had travelled extensively in Argentina and Bolivia before they'd fully realised the connection the whole area had with the outlaws' story.

My hosts had been over this ground before but, with great patience, they skilfully and swiftly wove together tales of the outlaws' time in Argentina, their subsequent robberies and their time on the run. I learned that the two men split up for a while after the Villa Mercedes job and that in 1906 Butch found work at the Concordia tin mine, 16,000 feet up in the Bolivian Andes. Sundance, meanwhile, secured a job looking after livestock for a contractor called Letson who was driving mules from northern Argentina to La Paz in Bolivia. Inevitably the two outlaws met up at Concordia where they both got jobs guarding, of all things, the mine's payroll.

'It was there, at Concordia, that they met a guy called Percy Seibert – he was the mine's assistant manager. It didn't take him long to figure out they were outlaws but he said he "never had the slightest trouble" getting along with either of them,' said Anne.

'Why didn't he turn them in?' I asked.

'Percy Seibert liked them. Even had them over for Sunday dinner – although Butch always took the seat facing the window in case they were joined by unwelcome company. In fact, most people who ever came into contact with Butch and Sundance really liked them – especially Butch,' remarked Dan. He pulled out a buff-coloured envelope and handed me a description which Percy Seibert had written about his outlaw employees:

> Butch Cassidy was an agreeable and pleasant person . . .
> He took well with the ladies and as soon as he arrived in
> a village he made friends with the little urchins and
> usually had some candy to give them. When he visited
> me he enjoyed hearing the gramophone records as I had
> a large selection of choice music. He allowed no other

bandits to interfere with my camp and told them when they needed an animal shod or they needed a meal I would take care of them, but that they should move on and keep their backs towards my camp and not give it the reputation of being a bandits' hangout. When he last visited me, he asked me a couple of times if I was sure he did not owe our commissary store anything more than the six or eight dollars I told him of and which he immediately paid . . . I never had the slightest trouble getting along with them [Butch and Sundance]. Cassidy purchased cattle and mules for us and always was scrupulously honest as far as we were concerned. He went to a mining camp owned by a pair of wealthy Scotchmen, to get the lay of the land and to learn when their payroll remittances would arrive so as to pick it up. They gave him a job as a night watchman and told him they really needed no one, but wanted to give him a chance to make a little money so he could continue to prospect for mines, as on applying for work he told them he was a prospector and had run out of money and supplies. They told him the meal hours, told him the sideboard had a supply of whiskey, appolinas water, gin and beer and whenever he felt like a drink to help himself. He told me after that he had not the heart to hold up people who treated him so kindly.

'After they left the Concordia mines – Sundance got drunk and bragged about something he shouldn't have – they headed south and on the way bumped into another guy who also took a liking to them. His name was A.G. Francis, a British engineer,' continued Anne.

She fished out a report Francis had written for a publication called *Wide World* Magazine which appeared in the May 1913 edition and handed it to me. It read:

One evening during the month of August 1908, I was enjoying a solitary meal, when a loud outcry on the part of my dogs announced the arrival of visitors. Going to the door of my house I was in time to greet two riders, who, from their saddles and general appearance, I judged to be Americans . . . During the next two or three days while the men were busy loading the carts for their next journey, Smith and Low [Sundance and Cassidy] proved very pleasant and amusing companions, and I was therefore not at all sorry when, as we were about to start on our trip to Esmoraca, they offered to accompany me. For the following few weeks the transport work went on as usual, Smith remaining with me and Low spending a good part of his time in visits to Tupiza. At the time I had no idea that he had any other motive in this but that of enjoyment . . .

'Enjoyment was the last thing on their minds – they were casing a robbery.' Dan sat back on the couch and laughed.

I read on. According to the testimony Butch and Sundance had just robbed a payroll and Francis found himself in an awkward position:

> After giving me these particulars, [Sundance] joined his partner in my room, and I returned to my hammock to pass the rest of the night. I thought deeply over the story I had just heard, and did not care at all for the position in which I found myself, practically the accessory of a couple of brigands . . .

After breakfast the next morning, which neither Butch nor Sundance seemed too inclined to hurry up despite being informed a posse was on its way, the two outlaws 'invited' Francis join them on their getaway: 'Needless to say, that was the last thing I wished to do,' wrote Francis 'but argument was useless . . .'

After spending the night in a village judged to be safe, the outlaws said goodbye to Francis:

> About eight o'clock that morning, after learning all the particulars I could give them regarding the road they wished to follow, [Sundance] and [Butch] suddenly pulled up their animals, and the former held out his hand.
>
> 'Well, goodbye, kid,' he said. 'You don't want to come any further with us. If you meet those soldiers, tell them you passed us on the road to the Argentine.'
>
> Exchanging farewells, I turned my horse and rode towards Tomahuaico catching the last glimpse I ever had of the bandits alive as they rounded a bend in the valley.
>
> The following day an Indian passing Tomahuaico informed me that two white men had been killed the previous evening at San Vicente . . . His descriptions of these men tallying with that of the robbers, I saddled up at once and rode to San Vicente, learning on the way further details which convinced me that it was indeed my late companions who had come to their untimely end.

The British engineer was quite sad when he learned the fate of his two erstwhile companions. He wrote about his feelings and stated the reasons the robbers said they had for living the life of outlaws:

> I must confess that it was with a feeling very much akin to grief that I wended my way homeward. [Sundance] told me once that he had made several attempts to settle down to a law-abiding life, but these attempts had always

been frustrated by emissaries of the police and detective agencies getting on his track, and thus forcing him to return to the road. He claimed that he had never hurt or killed a man except in self-defence, and had never stolen from the poor, but only from rich corporations well able to support his 'requisitions'.

'San Vicente – that was where they bit the big one,' said Dan, sipping his wine.

'That's where they died?'

'Yep. Tell him, Anne.'

'Let's see – okay, you've read from Francis's account how they robbed a payroll. The following is an account of how the robbery took place – it's from the man they robbed, one Carlos Peró, who worked for the Aramayo Francke y Companía, a large and profitable mining company located near Tupiza in southern Bolivia.'

Carlos stated on 4 November 1908 that:

> At 9.30 in the morning, we encountered two well-armed Yankees, who awaited us with their faces covered by bandannas and their rifles ready, and they made us dismount and open the baggage, from which they took only the cash shipment. They also took from us a dark brown mule ('Aramayo') which is known to the stable hands in Tupiza, with a new hemp rope. The two Yankees are tall; one is thin and the other – who carried a good pair of Hertz binoculars – is heavyset. They clearly came from Tupiza, where they must have been waiting for my departure to make their strike, because from the beginning they did not ask me for anything other than the cash shipment . . . One of them quickly began to search our baggage, specifying that they were not interested in our personal money nor in any articles

that belonged to us, but only in the money that we were carrying for the company. They knew that I spoke English, in which language they asked me if we were not carrying eighty thousand *bolivianos*, to which I replied that the sum was not quite as large as they believed. And when I saw that there was no point in hiding anything, a search of the baggage having begun, I informed them that it was only fifteen thousand. What I said caused great anguish, momentarily silencing the bandit nearest us . . . The two Yankees wore new, dark-red, thin-wale corduroy suits with narrow, soft-brimmed hats, the brims turned down in such a way that, with the bandannas tied behind their ears, only their eyes could be seen. One of the bandits, the one who came closest to and talked with me, is thin and of normal stature; the other, who always maintained a certain distance, is heavyset and taller. Both of them carried new carbines, which appeared to be of the Mauser-type, small-calibre and thick barrel . . . The bandits also carried Colt revolvers, and I believe they also had very small Browning revolvers outside their cartridge belts, which were filled with rifle ammunition.

'Well, after that, they headed for a place called San Vicente. It's a mining village 14,500 feet up in the mountains.' Anne sat back in her chair after she'd finished reading.

'Cold . . . Very cold.' Dan stared deeply into his glass obviously recalling many a chilly night he and Anne had spent in San Vicente.

'Yeah, cold, like Dan says. No holiday resort then, or now. At dusk on 6 November 1908 they rode into town. They were approached by an officer who asked them what they wanted – a room and food, they answered. The two robbers got off their mules and headed for the dingy room they'd been offered –

Sundance gave a local some money to buy food with . . .'

'Sardines and beer, their last supper – would you believe that?' Dan had come alive again.

'That's right. Sardines and beer. Near by a military posse was stationed – only four men though – who were on the lookout for the Yankee payroll robbers. They were informed by the officer who'd met Butch and Sundance as they'd entered the village that the North American bandits were under their noses. So, they gathered their guns and ammunition and headed for the room they were staying in.'

'Then what happened?'

'Butch approached the door and shot at the soldiers, wounding one of them. Fire was returned and Butch disappeared inside. More shots were fired. Then silence fell. Suddenly "three screams of desperation" were heard coming from the room Butch and Sundance were in. Then silence descended again. Forget the movie – there was no army, no volleys of shots and Butch and Sundance had plenty of ammunition left as well. At dawn the following morning, the authorities who'd laid siege to the place entered the room and found the Yankees dead. Butch was stretched out on the floor with a bullet through his temple and another in his arm. Sundance was on a bench with lots of bullets in his arms and one in his head. He was also holding a large ceramic jug close to his body. The police report stated that Sundance had been shot in the head by Butch. Then Butch must have killed himself.' Anne sat back and sighed.

'So much for going out in a blaze of glory like Paul Newman and Robert Redford, eh?' said Dan. He looked somewhat disappointed by the truth.

I knew how he felt.

My hosts had spent years going through files and letters and documents to piece together the South American end of the outlaws' last days. They were certain – as certain as anyone could be – that the two outlaws died that night in San Vicente. Dan and Anne told me that they were stripped and buried in the local cemetery the following day. Two weeks later they were dug up again so the man they robbed could double-check their identity. Once he'd confirmed they were indeed the men who robbed him the bodies were reinterred.

The deaths of Butch and Sundance in San Vicente didn't cause much of a stir for a while – which is not so surprising since they'd gone to South America to drop off the front pages and disappear. But, inevitably, that changed. In 1909, Frank Aller, the US vice-consul in Antofagasta, Chile, entered the picture. He'd helped the Sundance Kid with some problems a few years before – it had cost Sundance fifteen hundred dollars to make an unspecified, though clearly difficult, legal complication go away – and now, upon receiving unanswered letters addressed to Sundance, Aller wanted to know if the rumours concerning the outlaws' demise were true. He wrote:

> I have been informed that Boyd [Sundance] and a companion named Maxwell [Cassidy] were killed at San Vicente near Tupiza by natives and police and buried as '*desconocidos*' [unknowns]. I have endeavoured by correspondence to obtain confirmation and a certificate of death, but this has been impossible as it seems that the authorities are endeavouring to hush up the matter.

Aller eventually got his confirmation – which included a death certificate and a full report about the San Vicente killings – but all documentation and paperwork has since vanished. Aller's efforts to discover the fate of Butch and Sundance didn't make any headlines back in the States. No one really knew the truth. Even the Pinkertons, the main source of information about outlaws for pressmen, continued to believe the wanted men were still alive and kicking, and robbing.

It stayed that way for some time until the outlaws' old boss from their Concordia mine days, Percy Seibert, talked to journalist Arthur Chapman who wrote for the New York-based *Elks* magazine. The April 1930 issue told the story of the San Vicente shootout and the deaths of two of the West's most colourful and well-known outlaws. Other versions simply took the salient facts from Seibert's account and embellished them. The little book I'd treasured as a boy in Scotland, for example, had its own account which was basically the same as Seibert's:

A company galloped up to the barrio and one foolish young officer rushed in shouting to the bandidos yanqui to surrender. Cassidy had his gun out before he hit the ground. After the Kid got another trooper they ran for the hut. Just before he reached the doorway the Kid spun around and fell, shot through the chest. Butch scooped him up and rushed inside the hut. How long the Kid lived we don't know but Cassidy emptied both their six-shooters, knocking at least one more soldier from the wall. The gun battle lasted until darkness, the flashes lighting up the blackness while the acrid smell of gunpowder filled the warm night. The firing from the hut died down. The soldiers were reinforced and an older and wiser officer posted his men around the place to get the hut into a cross fire. But there was only silence, although they riddled the hut. All night they hugged the wall, their fingers on their triggers. In the early hours of the morning one shot shattered the stillness. At sun-up the officer led three of his men into the yard. He shouted to the americanos to surrender and throw out their guns but the hut was silent. They advanced cautiously and entered the riddled hut. Sitting on the shelf with his hand on his chest was Cassidy. In his stiffened hand was his single-action Colt .45. He had kept the last bullet for himself. The Kid lay on the floor with Cassidy's jacket under his head. It was evident Butch had done what he could for his friend. Then, with capture certain, he had killed himself.

The movie version, of course, came much later. Paul Newman and Robert Redford couldn't be seen committing suicide, for God's sake, so the film-makers sent them out – freeze-framed – in a true, bullets flying, blaze of glory. It was a good rousing ending for a film but more than a little misleading.

Shortly after the Chapman story appeared, people started saying that Butch (and, to a somewhat lesser extent, Sundance) hadn't died in South America at all. Without the bodies, photos of the bodies or identification by people who'd known the outlaws, a degree of doubt still remained. Some friends of Butch's from the old days are even supposed to have had a whipround and sent someone to South America to check and photograph the bodies. No hard evidence exists that this ever happened, however. No photographs, for example, have ever surfaced of that trip. Legend states that even after the delegated party came back armed with shots of the two bodies from San Vicente several of the financiers of the trip still disagreed over who was really in the photos. Confusion reigned.

Was the whole thing a case of mistaken identity? After all, Butch had been 'shot' more than once during his life back in the States and some said he'd even viewed a body on display that was supposed to be his. On that occasion, Friday, 13 May 1898, the dead cowboy propped up in a box was actually a man named Johnny Herring whom some said bore a strong resemblance to Cassidy. Killing famous larger-than-life outlaws was often more wishful thinking than accurate shooting.

I'd also heard about some other American outlaws who were in Patagonia at the same time as Butch and Sundance, so there was a slim possibility of a mix-up taking place. The most well-known Yankee outlaw double act in South America were Robert Evans and William Wilson. In several descriptions they sounded exactly like Butch and Sundance, using similar *modus operandi*, for example. According to Dan and Anne, though, there were witnesses who stated quite categorically that they knew Butch, Sundance, Wilson and Evans as four, quite separate, individuals. The fact that they may have consorted with one another at various times also caused confusion. Daniel Gibbons, who was Butch's best friend when he was at Cholila, had a son called Mansel who took up with Wilson and Evans around 1910. By then Wilson and Evans had already murdered the son of a prominent member of the Welsh community in Chubut whose name was Llwyd ap Iwan. The victim was cut down by gunfire during a botched robbery in December of 1909.

Two years later Wilson and Evans kidnapped forty-one-year-old Lucio Ramos Otero, a rich rancher from Chubut; their motive was probably murderous extortion. In on the job was Mansel Gibbon, son of Daniel. After being kept captive by the three outlaws for a month, Otero managed to burn his way out of his hastily constructed log prison and run to freedom. Once safely home he had to suffer the indignity of being accused of making the whole story up: 'He wasn't chained up in a log-cabin built by famous Yankee outlaws . . . He went to Chile or Paraguay and hid while everyone looked for him. Don't trust him. It was all a hoax!' whispered his jealous neighbours. Otero was so horrified by such scandalous rumours that he broke into print with a longwinded manifesto which told his side of the story The title of the publication was 'Son Cosas de la Vida, dijo Yake'. This referred to the reply made by Mansel 'Jake' or 'Yake' Gibbons' reply to Otero's weeping distress at being kidnapped:

'Hey, these things happen,' he'd been told by the cocksure outlaw.

Another American gunslinger knocking around Patagonia at the same time as Butch and Sundance was Andrew J. Duffy, who went by the alias Dientes de Oro, 'Gold Teeth'. The Pinkertons back in the USA managed to convince themselves that this man might be the murderous (resurrected or escaped) Harvey Logan. Dan and Anne were sceptical about this link and had produced fresh evidence which clearly suggested Duffy was someone else. But he *was* connected to Butch and Sundance, like Wilson and Evans, through Daniel Gibbons' son, Mansel. In August 1910 William Roberts, a British settler, came upon Mansel Gibbons' camp. The son of the Welsh settler invited Roberts to relax and take a seat and share some food. On sitting down, however, Roberts spotted the dead body of Andrew Duffy lying near by: 'That's Dientes de Oro,' he was told. 'We killed him because he was too cruel. The other day he wanted to murder a young boy just to see him fall.'

Another eerily similar pair of outlaws in Bolivia during the same period were two men who called themselves Ray A. Walters and Frank Harry Murray. Indeed, they were actually arrested for the Aramayo robbery and were jailed until the money was recovered from the two gringos shot and found dead in San Vicente. Eventually they were released. Walters and Murray, were described by Hiram Bingham, the archaeologist and explorer, as 'two rough-looking Anglo Saxons', and they spent time telling him:

> hair-raising stories of the dangers of the Bolivian roads where highway robbers, driven out of the United States by the force of law and order and hounded to death all over the world by Pinkerton detectives, had found a pleasant resting place in which to pursue their chosen occupation without let or hindrance. We found out

afterwards that one of our informants was one of this same gang of robbers . . . He put his case quite emphatically to us that it was necessary for them to make a living, that they were not allowed to do so peaceably in the United States, that they desired only to be let alone and had no intention of troubling travellers except those who sought to get information against them. They relied entirely for their support on being able to overcome armed escorts accompanying loads of cash going to the mines to liquidate the monthly payroll. This, they claimed, was legitimate plunder taken in fair fight. The only individuals who had to suffer at their hands were those who took up the case against them. Having laid this down for our edification, he proceeded to tell us what a reckless lot they were and how famous had been their crimes, at the same time assuring us that they were all very decent fellows and quite pleasant companions.

Were Walters and Murray actually Butch Cassidy and the Sundance Kid? No one knows. There are no other known references to them anywhere.

❁

Dan and Anne said that they too used to have doubts about the identity of the two men who died at the San Vicente shootout, but not any more.

'We're about ninety per cent certain it was Butch and Sundance who were killed there,' stated Dan. 'I know the evidence is all circumstantial but a shootout definitely took place there in November 1908; people met the Yankee outlaws before the robbery and identified them afterwards; Butch and Sundance stopped answering mail around the time the two outlaws were killed in San Vicente; the San Vicente outlaws' *modus operandi* was exactly the same as the one Butch and Sundance used; they went by known Butch and Sundance aliases; and the outlaws had a physical resemblance to Butch and Sundance. In our mind it's an open-and-shut case. There is the discrepancy of clothing – when they robbed the guy from the mines they were wearing dark-red corduroy suits but when they entered San Vicente one was wearing a light-brown cashmere suit and the other was wearing a yellow cashmere suit. But they probably just dumped their old outfits before going into the village, or the locals or army robbed them after they'd been shot. I believe it was Butch and Sundance who died there, all right.'

'Are their bodies in the graveyard in San Vicente waiting to be found?' I asked.

'Well, like everything else in outlaw history, it isn't as straightforward as it seems and you're rarely able to tie up all the loose ends. We went down there a couple of years ago to accompany the famous forensic anthropologist Clyde Snow who wanted to dig up the supposed grave of the outlaws,' said Dan.

I leaned forward on the edge of the chair listening intently as he spoke.

'Clyde has worked all over the world – Argentina, Bosnia, various Middle Eastern countries, you name it – and his speciality is digging up bodies people don't usually want found. He's done some very serious work for human rights groups like Amnesty International, that sort of thing. He was keen to take a "busman's holiday" and combine his love of outlaws with his work, and travel down to South America with us to search for Butch and Sundance's graves. Anyway, a local man in San Vicente claimed he knew where the grave was. We eventually found it and listened to his somewhat sketchy tale. The whole exhumation hinged upon this guy giving us accurate directions. The grave-marker was just a simple block of stone that had once held a proper cross and plaque — that's all there was. We got to digging. Eventually, we unearthed what we thought were the remains of two Caucasians and brought them back to the US for analysis. Clyde did his tests. DNA from two of Sundance's deceased relatives were compared to DNA extracted from the San Vicente skeletons we thought might belong to him.'

'And?' I waited hopefully.

'It wasn't Sundance,' he said. 'The guy in the village hadn't given us the right directions. His theories and stories, it turned out, were based upon other suggestions made by previous outlaw hunters who'd gone to the area years before we'd arrived on the scene. But he never told us that before we started digging and before we'd exhumed our bones for tests.' He smiled and scratched his head.

'So there is a chance, a very slim chance, that Butch, or to a lesser extent Sundance, may have survived the shootout and gone back to America?'

'Well, I don't think so. I think we just dug up the wrong body. I think they're in the graveyard in San Vicente somewhere. But I will say this; the best argument I can think of that Butch or Sundance could have come back to America to live out a normal life and vanish into thin air is the fact that that's exactly what Etta Place did. She did the greatest disappearing act in outlaw history. She left South America and . . . who knows? She dissolved into the background, leaving hardly any traces of her existence. There's always the possibility Butch and Sundance did the same thing. Highly unlikely in my view but not impossible,' said Dan.

'So who *did* the remains you found in San Vicente belong to?' I asked.

'Good question. One of the skulls we found which we thought belonged to a Caucasian outlaw — maybe Butch — turned out to belong to a Native American. The one we thought belonged to Sundance *was* Caucasian and it probably belonged to one of two people who visited San Vicente and died there – either a Swede or a German,' said Anne.

'And what happened to them?' I asked.

'Well . . .' said Dan running his hands through his hair, 'we believe the Swede accidentally shot himself getting off his horse. And the German –'

'We think the German,' interjected Anne, 'accidentally blew himself up when he was trying to defrost dynamite in his oven at home.'

15. Hi, I'm Butch

'Uncle Butch didn't die in Bolivia – he survived. I'll meet you in his home town of Circleville, Utah, at noon on Sunday and I'll tell you all about it.'

Bill Betenson is the great-great-nephew of Butch Cassidy, known in the family as Robert LeRoy Parker. His great-grandmother was Lula Parker Betenson, Butch Cassidy's sister. I'd spoken to Bill by telephone from Las Vegas. He sounded like a nice guy and seemed enthusiastic about chatting to me. He promised to explain why Cassidy's family have always maintained that Butch came back from South America alive.

I was genuinely intrigued about this part of the outlaw's saga. Various books and documents I'd come across had mentioned in some detail the tales that had begun almost as soon as Arthur Chapman's 1930 *Elks* magazine article reported Butch and Sundance gunned down in San Vicente. 'Butch can't be dead,' said people in various parts of the West. 'We saw him last week!'

People had spotted him in hotel lobbies, driving a car in Rock

Springs, getting on a train in California, walking down a street, having meals in diners. He was seen camping, he was spotted in a powerful boat on a river, prospecting in Alaska, living and dying in the Nevada desert, visiting old girlfriends in Wyoming. Someone waved to him at a rodeo and others shook hands with him. Reports surfaced alleging Butch had even met and chatted with friends who'd known him long before he went to South America. Contradictory statements came from some of his old friends, the very ones you would imagine Butch, had he lived, would have looked up first. Matt Warner, for example, allegedly pointed out a guy in a bar some time between 1915 and 1919, saying: 'That's Butch Cassidy. He's staying with me for a while, but keep it under your hat.' But in a note to western writer Charles Kelly in 1937, Warner stated: 'There is no such man living as Butch Cassidy. His real name was Robert Parker, born and raised in Circleville, Utah, and killed in South America. He and a man by the name of Longbow were killed in a soldier post there in a gunfight. This is straight.' And in 1938 the same Matt Warner said: 'A lot of false legends about what became of Butch [exist]. Some believe today that he is still alive. Some men claim they have seen Butch recently. Once in a while some hombre claims he is Butch. It's all poppycock.'

But the Butch-came-back-alive claims still persisted. Some even mentioned the new occupations the former outlaw was engaged in – everything from trapping in Alaska to gold-mining in Nevada to being an extra in Hollywood westerns. Others said he'd been to Europe to have plastic surgery, spent time in Britain looking up old Mormon relatives, walked the length and breadth of Spain (attending the running of the bulls in Pamplona and subsequent bullfights during the festival of St Fermine which he didn't care for) and spending a lot of time in Italy (which he'd loved).

In the various states Butch had once robbed it was something of an accepted open secret that he had returned from South

America. Everyone knew someone who'd met him post-1908. Or so they claimed.

Sundance too did his fair share of appearing after his alleged demise in San Vicente, although a lot less than Butch did. He supposedly joined Pancho Villa in Mexico before he travelled through Europe and India. He was also spotted in the Middle East showing T.E. Lawrence how to dynamite trains properly during the Arab–Turk conflict – something for which, by all accounts, the diminutive Lawrence was eternally grateful. But he fell on rough times and was next heard of in San Francisco in 1919, calling himself George Hanlon and being arrested for rolling a drunk in a street brawl. Hanlon, who also went by the alias of Hiram BeBee, died in a Utah prison at the age of eighty-one in 1955. He allegedly told his fellow inmates that he was indeed the infamous and deadly Sundance Kid. Most chose not to believe him, if only because he was a good six inches too short to be the strapping Harry Longabaugh. Others convinced themselves it was him and that the old man had shrunk with age. Researchers eventually turned up evidence that Hiram BeBee in his prime in 1919 was only five foot three inches tall. No way was he Sundance. Anyway, as my Washington informant, Dan Buck, had pointed out, the jailbird looked more like the comedian Jimmy Durante than Butch's handsome sidekick.

Another Sundance connection cropped up shortly after the release of the Hollywood movie when a character calling himself, amongst other variations, 'Harry Longabaugh Jnr' turned up. He gave lectures claiming to be Sundance's son, saying his mother was named Ann Marie Thayne, a schoolteacher, who was related in some way to Etta Place. Sundance had married then divorced his mother, claimed Harry Jnr, before leaving for South America with Etta. He said he met his famous father either in 1937 or 1940 – his dates and information often changed. His father gave him a map to find $300,000 in buried loot but he was afraid to search for it because the US Treasury was on his trail. He claimed on several occasions that Sundance died in Casper, Wyoming, in the late 1950s, something no one has ever been able to verify. Most people dismissed Harry Jnr as a crank but a few researchers were shaken by the odd detail he managed to produce which suggested he knew more than many gave him credit for. He died in a mysterious hotel fire in Montana in 1972. All his papers, documents and, presumably, treasure maps, went up in flames with him.

Most of the tales told about Butch and Sundance after 1908 hinged on the fact that the two ageing outlaws used the San Vicente rumours as a cover to escape from a life of crime and go straight. The shootout had wiped the slate clean and they could begin again with new identities. But, as Dan Buck and Anne Meadows pointed out, the only flaw in this line of argument was that no one in the USA knew of their alleged deaths until 1930. If they had planned on using the shootout as a cover it *failed*, simply because it took so long for Seibert to get the story to Chapman and into print. But even the Pinkertons, who'd chased the outlaws from coast to coast and then down into South America, never really believed they'd been shot in San Vicente. As late as 1921 the agency was convinced that Butch and Sundance were still up to their old tricks in South America. The files remained open for years after that and were never, to all intents and purposes, properly closed.

Theories about *how* the two men had survived were interesting. Some said it was a straightforward case of mistaken identity – two other outlaws had bitten the dust in San Vicente, not Butch and Sundance. Others suggested they were involved in the shootout but managed to avoid being killed. Most of the stories focused on Butch. He'd been injured in the gunfight but, after seeing Sundance killed or after shooting his friend himself to end his suffering, he'd managed to sneak away to safety, either dressed in the uniform of a dead Bolivian soldier or under the cover of darkness.

The most persistent rumour involved a guy named William T. Phillips from Spokane in Washington. Countless people muttered that old Butch had come back from South America and settled in Washington state calling himself by that name. One of the earliest outlaw writers, Charles Kelly, followed up the rumour, tracing a by then deceased William T. Phillips in Spokane and contacting his widow, Gertrude. She said her husband and Butch Cassidy were two different men but that before his death in 1937 William had claimed to know the famous outlaw 'very, very well'. Phillips wrote a manuscript called *The Bandit Invincible* which told Butch's life story. Some, believing the two men were one and the same, even regarded this as Butch's story as written by the outlaw himself. If it was, it was bad. And full of holes. Phillips certainly looked sufficiently like Cassidy to fool a few old-timers into thinking he was the real thing. The whole affair was complicated by the fact that Phillips took several trips back to Cassidy's old haunts. Some speculated that it was Butch back to find his buried gold – Phillips encouraged them by dropping the odd remark along the lines of 'if we can find that cabin, we'll all be fixed'. Various characters came forward to attest to his identity but none was completely reliable. Phillips himself, a qualified engineer, remained tight lipped. He was probably scared of being rumbled by anyone who knew Cassidy well. It was claimed he'd given a ring to an old girlfriend with the outlaw's name inscribed on it – 'Geo C to Mary B' – but the whole exchange reeked either of a married man trying to impress an occasional girlfriend with an alleged double-identity, or of a private joke between two lovers. Phillips's son claimed 'the fact that his father was Butch Cassidy was accepted in their home . . . It was, however, a well-guarded secret.' Phillips's son also said that his mother misled Charles Kelly about his father's identity because 'she just didn't want the notoriety'.

Some handwriting experts claimed letters written by Phillips were in the same hand as those penned by Butch Cassidy. But the theory didn't really hang together. Buck and Meadows eventually pulled the rug from under the Phillips story when they successfully unearthed a picture of Phillips's mother – he was her spitting image. Thus, there was no way he could be Butch Cassidy.

In reality William Phillips was probably just a western history buff, who may have once met the real Cassidy. Being mistaken for Butch, especially after immersing himself in the writing of a book about him, was the ultimate compliment – one he never really acknowledged as being true or went out of his way to deny. He simply played along with it.

The claim that intrigued me most was the one made by Butch's sister Lula. She said he came back to Circleville long after San Vicente – alive and well enough to eat home-made blueberry pie she'd baked for him. She also stated, quite categorically, that he wasn't 'the man known as William Phillips, reported to be Butch Cassidy'. It was a hell of story – and certainly worth the long drive from Las Vegas to Utah to check out. Lula Parker Betenson died in May 1980 at the age of ninety-six. Right up to the end she'd claimed to have met her brother long after he was reported dead in South America. Her great-grandson, Bill Betenson, was now the main propagator of this claim and it was him I was going to meet the following day.

❀

After leaving behind the lights and casinos I headed north through the desert – where most of the Mafia's former Las Vegas middle-managers are supposedly buried standing up in unmarked graves – and followed the route on my map to Utah.

Three hours later I pulled into St George, Utah. It was my stopping-off point for the night *en route* to Butch's home in Circleville. I consulted my guidebook for information:

In the fall of 1861, Brigham Young sent 309 families to establish a cotton-growing community in the semi-arid Virgin River Valley; today, St George has almost 40,000 inhabitants. Known as one of Utah's more conservative communities, life in St George is strongly influenced by the Mormon Church; it is also a winter home to many snowbirds and retirees, who love the hot, dry summers and mild winters. Despite the climate, this desert city appears quite green, with tree-lined streets and lovely grassy areas. There are eight golf courses, with more in the planning stages, and recreational and cultural facilities to suit every taste.

I'd spotted the burgeoning golf-course industry on the way into St George. One minute there was desert – the next golf-course green grass. Not the natural, light-coloured, mottled grass which nature produces but instead a thick, St Patrick's Day green carpet stretching as far as the eye could see. Puffs of smoke from earth-moving equipment wafted into the blue sky. RV or caravan parks for older travellers who'd just sold up and hit the road in search of optimism and youth and sunshine were everywhere. It was boom time in the West again. Only this time, the average age of those doing the booming was around seventy.

One hotel had a huge fountain in front of it. Gallons and gallons of dyed blue water gushed and spiralled into the sky. It looked stupid and wasteful and above all tasteless. Still, I loved it. It summed up everything about the American 'bigger is always better' mentality. If someone had asked me what I thought about this aspect of American culture I wouldn't have needed to say anything – I'd just pull out a picture of this awful fountain in the desert and point to it. As darkness fell in St George I stood on a hill and looked at this monstrosity. From a distance it resembled a large, neon-pink lavatory which couldn't stop flushing.

I'd promised a friend that I'd visit their relatives when I was in St George. I drove down the main drag towards where they lived, in a development not far from the town. I noticed a lot of really beautiful old buildings. On closer inspection I saw that every single one of them housed funeral parlours. It ranked alongside golf as the main industry.

When I arrived at the home of the people I'd promised I'd call in on, I stood for a moment looking up and down the rows of identical houses. Everything was neat and tidy. The gardens were spookily manicured and clipped to perfection. It gave me the chills just looking at it. I even spied some white picket fences. The street looked like a home for the retired, built by Disney.

The couple I was visiting had retired to the St George area because of 'the climate' I was told. She was American, he was Swedish. They were rich. The conversation started slowly.

'One of my neighbours was found lying in the desert recently. She tends to wander off by herself. She's seventy-six. Probably slipped or something. Anyway, she nearly died. Old fool. It could have been a snake, I suppose. That's the only drawback of the desert – snakes and the like – *deserty* things that get in the way.' Max rubbed his rubbery old lips and shook his head. He was in his seventies and dressed from head to toe in white. Everything matched his white hair, even his sparkling, box-fresh Nike trainers.

'Have you seen our kitchen? Nice and airy.' His wife pointed to the kitchen. It was indeed nice and airy. She was a tall, sincere woman who was either trying to impress me quickly or get rid of me quickly. She was also dressed in white.

'Europe's going down the toilet – the unions have wasted everything – and your health service in Britain doesn't work either. Socialised medicine is doomed. Here is where it's at.' Max had a slightly collapsed air about him. He was shrinking but fighting it.

'Have you seen our garden?' asked his wife. I stood up and peered into the darkness. A small lake was outside their back door. It was shared by all the other residents who lived in the white houses. A large white dog with luxuriously long fur stood up and yawned when it saw us.

We sat back down again.

'Hey, and what about black people!' Max hadn't risen from his chair while I'd been shown the garden, the lake and the dog.

'What about them?' I said.

'Don't you think they have genetically inferior intellects to us?' His eyes screwed up and he smiled slightly as he spoke.

'No, I don't. That's total crap.'

'I'm just asking you. What's your problem?' He smiled and flapped his thin hairless arms like a skinny seagull trying to take off.

I'd been in the house less than ten minutes.

'Have you seen our bedroom – we liked it because it was big.' I accompanied his wife into their bedroom. It was big. And white.

'People in the northern, colder hemisphere have better brains than those nearer the equator. They don't have winters like we do. That means we think better. They are lazier.' Max had started talking again the moment I'd sat back down.

'They do have winters. Different seasons. Look, what are you trying to say?' I was bloody angry with him.

'Hey, cool it. You could do with coming to St George for a while to chill out my boy! Kick back, smell the good desert air, relax, play some golf or something . . .' Max looked at me like a benign old uncle.

I stared out the window.

'I'm just wondering what you thought about these things, that's all,' he said. 'That's all . . .'

I looked at him. 'Do you really want to know what I think?'

'Yes.'

'I think you're about to sprout a small moustache under your nose and find a swastika armband around your arm. That's what I think.'

He stared into space. There was silence for a moment or two.

'You write don't you – a journalist?' he said eventually. 'Why are you all so left wing? Why do you write negative stories? I only read *Forbes* magazine – it's full of financial success stories. They even had a black guy on the cover recently. That's what I like to see. Positive thinking.' He raised his eyebrows in a 'I-rest-my-case' kind of way.

'Have you seen our second bathroom yet? It's really nice. It was one of the main features that caught our eye when we were thinking about buying this house,' said his wife. I went to inspect the bathroom. I even used it. I noticed the new bar of soap had dust on it.

'I arrived in this country with only a big sausage under my arm and fifty dollars. Now look at me. If you want work, you'll find it. You can make it happen! It's all here for the taking. Look at us. We're an example. We're a success!'

I looked at them. They looked at me. If they were an American success story, I'd gladly die a snivelling, failed, miserable, impoverished wreck – who owned no white clothes.

A noise at the sliding back-garden window broke the silence. Max and his wife peered out to inspect the source of the scratching.

'Oh!'

The dog had shit itself.

I arose early for my journey to Circleville. On my way to the diner in St George for breakfast I passed a group of four people in their late sixties, maybe early seventies, who were striding quickly up a steep hill. They wore little stereos and headphones.

and white clothes. Every so often one of the men in the group stopped and angrily gestured at a figure behind him.

I glanced back and caught sight of an ancient old man silently floating along behind the walkers in what looked like a golf buggy. He was wearing an oxygen mask that was attached to a large tank via a long piece of frosted-plastic piping. Everything on the buggy was wired up to a battery. In the early-morning light he looked like something out of a science-fiction novel – apart from the tartan bonnet clapped on his head. He studiously ignored the man waving at him whom I'd already decided must be his impatient seventy-year-old son.

Fifteen minutes later as I ate breakfast in the diner I overheard two Mexican dwarfs seated behind me. When I heard them speaking I carefully positioned myself in my seat to get a better view of them. They were engaged in a heated argument. They spoke in heavily accented English and their raised voices clattered and echoed around the almost empty restaurant without a hint of embarrassment. They seemed completely oblivious to my presence. A few other solitary diners seemed to know them, and the waitress occasionally addressed them by their names when she buzzed by the table to refill their coffee cups. Neither was more than three feet tall.

'She always acts like that when I'm around her. Your mother doesn't like me. She shows no respect!' The man munched on his bacon and stared out of the window with hurt eyes.

'She does, baby. Oh, my mother does like you. Oh baby! It's just that you never cook anything for dinner except pasta, that's all. Change the menu and she'll show you respect.'

He ignored her and kept eating.

'Now can we talk about our investments?' she said rustling a newspaper.

'We need to be more aggressive . . .' Her husband wiped his greasy mouth, slurped down some coffee and continued to stare out the window.

'Aggressive?'

'Yeah, aggressive. You know. Like your mother.'

❋

I left the diner and drove north through the canyons of Utah. The red sandstone cliffs were painted with shadows and sculpted by the morning light. Mine seemed to be the only car on the road.

The dark-red stone gave way to more and more snow. I climbed high over a very steep pass, through a dense forest, until I eventually emerged on top. The view was stunning. Beneath me lay a scene from a Christmas card. A little wooden ranch, with heavy rugs of snow on its logs, lay in the middle of deep valley that stretched for dozens of miles in both directions. To the east was a range of tall mountains that disappeared into mist at their highest points. The floor of the valley was level and white and perfect-looking. The branches of the trees bent under the weight of the snow which clung to them. It dropped off in large clumps which glinted in the bright, warm, morning sunshine.

I stood at the top of the valley and traced the road I'd be driving on. The distance was deceptive. A mountain that looked close actually took me an hour to reach. But it was worth it.

Along the way I spotted an old silver mine. I stopped the truck and hoofed it over a field and a river to inspect it. Ancient timber beams held the earth back and large rocks lay at its entrance. It could almost have been something out of an old movie set – unreal and deliberate. I suddenly felt uneasy, as if I was being watched, so I returned to my truck.

The snow-covered hills gave way to lower-lying slopes that were damp and mossy-looking. The fields seemed muddy and aching for some dry weather. A few horses stood around in stabled areas, huddling together for warmth, their breath puffing out in the cold air when they snorted or moved.

Eventually I drove into Circle Valley, also known as Circleville. This had been home to the young Robert LeRoy Parker. It was the place he'd left to pursue his life as an outlaw, the place he'd first met his mentor and namesake Mike Cassidy.

A new diner-cum-motel had opened up in Circleville. Butch Cassidy's Hideout it was called. It had four or five bedrooms attached to it. Inside the diner they sold T-shirts with Butch's face on them — they'd used his picture from the Fort Worth photograph. The diner's menu was printed in old Wild West lettering, the kind I'd seen on fake WANTED posters at the seaside when I was a kid. A few locals from Circleville were dotted around the diner when I walked in at lunchtime. It smelled of coffee, cigarettes and grease. I ordered some soup and a sandwich and waited for Bill Betenson to arrive.

As I ate I watched two customers opposite me. Both were in their forties and both wore nice fur cowboy hats. The man facing me had only one arm. He stirred his coffee and looked out the window. His friend shuffled around in his seat then hopped off to pay their bill. It was then that I noticed he had no legs from the thighs down. He waddled over to pay for their meal on two metal-soled flesh coloured plastic stumps. They hit the floor with a sharp crack when he put his weight on them. His friend nodded to me when he saw me watching. He knew what I was thinking. One word had entered my head when I saw them. Vietnam.

On cue Bill Betenson entered and made straight for my table. A large man with a very open, smiling but watchful face, he shook hands with me and sat down. 'All the way from Scotland, huh?' He laughed as I nodded. His face was red. 'Don't tell me — you liked cowboy books and films when you were a kid!'

Again he laughed as I nodded once more.

'I've been to Edinburgh once — I was doing my church missionary work and I had some time to visit some places. It was nice. Wet, though. And that's where Butch Cassidy's maternal grandfather came from – you know that? Cassidy was just the alias – made him sound Irish. In fact, he was as Scottish as you are!'

I told him I was first-generation Irish.

'Oh, well . . . give me a break! You have a Scottish accent!'

We chatted for an hour or so and I looked through a large family photograph album that he'd brought with him. It was like any other family keepsake, full of snaps of gatherings, holidays and weddings. The only difference was that every so often the unmistakable image of Robert LeRoy Parker would pop up. Uncle Butch in all his glory when he was a young man.

'Some of my family are still a bit, well, sort of "funny" about Butch being part of the family, if you know what I mean.' Bill squinted when he spoke. He seemed very serious all of a sudden. 'Butch was, after all, a criminal. Our family, me included, are Mormons; we believe in certain things and breaking the law is not exactly conducive to our way of life.'

'How much did the family really know about his outlaw goings-on?' I asked.

'Little. He kept himself to himself. Of course his brother Dan was an outlaw too, which not many people really knew about, which made it even worse. So the family must have thought, "Where did we go wrong?" It was awkward all round,' said Bill flatly.

'So tell me – did he really come back alive after the San Vicente shootout in 1908?' The sun streamed in through the window.

Bill closed the large photo album and put his hands under his chin. He smiled silently. 'You finish what you're eating and then we'll go for a little tour. But first I want to buy something.'

'What?'

'A Butch Cassidy T-shirt.'

❁

The old Butch Cassidy cabin was falling down. The roof had caved in and the door was off its hinges. It looked like a broken-down old barn. It was five minutes south of the town. I'd passed it on the way in without even noticing. It looked sad and lonely. A forlorn-looking metal donation box stood guard at the door. A few rusted old pennies sat in a puddle of water at the bottom of it.

'People broke into this place and robbed it. The family had it fixed up after all the publicity when the film came out, but now it's gone to ruin.' Bill walked around the interior, touching the walls and picking at the crumbling wood. 'I wish I had the money to do something with it,' he said to no one in particular.

Crow-black smoke stains from the old chimney could still be seen halfway up one of the walls. This was the place Butch had grown up, the large Parker family squeezing themselves into two rooms. It was tiny by any standards, absolutely impossible for a family of thirteen. No wonder young LeRoy had been keen to strike out on his own.

'That's some of the old farm equipment Butch's father had,' said Bill pointing to some big old wheels and tools that lay rusting on the grass outside. We looked at the ancient hulks for a few moments then walked in silence over to some trees that stood next to a little stream.

'Butch planted these with his mother when he was a boy – they're poplars.' The trees towered above us, swaying gently in the wind. The thick, overgrown grass under our feet washed backwards and forwards over the heavy, twisted roots.

We inspected an old shed. I hauled open the same doors Butch himself had opened when he'd dragged himself out of bed to do the early-morning chores. Inside it smelled musty and oily. Old newspapers from half a century ago had been used as wallpaper. Chinks of blue light from holes in the walls pierced the darkness. The timbers groaned in the wind.

❀

Five minutes later I was standing at the brick house in the middle of Circleville the Parkers had built for themselves after they'd left the old timber cabin for good.

'This was where Butch came back to in 1925,' said Bill. He pointed to the left-hand side of the building. 'That's where the porch used to be. Butch's father was sitting there when two men drove up in a Model-T Ford. One of them was Butch.'

I already knew most of the story.

Bill's great-grandmother, Butch's sister Lula, claimed she was told to come down to the house to cook supper for the guest. When she arrived she didn't recognise the man – she'd only been an infant when he'd left – but he did have a familiar family grin, she recalled in her book. Her father introduced the man as LeRoy, her long-lost brother. For hours, she said, he sat and talked of his life as an outlaw. He said that he and Sundance had wanted to go straight in South America but that 'When a man gets down, they won't let him up. He never quits paying his price.' Butch went on to say he had heard more about his alleged death in San Vicente in the United States than he ever did when he was down in South America. He'd even heard wild stories about how he was supposed to have escaped by dressing in a dead Bolivian soldier's uniform. He and Sundance had gone in separate directions before leaving South America and had never met again, apart from one chance encounter in Mexico City, where he claimed Harry and Etta were now anonymously living their lives out. As for San Vicente and the alleged identification of the two bodies as Butch and Sundance, he didn't know what had happened but he did have a theory:

I heard they got Percy Seibert from the Concordia tin mines to identify a couple of bodies as Butch Cassidy and the Sundance Kid, all right. I wondered why Mr Seibert did that. Then it dawned on me that he would know this was the only way we could go straight. I'd been close to Seibert – we'd talked a lot, and he knew how sick of life I was. He knew I'd be hounded as long as I lived. Well, I'm sure he saw this as a way for me to bury my past along with somebody else's, so I could start over.

'He stayed for a while in the town, met some more relatives, took off into the hills to meet some brothers and then disappeared,' Bill told me. 'He stayed in touch with his father via mail for a while but the letters were always carefully destroyed after they'd been read. According to Lula, he died in the fall of 1937 somewhere in the north-west. Someone called "Jeff" wrote a letter to the family saying he'd been "laid away very nicely". No one ever divulged where the grave was, although Lula definitely knew.' Bill shrugged and looked at the old brick-house.

'Do you know where he's buried?' I asked.

He smiled and said nothing.

'C'mon, I won't tell anyone,' I said.

'Yeah, right!' He laughed loudly. 'When the old cabin was being done up, one of the family asked some workers not to disturb a specific spot near by where he said there was a grave. Within hours there were rumours flying around that Butch was buried there. It was, would you believe, an old dog that we'd been fond of. But it shows you how desperate people still are to find him. In fact, shortly after Lula died in 1980, a local historian went to Nevada with a TV crew and pointed to a pile of rocks: "That's Butch's grave right there!" this guy said. "I know because Lula told me so from her hospital bed!" Hardly likely, given she was paralysed with a stroke and couldn't even talk.'

'Did any other members of the family see Butch apart from Lula?' I asked Bill this because I'd read that Lula's views had been described as being 'controversial within the family' by a niece.

'Yes. Mark Betenson, Lula's son, who was only eleven at the time, saw him. Butch's brother Eb told him who the stranger was. Mark's widow, who lives right here in Circleville, and my grandfather Scott Betenson both confirmed this,' answered Bill.

'Do you believe that he came back?'

'Yes. Why would Lula lie? She was a Christian lady. She wouldn't have lied about something like that,' said Bill seriously.

'Did she offer any other evidence that he'd come back?' I pressed.

'No. But after she made her story public she was inundated with letters from people who'd also seen him at one time or another. She went public to set the record straight – especially after the movie came out.'

'Did that make her happy?'

'Oh, yeah . . . she'd finally taken this burden off her shoulders. People now knew the truth, that Butch Cassidy had come home. He hadn't died like the movie said, he'd lived. And all he wanted to do was to settle down and be left alone. It must have been hard for him at the time and then hard for Lula carrying that secret for years.' Bill shrugged his shoulders.

'What did she think of the film? I asked.

'She enjoyed it apart from the ending which, obviously, bothered her a great deal. In fact, at the age of eighty-five, she even went to visit the set where they were filming it. She met Robert Redford who played Sundance and then she was introduced to Paul Newman. Can you imagine it? This old lady in her eighties from Circleville, Lula Parker Betenson, and probably the biggest star in Hollywood at the time, Paul Newman!'

'What did she say to him?'

'He grinned and said to her: "Hi, I'm Butch!" She answered as quick as a flash, "Hi, I'm your sister!"'

We laughed and chatted for a little while longer, then said our goodbyes. We both had long drives ahead of us.

I headed out of Circleville, going past the old Parker cabin again. I wanted to visit it on my own before I left. As I neared it I pulled the truck off the road and parked on a muddy grass verge. I rolled the window down and sat looking at the little ranch for a few minutes.

This had been the first place Butch had stopped at during his alleged return visit in 1925. I'd been told that when he'd driven into town in his new Model-T Ford he'd pulled off the road and walked across the fields looking for the home he'd once known. Instead of hearing familiar voices and seeing familiar faces, he'd found the same thing I did: a broken-down little shack. It must have seemed tired and old even then. Everything had changed; nothing was the same anymore. Butch's restless instinct may have been to keep going, to turn his back on the past and search elsewhere for that which mattered to him. Or he may have lingered for a moment or two, just this once, and allowed himself to think over his life. He may have contemplated the other roads he could have taken. How many different outcomes could his life have had? Only God knew the answer to that. He'd have silently walked away, a solitary, doubt-filled man whose only remaining request was to be allowed the quiet privilege of anonymously fading into the background of life like a spent ghost.

I started the engine of my truck and took one last look at the old cabin. Framed against the trees and the hills, it looked like an old postcard as the first snowflakes of the day gently started falling.

I pulled out on to the road and drove slowly away with the image imprinted on my mind like a carefully executed sketch.

❊

Several hours later I was standing in the canyons near the ghost town of Grafton where the movie *Butch Cassidy and the Sundance Kid* had been shot decades before. This was the remote location where Lula Parker Betenson had visited the film's stars. The road to the movie-set had been bumpy and uneven. It had taken me a while to find it – one dirt-track had even been marked 'This is *not* the road to Grafton'. When I'd finally found the correct route I bumped and thudded my way along it. Winter storms and age had corroded its surface and it had been almost thirty years since the film-crew with their lights and cameras and caravans and heavy equipment had rolled past this place.

I walked around some of the few remaining buildings in Grafton. Old doors hung on rusting hinges and even floor-boards were sprayed with graffiti. The house where Butch and Sundance had supper with Etta Place was still standing and so were a few others that I recognised from the film. The wind whistled through the trees and blew some pieces of cardboard down the empty, dusty street.

I was completely alone.

A short walk away was an old, forgotten graveyard. Symmetrical mounds where bodies had been laid generations before slumbered in the fading afternoon sunlight. Several markers said the deceased had been 'killed by Indians'. One was for a man only known as 'Cedar Pete'.

I sat on a rock and looked around me. My book about the Wild Bunch that I'd first read in Glasgow twenty years earlier lay beside me. There wasn't a sound. I gazed across at the old set – the faded plasterwork, the brickwork and the collapsed roofs. It was hard to tell which buildings belonged to the real ghost town and which had been built by the Hollywood carpenters. It was impossible to distinguish between fact and fiction.

High above me, above the houses and above the graveyard, I spied a large eagle. It was silhouetted against the dark-blue sky, perched proudly on a towering pinnacle. It turned its head slowly from side to side as it kept an eye on the scene below. I watched it for a while to see how long it stayed there. It didn't move for what seemed like an eternity. Then, quite suddenly, it was gone.

All that was left were the old buildings, the weathered canyons, the swaying trees and the faded memory of people like me who had once passed this way.

This was the place where the cowboys had lived.

Both real and imagined.

Acknowledgements

This book, although written by me, was in the best of senses a collaborative exercise. I'd like to thank the following, in no particular order, for the various roles they played during its writing: Bill Campbell and Peter MacKenzie at Mainstream for taking a chance and commissioning the work in the first place; Jerry Carpenter and Esther Nui of Apalachin, New York, for their kindness, hospitality and generosity; Jan Peterson-Sterling and Professor David Sterling of Port Crane, New York, for the use of their library; Dan Buck and Anne Meadows of Washington DC for their time, practical help, advice on South America and friendship; Ross Wilson at Scottish Television Enterprises for, as always, his sound judgement and valued friendship; George Rose, colleague and friend, for listening and encouraging me to write about Cleland; Philip Watson at GQ magazine in London, a fine editor and a good friend; the family of the Sundance Kid, Paul and Donna Ernst in Souderton, Pennsylvania; the family of Butch Cassidy, especially Bill Betenson in Salt Lake City, Utah; my own family, the O'Neills, in Scotland,

251

England and Ireland, and their respective spouses; my mother and father of Daingean, Co. Offaly, Ireland, especially the latter, with whom I enjoyed many a good cowboy film; the various staff members of the State Archives in Cheyenne and Casper College, Wyoming; Gerry Turnbull and John MacDonald, two valued friends; all the people I met and chatted with on my long trip across the USA; and, finally, my wife Sarah my companion and co-conspirator – to whom this book is dedicated with much love.

Bibliography

I used the following publications for research and background reading when I was writing this book. Some were more enjoyable to read than others but I would certainly recommend all of them to anyone interested in either the history of outlaws in general or the criminal careers of Butch Cassidy and the Sundance Kid in particular. Three of them merit special mention: firstly, the book I read as a boy which hooked me on this subject was James D. Horan's classic *The Wild Bunch* published in 1958 by Signet. A great little book, it's probably out of print by now, but I have no doubt copies can still be found if you are willing to hunt through second-hand bookstalls; secondly, there was a very good *National Geographic* article in November 1976 written by Robert Redford (later expanded into a first-rate *National Geographic* book which looked at the outlaw trail; thirdly, and finally, I'd encourage anyone interested in the subject to peruse the excellent *Encyclopedia of Western Lawmen and Outlaws* which was edited by Jay Robert Nash and published by Da Capo. This is full of wonderful biographies, anecdotes and a wealth of photographs which leads me to assert that nineteenth–century outlaws seem to have been a lot uglier and scarier than their twentieth-century counterparts. The others, in no particular order, are:

Triggernometry: A Gallery of Gunfighters with Technical Notes on Leather Slapping as a Fine Art, gathered from Many a Loose Holstered Expert over the Years by Eugene Cunningham (The Caxton Printers, 1934)

The Wild Bunch by James D. Horan (Signet, New York, 1958)

Butch Cassidy, My Brother by Lula Parker Betenson (Brigham Young University Press, Utah,1975)

The Outlaw Trail by Charles Kelly (University of Nebraska Press, 1938)

Digging Up Butch and Sundance by Anne Meadows (University of Nebraska Press, 1994)

The Best of the West, edited by Tony Hillerman (Harper Perennial, 1991)

Wondrous Times on the Frontier by Dee Brown (Harper Perennial, 1991)

In Search of Butch Cassidy by Larry Pointer (University of Oklahoma Press, 1977)

Sinners and Saints by Gladys S. Beery (High Plains Press, Laramie, 1994)

The Outlaw Legend by Graham Seal (Cambridge University Press, 1996)

The Log of a Cowboy by Andy Adams (Senate, n.d.)

Butch Cassidy and the Sundance Kid – Screenplay by William Goldman (Bantam Books, New York, 1969)

In Patagonia by Bruce Chatwin (Jonathan Cape Ltd, London, 1977)

Sundance: My Uncle by Donna B. Ernst (Creative Publishing Company, Texas, 1992)

Tom Horn by Chip Carlson (Beartooth Corral, Cheyenne,

Wyoming, 1991)

Joe LeFors by Chip Carlson (Beartooth Corral, Cheyenne, Wyoming, 1995)

The Cowboy Encyclopedia by Richard W. Slatta (W. W. Norton & Co, New York, 1994)

Cowboying – A Tough Job in a Hard Land by James H. Beckstead (University of Utah Publications, 1991)

The Outlaw Trail by Robert Redford (Elm Tree Books, London, 1978)

The Wild West (Warner Books, USA, n.d.)

The West – An Illustrated History by Geoffrey C. Ward (Little, Brown, New York, 1996)

The Encyclopedia of Western Lawmen and Outlaws by Jay Robert Nash (Da Capo Press, New York, 1994)